TEACHING THAT
TRANSFORMS

TEACHING THAT
TRANSFORMS

WORSHIP
as the Heart of
Christian Education

Debra Dean Murphy

BrazosPress
Grand Rapids, Michigan

For My Parents
Elmer Lowell Dean and *Judith Shaw Dean*

And in Memory of My Sister
Kimberley Susan Dean

© 2004 by Debra Dean Murphy
Published by Brazos Press
a division of Baker Publishing Group
P.O. Box 6287, Grand Rapids, MI 49516-6287
www.brazospress.com

Printed in the United States of America

Library of Congress Cataloging-in-Publication Data
Murphy, Debra Dean, 1962–
    Teaching that transforms : worship as the heart of Christian education
/ Debra Dean Murphy.
        p.   cm.
    Includes bibliographical references.
    ISBN 1-58743-067-3 (pbk.)
    1. Christian education. 2. Public worship. I. Title.
BV1471.3.M87 2004
268—dc22   2004007725

Scripture is taken from the New Revised Standard Version of the Bible, copyright 1989 by the Division of Christian Education of the National Council of the Churches of Christ in the USA. Used by permission.

Chapter four, "Worship as Catechesis: Knowledge, Desire, and Christian Formation," originally appeared in the journal *Theology Today*, October 2001, pp. 321–332. It is reprinted here with permission.

CONTENTS

Prologue 9

Part One: The Problem with Religious Education

1. Understanding Religion: Religious Education as Quest
for Transcendence 29
   Introduction
   The Invention of Religion
   Getting Outside Ourselves: The Fallacy of Perspective
   Splitting the Difference: Jews and Christians in Dialogue
   Summary

2. Freedom and Justice for All: Religious Education as
Modern Project 49
   Introduction
   Religious Education as Spiritual Endeavor
   Christian Education and the Kingdom of God
   Freedom For and Freedom From
   Christian Religious Education and the Cause of Justice
   Justice, Love, and the Common Good
   Summary

3. Faith and the Public Good: Religious Education as
Responsible Citizenship 73
   Introduction
   The Bible and Religious Education
   "Has God Only One Blessing?" Judaism in Christian Terms

Knowledge of a subject mostly means knowledge of the language of that subject.

Neil Postman
The End of Education

Learning takes place when words are used, either aloud or privately, in the context of particular acts of attention.

Iris Murdoch
The Sovereignty of Good

Why do we praise God?
We praise God, not to obtain anything, but because God's being draws praise from us.

From the Catechism of
The Book of Common Prayer

PROLOGUE

The church I grew up in is a small, white clapboard structure with long, narrow, clear-paned windows framed by green wooden shutters, a set of high front steps—their elevation lending a dramatic effect to the church's entrance—and a simple yet beautiful cupola roofed with green tile. The church stands against a backdrop of stunning natural beauty in the remote Allegheny Mountains of southeastern West Virginia. When I was a child, Sunday mornings at Huntersville United Methodist Church consisted of Sunday school at 10 a.m. and worship (or "preaching" as we liked to call it) at 11 o'clock. Since our church was on a "circuit" with three other Methodist churches, our minister (or "preacher" as we liked to call him) came to us only two Sundays a month. Because worship was rather infrequent, it was Sunday school that was the heart and soul of our little church. We would meet in the church's damp, cramped basement, each class's space defined by a set of temporary partitions that could easily be removed for potluck suppers, the Wednesday afternoon 4-H club meeting, and visits by Santa Claus at Christmas. There we, like dutiful Protestant children everywhere, would memorize Bible verses, read inspiring stories from our Sunday school quarterlies, be rewarded for faithful attendance, and occasionally ask the unexpected and sometimes exasperating question of our long-suffering teacher, Mrs. Sherbs. When the Sunday school hour was over, we would emerge from the dim,

dank basement into the light of the sanctuary. The preacher
would arrive (sometimes late because of his earlier duties at the
Minnehaha Springs Methodist Church just up the road), and
worship would commence.

If we ever used the term *Christian education* in my hometown
church, which I suspect we did not, we would have meant by
it those activities involving children occurring in the basement
on Sunday mornings between 10 and 11 o'clock. We would not
have used the term in connection with anything that occurred
upstairs during the worship hour. What we did when we entered
the sanctuary at 11 o'clock, we would have said, was something
else altogether. Not only was a physical boundary traversed in
mounting the steps into the worship space, but another kind of
threshold was crossed, for we all knew that we had school in the
basement and church in the sanctuary. These were fundamentally different kinds of activities, categorically distinct realms
of experience, with different means and ends, procedures and
purposes. And whether this kind of scenario occurs in a small,
working-class community in Appalachia, a midwestern suburban
congregation of thousands, or an inner-city mission church, the
assumption that worship and education are categorically distinct remains deeply embedded in the theologies and practices
of American Protestantism.

In contrast, the starting point of this book is that it is in corporate worship that the lives of Christians are most acutely formed
and shaped. Worship, as theologian Don Saliers has noted, is a
"characterizing activity." In worship "people are characterized,
given their life and their fundamental location and orientation in
the world."[1] While our formation as Christians also takes place in
extraliturgical settings, all efforts at forming and discipling Christians should presume the centrality of worship. And because
the argument of this book is that the formation of Christians is
integrally linked to worship, praise, and doxology, I prefer the
term *catechesis* over the more familiar *Christian education*.

Now *catechesis* is a word that most certainly was not uttered
in the church of my childhood, but historically it has signified
the deep unity between Christian formation and worship, between discipleship and doxology. *Christian education*, by comparison, is a term rooted in the schooling model of modern
pedagogy, with its emphasis on classroom instruction, teaching

techniques, theories of human development, and the designing and implementing of curricula. Moreover, the term *education* is increasingly characterized in economic images and metaphors (schools as marketplaces, teachers as managers, learners as consumers, and so on). Such troubling images and metaphors can (and have) become literal descriptions of the learning process itself.[2] I will direct a good deal of attention in this book to the disciplines of Christian education (and religious education) and the assumptions inherent in many of their practices, but for now it is enough to say that because of its historical associations and its indebtedness to certain (questionable) philosophical and social-scientific premises, the term *Christian education* continues to perpetuate, however unwittingly, the false divide between worship and Christian formation.

It should be noted that my appeal for a recovery of the term *catechesis* is not new. Writing a generation ago, John Westerhoff challenged Christians in both Protestant and Catholic traditions to reclaim "our educational ministry in the church as 'catechesis,' and [to] direct our attention to the nature of catechesis."[3] Westerhoff's work through the years, within the academy and in parish settings, can be seen as an attempt to help churches learn to carry out the task of catechesis and to understand that such a task is derived from and dependent on the church's worship. I see my own efforts here as congruous with, though not identical to, Westerhoff's—and perhaps all the more urgent, given that in the years since Westerhoff first insisted that the practices of Christian formation are linked fundamentally to the church's liturgical life and are best named *catechesis,* little progress toward such a recovery has been realized, at least within most Protestant traditions.

And so this book seeks to develop an understanding of Christian catechesis as a practice, or set of practices, informed at heart by doxology. The term *catechesis* can be a slippery one. For some within the Roman Catholic tradition, the word may conjure unpleasant childhood memories of lifeless, unimaginative instruction in the doctrines of the Catholic faith. For a great many Protestants, as I suggested above, the word and its meaning are simply unknown. The earliest Christians used the term, from the Greek word *katēkhēsis,* meaning to "teach by word of mouth," to refer to the oral instruction given to new converts who were preparing for baptism. In the early centuries of Christianity and through the medieval period, it was common for these new converts, "catechumens" as they were called, to receive anywhere from eighteen months to three years of doctrinal training. During this period, the baptismal candidates had their lives scrutinized, they memorized the creed and the Lord's Prayer, and, following participation in the rites of initiation (baptism and Eucharist), they received further instruction on the character of the Christian life and the mysteries of the church. Catechisms—training manuals whose contents were organized variously around the creeds, the sacraments, the Ten Commandments, the seven deadly sins, and the classic Christian virtues—were developed in the late Middle Ages as pedagogical tools for the moral and spiritual development of new Christians.

My own use of the term *catechesis* both departs from and draws on the traditions of early and medieval Christian practice. It departs from the earlier traditions in that I want to broaden the understanding of the term to include more than the oral and written instruction given to new Christians. Following Pope John Paul II's description in *Catechesi Tradendae*, catechesis is "the whole of the efforts within the Church to make disciples."[4] These efforts, as such a sweeping summation makes clear, are not limited to, nor even defined by, the earlier didactic methods of memorization and recitation, question-and-answer tutorials, and so on (though such pedagogical practices are not unimportant). Catechesis, more broadly conceived, cannot be separated from the church's liturgical, pastoral, and missionary activity as a whole—from the material, embodied witness of Christian communities actively engaged in ministry in the world. And so catechesis in this book is understood to be much more than verbal instruction in church doctrine and dogma.

But I will also draw on and aspire to the earlier traditions of Christian catechesis in that I hope to demonstrate the importance of intentional, sustained, communally centered, liturgically driven efforts at forming Christian disciples. Just as the earliest Christians insisted that the training of a Christian was an ongoing process of conversion, accomplished only within the worshiping community and dependent upon the cultivation of certain habits, skills, and dispositions, I hope to show that contemporary catechesis is best understood as a journey of transformation—a journey in which the destination and the means of arrival are one and the same: the praise and adoration of God. Like Augustine, we learn that the self is disclosed only in and through the doxological. Thus catechesis does not begin with "the individual," for there is no "self" prior to its doxological performance (an idea that will be developed in more detail later); nor does it begin with "method" or "technique," the application of which is meant to result in something called "education." It begins, rather, with worship.

But what does *that* mean? What does it mean to insist that both the origin and the ultimate aim of Christian catechesis is doxology? One implication of such a claim is that our conceptual framework for thinking about what it means *to know* is called into question. As heirs of modernity, we are accustomed to thinking that our coming to know something is a matter of acquiring information, absorbing data, and so on. Knowledge is thought of as a kind of repository of neutral facts, and the mastery of these facts is deemed the process and ultimate goal of coming to know. Efforts at Christian catechesis, at their worst, have perpetuated this model of efficient neutrality—assuming that our coming to know the truth of the Christian faith is an intellectual exercise in the mastery of ideas, independent of the social, linguistic, theological, and liturgical contexts that give such ideas their coherence and legitimacy. But if, on the most basic level, the knowledge that Christians aspire to is, as it was for Augustine, knowledge of God and knowledge of self, then such knowledge will not leave us unchanged. As long as our understanding of what it means to know and learn remains wedded to the modern fiction of the cool, clinically detached observer and to a view of the end of knowledge as the technical mastery of information, we fail to recognize that to learn, to know, is to be *transformed*—it is to implicate our selves, even our very bodies, in the actions and practices of our learning and coming to know. Corporate worship, then—the local, bodily gathering of the church in time and space—is where our lives as Christians are shaped, where we come to know who and whose we are. And so catechesis begins (and ends, we could say) with liturgy.

But more must be said at the outset about worship and liturgy. First, it is important to insist, as many writers have, that worship is not a tool for the catechizing of Christians. Worship is, first and foremost, *gift:* the gratuitous offering of ourselves, the sacrifice of praise rendered to God by God's people (and, paradoxically, made possible only *by* God). Worship, as Marva Dawn has noted, is a "royal 'waste' of time": it accomplishes nothing; it is not a means to any end except that of praising and adoring God.[5] This is in many ways a startling claim, for most of us live in a world (and a church) that measures human activity by its usefulness and practical worth. We sometimes, in fact, speak of worship in starkly utilitarian terms, thinking of it and describing it as an instrument for personal growth or evangelistic outreach or moral exhortation or the stirring of our souls. But its purpose is not any of these. Its only aim? *Soli Deo gloria:* to give glory to God alone.

This gift that we offer as our common worship is the liturgy of the church, the "work of the people" (from the Greek *laos* = people, *ergon* = work) gathered up into the presence of God by the power of the Holy Spirit. The term *liturgy,* as I will use it in the pages that follow, is not to be understood as simply any order of worship or any service that follows a regular, predictable pattern. Rather, by *liturgy* I mean the identifiable, recognizable continuation of the historic forms of Word and Table. This was not the worship of my childhood. Those of us whose heritage is the evangelical traditions of American Protestantism have often found ourselves situated, precariously at times, between the minimalist piety of American frontier religion and the relatively recent efforts at liturgical renewal within those evangelical traditions.

The liturgical renewal movement of the middle to late twentieth century helped many churches to recover the classical substance of early Christian worship, which placed the Eucharist at the center of the liturgy. This recovery has not been a mere return to earlier liturgical forms, as if the church could simply go back in time, as if liturgies themselves were not connected to time, place, language, culture, and history. Instead, the renewal of ancient traditions is rooted in the conviction that the early church understood well the centrality of the sacraments for authentic worship, for cultivating and shaping Christian identity, and the importance, even necessity, of the active participation of the people of God in corporate worship.

But of even more significance, the liturgy reminds us that we are liturgical beings, created for the purpose of praise and worship. What the liturgy does, through its movements and gestures, music and silence, texts, prayers, creeds, offertories, and responses, is to teach us a new language—or perhaps to call us back to our native tongue as those whose speech is directed toward our Creator, the Triune God, in whom we live and move and have our being. And yet it is after all a new language—foreign speech—for we live in a time (as all Christians have) in which we are named and claimed, created and shaped by other languages and systems of meaning (such as consumerism, capitalism, nationalism, individualism—each one, in varying ways, dependent on or constitutive of the others).

If doxology is the purpose of worship, insofar as we can say that worship has a purpose, it is in and through the doxological that the shaping and ongoing training of the Christian self occurs. Again, this is an unusual claim, for though we might not articulate it quite this way, many contemporary Christians regard the liturgy as a kind of enacted *symbolism:* rites, rituals, speech, and gestures in need of decoding or deciphering. That is, worship is understood as a medium for communicating or mediating particular truths or metaphors. For example, it is common in many Christian communities to say that the breaking of bread together in the eucharistic celebration *means* economic solidarity with the poor and suffering for those who partake of it. But such a view is a peculiarly modern reading of the liturgy and the function of the church's sacraments; it presupposes an unnecessary—and thoroughly rationalist—separation of act and meaning. For when worship itself has been turned into a set of acts *that mean something else,* which are independent of the identity and activity of the worshiper, it becomes difficult if not impossible to see that the performance of the liturgy involves not symbols to be interpreted but abilities to be acquired. Worship is the site at which we are trained in particular skills, physical and linguistic; the site at which even our very bodies are engaged and produced. So the breaking of bread together in the Eucharist does not *mean* that Christians are called to be in solidarity with the poor; the act itself *constitutes* a people so defined.

In *The Rule of St. Benedict,* a sixth-century primer for monastic living, doxology is understood perforce as a *mode of existence*—liturgy and life, worship and morality, are of a piece. Instructions for how to cultivate humility, embrace suffering,

and tend the sick are interspersed with directions for the appropriate number of psalms at Vigils and the proper decorum
for celebrating Lauds on Sunday.[6] All deeds are doxological,
performed in service to and in praise of God. For the Benedictines the "everyday" was, as Catherine Pickstock has observed of
the medieval church generally, a thoroughly *liturgical* category.[7]
Which is not to say that the disposition of the worshiper was (or
is) constant cheerfulness and unwavering certitude. We are not
liturgical creatures because we always *feel* like worshiping God.
The authenticity of our worship can never be measured by our
moods, as Christians who daily observe the liturgy of the hours
well know. (As a priest in one of Gail Godwin's novels remarks
when asked what he would do if he ever stopped believing: "make
a fist in my pocket and go on with the ritual").[8] Rather, to say
that we are liturgical beings is to recognize that what we *do* has
everything to do with who we *are*, that the liturgy itself is a kind
of script to be performed for the shaping of the self.

This appeal to the *Rule* and to other early Christian traditions should not be viewed (or dismissed) as conservative or
nostalgic. I am not advocating a mere return to the past (as if
that were even possible) but am suggesting that we proceed
with our examination of catechesis and worship with a fresh
awareness of how our language has shifted, how conceptual
categories have changed, and how it is that what we assume
worship and catechesis *do* has undergone monumental shifts
in our thinking and practice. Only by recognizing worship's
gradual (and problematic) transition from the formative to the
figurative can we hope to recover the doxological character of
Christian catechesis and Christian living—not as an exercise in
nostalgia or as an uncritical embrace of the past for its own sake,
but that we might learn what it means to be worshipers of God
whose entire lives are acts of praise, who speak, act, and live in
the world doxologically.

It is this sense of the catechetical force of worship and liturgy
that I wish to communicate in the pages that follow. In corporate
worship the lives of Christians are formed and transformed,
Christian identity is conferred and nurtured. Thus I will take
up questions like these: How is it that Christian worship offers
a kind of privileged contrast to the ubiquitous and deeply seductive myth of the unencumbered modern subject within the

capitalist-driven, consumer-oriented, media-saturated cultures of the West? How does worship form, shape, and catechize in countervailing ways? How does catechesis create a community of worshipers who *know differently*, who are constituted contrarily to the dominant ways of thinking, acting, and being in the world?

Before such questions can be answered and this vision of catechesis and worship set forth, it is necessary to look broadly and critically at the current discipline of religious education. Part 1 of the book—"The Problem with Religious Education"—undertakes an examination of the writings of Gabriel Moran, Thomas Groome, and Mary Boys, whose work is both highly regarded and classically representative of the field. I will begin by suggesting that the very term *religious education* is problematic and in need of careful scrutiny. To posit something called "religious education" is to betray an indebtedness to modernity's uncritical embrace of religion as a self-evident category of human experience. That is, the modern enterprise, undertaken by thinkers such as Descartes, Kant, Hume, and Locke, was founded on the notion that religion is a universally recognized phenomenon that transcends history, culture, and language and that is quite distinct from other (equally transcendent) realms of human experience and activity such as politics, art, law, and science. In contrast, following the work of Talal Asad, Immanuel Katangole, Stanley Fish, John Milbank, and others, I will maintain that the category of religion is not a natural, necessary, inevitable given but rather is the product of a unique confluence of ecclesiastical, philosophical, and cultural forces that merged in the making of the modern West. The power of such a confluence of forces is evident in that we in the church (and in the wider culture) rarely question the existence or legitimacy of the concept of religion, and thus the term *religious education* seems not only plausible but essential for defining what it is that teachers of religion do. However, once we see that modernity's construal of religion as transparent and universal is deeply suspect, it becomes possible to detect the flawed (though well-intentioned) premises at the heart of the religious education enterprise.

Part and parcel of that enterprise has been the positioning of Christian education as a subset of religious education and the assumption that in order to evaluate one's beliefs and practices (one of the cardinal tasks of religious education) it is necessary to step outside of them. Thus, the argument goes, in order to neutrally assess the claims and customs of Christianity (and to impart those claims and customs to the faithful) one must situate them within the broader context of religious claims and customs generally. I will criticize this notion that Christian education should be conceived of as simply one of the many varieties of religious education and will argue that it is not only undesirable but impossible to step outside of one's beliefs and practices in order to neutrally evaluate them. We have no standpoint from which to regard, observe, assess, or evaluate *anything* except that point where we stand.

Stemming from this idea that Christianity is one religion among many and that Christian education is a subset of religious education is the conviction that to be religious is to be concerned primarily about matters of justice, freedom, and equality. As we will see, it is a commonplace assumption in much of the writing of those in the fields of religious education and Christian education that Christianity is first and foremost about the cultivation and actualization of human freedom and the promotion of justice, equity, and social harmony. I will suggest that the deployment of such terms owes more to liberalism's construction of the "human" than to historic Christianity's doctrine of God, the nature of Christian community, or the church's witness of the gospel. Moreover, the call by many Christian educators for a more "public" theology and a more public religious education will be shown to be part of this same problematic alliance with the liberal orthodoxy of modern social orders.

Part 2, "Pedagogy without Apology," takes up the constructive task of attempting to formulate an account of Christian catechesis that does not make excuses for its necessarily parochial character. That is, the distinctive truth claims and specific practices of the Christian faith are not liabilities to be overcome in the "quest for transcendence," nor are they particular expressions of a more general, universally available phenomenon known as "religion." Rather, they are the heart and soul, the basic raw materials, of the educative enterprise itself. The *content* of catechesis is the story that Christians are called to live by and to embody in their common life: the ever-unfolding drama of God's redemptive purposes as revealed in the people Israel, through the life, death, and resurrection of Jesus of Nazareth, and in the ongoing mission and ministry of the church. The *task* of catechesis is to create the conditions in which this story can do its transformative work.

Moreover, Christians believe that the God revealed to us in Israel, Jesus, and the church is a community of persons—Father, Son, and Holy Spirit. To speak of the importance of the Trinity for Christian catechesis is to say something about the significance of the grammar of Christian discourse that regulates life together in the body of Christ. That God is triune is significant for catechesis (and for the church as a whole) not because such language gives us a grasp on the nature and being of God but because it reminds us that no such grasp is possible. As Nicholas Lash eloquently puts it:

> We *require* some such grammar for our pedagogy, because all the pressures—outside and within—both pressures applied by the structures and mind-sets of individualism and collectivism alike, and the pressures derived from fear and egotism, homelessness, ambition, and despair, incline us to opt for "irrelation": to treat persons as things, and to bind the mystery of God into the It-world by mistakenly identifying some feature of the world—some individual, some nation, some possession, some dream, some project, or some ideal—with divinity, with the "nature" of God. We require some "set of protocols against idolatry," against the manifold forms of the illusion that the nature of God lies within our grasp.[9]

Thus the Trinity matters for Christian catechesis because this way of speaking about God—as Father, Son, and Holy Spirit, each in eternal communion with the other—reminds us that the truth we teach, the mystery we communicate, can never be definitively possessed; it can only be witnessed to.

The use of the word *apology* in this section of the book is dual-edged. First, to speak of a "pedagogy without apology" is to insist that there is no "catechesis in general" that can be separated from the practices of the church at worship through time and space; catechesis is unavoidably particular and parochial, and not—as some have suggested—general and universal. Second, and conversely, the argument here is in fact quite apologetic, in the more formal sense of arguing in defense of a position or system. What I endeavor to do is argue for the necessity of the Trinity and worship of the triune God for conceiving of, writing about, teaching, and implementing Christian catechesis.

After surveying the current landscape of religious education in the work of three of its most prominent architects, I argue in the book's second half that catechesis must begin not with *experience* (à la Moran, Groome, and Boys) but with *practice*. While Christian catechesis is perhaps best thought of as an ecology of practices whose aim is the formation and ongoing nurture of Christian disciples, any and all such practices derive their intelligibility and legitimacy from the church's worship. And while catechesis assumes a variety of forms, from the intentionally didactic to the more experiential and praxis-oriented, the formative power of worship must be maintained as the center from which all other catechesis emerges. What we do and how we act in the liturgical assembly shape us in particular and powerful ways and are formative of identity and catechetical in the most basic sense. In and through the doxological, the shaping and training of the Christian self and community occurs.

Part 2 begins by examining the connections between knowledge, desire, and Christian formation, drawing on historical, philosophical, theoretical, and theological sources to undergird a set of assertions meant not only to foreshadow but also to fortify the remainder of the book's contents: a descriptive account of the formative and catechetical character of the elements of Christian worship—from Entrance, to Proclamation and Response, to Thanksgiving and Communion, through the Sending Forth. When we pay attention to the narrative progression of the basic Sunday pattern and its constitutive practices, the formative power of worship is revealed, and catechesis is located in its proper doxological setting. And in and through this close reading of Word and Table, it becomes evident that knowledge and truth—the aims of catechesis—are never finally achieved; rather, they are continually sought within communities whose desire is ordered toward participation in the very life of the Triune God.

Finally, let me say outright—as I have been suggesting all along—that this book is written out of the conviction that much of what constitutes the discipline of Christian education, both historically and at present, is lacking in serious, thoughtful engagement with the theological traditions of the church. An example of what I mean by this is found in Norma Cook Everist's 2002 book on Christian education, in which she maintains that "the goal of education is to facilitate learning experiences." Part of my task in this book is to show, first, why this statement and others like it have been favorably received by the general readership of Christian education texts, and second, why they should not be. In the preface of her book Everist tells the reader that her book "does not debate doctrine, nor does it engage in extensive biblical exegesis. It does not present a history of the church. If one begins and ends with biblical and theological content, the educational process is seen merely as the delivery system for doctrine."[10] Many who read, write, and work within the field of Christian education would consider Everist's statement not only apt but admirable. My aim is to demonstrate that it is neither. Despite the worthy attempt to enlarge the church's vision of teaching and learning (Everist's overall purpose), to assume as she does that one can and should bracket Christian education apart from doctrine, Scripture, history, and theology is to misconstrue the very nature and purpose of catechesis. In contrast to Everist, I will insist that "biblical and theological content" (which necessarily includes the church's worship and liturgy) *is* the beginning and ending of Christian education.

Few outside the discipline of Christian education/religious education will contest my assessment of the field's lack of theological weight; many on the inside will see it as an unfair criticism. Theology, after all, is another (though perhaps related) field of inquiry; educators, like theologians, have their own vocabulary, theories, rules, and agendas with which to ply their craft. But such a distinction is at the heart of my critique here, for I will maintain that Christian education (or catechesis) is bound up entirely with doxology—with the praise and adoration of the Triune God—and therefore cannot be separated from the worshiping life of Christian communities. Thus theology and ethics, worship and liturgy, prayer and sacraments, mission and witness are all implicated in the practices of Christian catechesis, and those who write within and speak for the discipline of Christian education must take account of this utter continuity. It is my position in this book that, for the most part, they have not.

In many ways Christian education is a discipline struggling for credibility. Its marginalization both intellectually and institutionally is the result of a complex history that cannot be rehearsed in its entirety here. Some within the field are oblivious to this marginalization; others, aware of it, struggle to know what to do about it. One of the reasons Christian education finds itself in a battle for respect and legitimacy is that much of its scholarship has been heedless of the historical presuppositions on which it was founded and by which it continues to exist. It has paid insufficient attention to the philosophical assumptions at the heart of its enterprise. As I will show, it has embraced without reservation (without awareness?) the orthodoxy of liberalism and has sanctioned and promoted the politics of modernity, rather than naming catechesis itself a kind of counterpolitics. What has gotten the field of Christian education into this kind of difficulty is also, paradoxically, what it has assumed to be the cure for its troubles: the appeal to a transcendent, self-evident category of human experience called religion, the naming of Christian education as a subset of religious education, and the insistence that one must step outside of one's beliefs and convictions in order to gain perspective on them.

Throughout this book, and especially in my critique of Moran, Groome, and Boys, I hope it is evident that while I am sharply critical, I am not scornful; my intent is not to be inflammatory (or unkind) but to read the discipline of religious education through a hermeneutic that combines the freshest insights of contemporary theology and philosophy with the practical wisdom of the early church. My modest hope is that this project will help initiate conversation within a discipline struggling for legitimacy and respectability, a discipline whose intellectual complacency and lack of critical awareness have not only led to its marginalization in the academy but also left it bankrupt of the necessary resources to carry out the urgent task of forming and transforming the lives of Christian women and men, children and youth, in the complex times in which we live. Moran, Groome, and Boys, despite the contributions they have made to the practice of Christian education—and I do not deny that their efforts have been considerable and their influence, in many ways, a positive force—continue to perpetuate a pedagogy undergirded by assumptions and premises now widely discredited. The liberalism at the heart of each of their projects is fundamentally at odds with an account of Christian catechesis that takes as its *telos* not the "facilitating of learning experiences" but the very reordering of human desire, the shaping of the self into the image of the crucified and risen Christ, and the formation of worshipers of the Triune God. A doxological catechesis cannot be fashioned from a vision of Christian education that takes as its starting point the necessity of understanding religion (Moran), the primacy of human freedom (Groome), or the cultivation of responsible citizenship (Boys).

I realize that this is a harsh indictment of the field of Christian/religious education, both as a scholarly discipline and as a ministry of the church; I am keenly aware that my efforts are likely to be (at best) dismissed or (at worst) disdained by many who work, write, and teach in the field. But I am also convinced that these issues need to be raised and addressed because of the current state of affairs in North Atlantic Christendom: the market-driven character of much of our worship; the dumbing down of the church's historic liturgy; the thoughtless capitulation by Christians to consumer capitalism; the extolling of managerial models of ecclesial leadership; the view of the church as the promoter of "family values" and defender of the principles of love, justice, and freedom; the facile identification of Christianity and nationalism; the failure to train the imaginations of the young; the devolving of rigorous Christian discourse into pious sentimentality; and the growing trend across Christian traditions toward a vacuous, generic, benign pop spirituality. These troubling patterns reveal that at the heart of our ecclesial crisis is a momentous failure of catechesis.

Because the argument put forth here assumes a bridging (or blurring) of disciplines habitually conceived of as separate and distinct, I envision a broad-based readership composed of educators, theologians, preachers, teachers, and liturgists. Certainly professional Christian/religious educators will be interested in, if not entirely sympathetic to, my treatment of the work of Moran, Groome, and Boys in part 1. Persons presently engaged in leading worship and in teaching about worship may be especially drawn to part 2's emphasis on liturgy and formation. But the two parts that make up the whole are mutually dependent, and neither can be read profitably without the other. Thus readers interested primarily in liturgy and catechesis will need to attend to my critique of academic religious education in order to fully situate the constructive proposals regarding worship and formation. Similarly, professional/academic educators concerned with my critique of the discipline will not appreciate the full force of my analysis (and its implications for educative practice) without following through to the treatment of liturgy and catechesis.

Moreover, because I advocate the term *catechesis* in place of *Christian education*, at various points throughout the book I use the term *catechist*. Such a locution can refer formally to a professional staff person charged with overseeing teaching and training in a congregational setting. But I want to challenge the common assumption—indeed this book is predicated on such a challenge—that only educators do the educating. So *catechist* is deployed throughout the text more broadly and generally, in recognition that all those engaged in leadership in the worshiping body (preacher, presider, liturgist, musician, etc.), by virtue of their distinctive gifts and tasks, catechize those under their influence. That is, they form and shape not only the worship itself but the worshiping body that participates in the liturgy.

What I hope to put forth in these pages is a vision of Christian formation that takes as its starting point the trinitarian character of the Christian life and the centrality of worship for forming and reforming Christians in the life pilgrimage from baptism to death. As such, this vision necessarily involves the recovery of a vocabulary (and an accompanying set of practices) currently absent from the writings of prominent Christian educators: the language of *holiness* and *witness, discipleship* and *doxology, gift* and *grace.*

A word of clarification about my use of the term *theological* is in order. It is arguable, of course, that the writings of Moran, Groome, Boys, and others under scrutiny here are all theological in that they presuppose a certain vision of God, humanity, church, the moral good, and so on. It is also true that Christian education as an academic discipline is indebted to particular theological positions and orientations, for example the neo-orthodoxy of James Smart and the evangelical Protestant theology of Robert Pazmiño. My point, however, is that the work of most Christian educators promotes, sometimes knowingly and sometimes unknowingly, a classic modern theism that betrays historic Christianity's particular (and peculiar) assertion that in order to speak of God we must speak of a first-century crucified Jew who, as the risen Jesus, makes manifest to the world the nature and being of God as Trinity. In examining the work of Gabriel Moran, Thomas Groome, and Mary Boys, I will challenge this loss of theological language and the tendency toward the grammar of liberalism, toward a substitution of the politics of modernity for the politics of the cross.

THE PROBLEM WITH RELIGIOUS EDUCATION

1

UNDERSTANDING RELIGION

Religious Education as Quest for Transcendence

Religious education can be seen as the attempt to bring into one conversation, many religious languages.

Gabriel Moran

Introduction

Gabriel Moran has written widely in the field of religious education since the early 1960s. Exploring a broad range of subject matter—including developmental theory, philosophy of education, Jewish-Christian dialogue, death and dying, and curriculum and pedagogy—Moran has sought in recent years to formulate a "language of religious education" that he hopes will contribute to "tolerance, understanding, and peace in the world."[1] One of his primary concerns has been to promote religious education as a means of healing the wounds of prejudice, hatred, intolerance, and fanaticism that have given religion a bad name. To that end, he has attempted to prod the practitioners of various religious traditions to rethink their relationship with each other, to become more aware (and accepting) of their similarities and differences, and to recognize that a workable, successful religious education must be interinstitutional, intergenerational, interreligious, and international. In the book *Reshaping Religious Education,* coauthored by prominent Christian educator Maria Harris (who is Moran's spouse), Moran makes this observation:

> Throughout the centuries there have been Jewish education, Christian education, Muslim education, Buddhist education, to name several. None of these names necessarily involves references to any other religion than that of the learner and the teacher. Today the need remains for Christians to teach Christian practice and Jews to teach a Jewish way of life. The twentieth century, however, has also seen the beginning of another educational enterprise, one that overlaps and transforms Jewish, Christian, and other particular educations. A *religious* education does not simply add something to these educations nor is it their sum. Instead, religious education situates the work of the Jewish or Christian educator in the worldwide conversation of today. . . . For the first time one fully recognizes that Christianity is "a religion," utterly unique but comparable to every other religion.[2]

This passage is noteworthy because it captures so succinctly the supposition at the heart of the religious education enterprise as formulated by Moran and many others—that despite the various ways one might qualify the term *education* (e.g., "Christian" or "Buddhist"), there exists a larger entity, a kind of host repository into which all of these particular educations are neatly situated and sorted. Religious education is conceived of in almost spatial terms—as a *place* from which one can survey the particularities of, say, Muslim education or Jewish education, and yet remain unencumbered by those particularities for the sake of something grander and purer.

Moran almost never defines the terms *religious* and *religion;* he simply assumes that they circulate in the discursive space inhabited by enlightened, educated individuals. The closest Moran comes to a definition of religion is to say, circuitously, that he understands "religious education to be that part of education concerned with religious attitudes, ideas, and practices."[3]

Elsewhere he says that "religious education emerges with the first stirrings of comparisons between religious languages" and that "religious education can be seen as the attempt to bring into one conversation many religious languages."[4] According to this logic, to do *Christian* education is to identify Christianity's "uniqueness" as something to be admired, celebrated, and systematically imparted to the faithful but also, ultimately, as something to be transcended. It is never questioned that the historical particularities and material contingencies of Christianity *can* be transcended, because it is taken for granted that their significance lies in their function as symbols that point to, represent, or otherwise legitimize a universally human experience of "faith" or "transcendence" or "ultimate value."

For example, James Fowler, whose work has been widely influential among religious and Christian educators, has argued that there exists a universal human quest for transcendence, that persons everywhere in all times and places have a primordial longing for an experience of the divine. This desire is natural and innate, and the faith it produces, understood as trust in and loyalty to a transcendent center of value and power, is "generic, a universal feature of human living, recognizably similar everywhere despite the remarkable variety of forms and contents of religious practice and belief."[5] Various religions or religious traditions, then, are understood to be concerned about matters of faith in ways that make this universal phenomenon visible. As George Lindbeck puts it, speaking critically of positions like Moran's and Fowler's: "Religions are seen as multiple suppliers of different forms of a single commodity needed for transcendent self-expression and self-realization."[6] Lindbeck calls this the experiential-expressivist approach to religion, in which various religious traditions are understood to be differing manifestations or symbolizations of the same core experience (or desire for experience) of the Ultimate.

Moran follows this way of thinking when he says that a "religious" question is one concerned with "the nature of infinitude and the relation of human life to some unimaginable unity."[7] Like Fowler, he prefers to speak of faith as generic, primal, and everywhere the same. "The most important religious terms," he contends, should be used "in the singular without qualifying adjectives. The oneness of faith, revelation, grace, covenant, and the rest is complemented by a multiplicity of forms. . . . The term faith, without qualification, is a daily challenge to live faithfully."[8] Further, Moran's way of articulating the nature and purpose of religious education shares the view of religion as a conduit through which flows the universal desire for transcendence and of faith as an inherent property or capacity of all human beings. *Religious education* names the processes of socialization that transcend or sidestep the particular pedagogies of local and historic traditions. For Moran this means that religious education is concerned with cultivating across religious traditions and boundaries a sensibility informed by the hope, necessity even, of mutual respect, mutual learning, and mutual enrichment. This is accomplished by comparing and situating, by locating particular religious traditions within what he calls "the worldwide conversation of today."

In contrast, I contend that the idea that it is necessary to step outside of one's beliefs and convictions in order to get perspective on them (and thus identify them as "religious") *and* that Christian education is a subset of something called "religious education" is not only ecclesiologically undesirable but epistemologically incoherent. For Christian education to maintain any integrity as a practice of the church and to recover (or establish) its credibility as a discipline of the academy, it must embrace its embarrassing particularity.

As John Paul II has put it, "The definitive aim of catechesis is to put people not only in touch but in communion, in intimacy, with Jesus Christ: only he can lead us to the love of the Father in the Spirit and make us share in the life of the Holy Trinity."[9] From Moran's perspective, the pope's statement cannot help but sound quaint, anachronistic, and not a little triumphalistic. Indeed, to begin this project by favorably citing John Paul II is to risk losing the very audience I am trying to persuade. But as I hope to show, a position like John Paul II's is more generous and open to difference than those under scrutiny here precisely because it refuses to abstract religious traditions from the practices, doctrines, and forms of life that give them their coherence.

The Invention of Religion

Defenders of Moran's position might counter this opening argument with the claim that Moran himself does not advocate or urge such abstractions; he would be quick to acknowledge, one might suppose, that one is religious in specific and particular ways, not in general terms. But such a rebuttal would not go far enough; indeed this way of responding fails to recognize the suspect agenda attached to the very word *religious*. To promote something called "religious education," I am suggesting, is to refuse to acknowledge the very specific history of power and knowledge that produced religion as an ostensibly universal phenomenon, as an abstraction stripped of all distinctiveness and particularity. That we have come, in the last four hundred years or so, to regard religion as a self-evident category of human experience does not negate such history. What has been assumed to be inevitable, natural, and necessary (i.e., that there exists an isolatable phenomenon called religion and that it contributes either positively or negatively to something called the secular order or the larger public) is in fact the product of a unique post-Reformation history that has everything to do with the making of the modern West.

In his book *Genealogies of Religion: Discipline and Reasons of Power in Christianity and Islam,* Talal Asad makes subtle and skillful use of the important work of French social theorist Michel Foucault in order to dislodge long-held assumptions regarding the autonomy and essence of the signifier *religion.* Asad is an anthropologist, and his use of Foucault is insightful and fitting, for Foucault's work (on human sexuality, the clinic, the prison, and madness) delves not into the essences of things—things as they are in themselves—but into the ways our discourse (how we talk, write, and behave in social groups) *produces* the things we talk about, write about, and act on. Foucault in fact wrote very little about religion, since for him religion is but one of many sites at which humans create and ultimately contest knowledge, privilege, and power. A Foucauldian critique of religion recognizes that the attempt to hypostasize "religion" by thinking of it in isolation from social contexts, material conditions, and systems of meaning—that is, positing religion as something more fundamental than these things—is a futile task, a hopeless fiction. Foucault's "genealogical" approach to historical and social analysis "can account for the constitution of knowledges, discourses, domains of objects, etc., without having to make reference to a subject which is either transcendental in relation to the field of events or runs in its empty sameness through the course of history."[10] For the genealogist "there are no fixed essences, no underlying laws, no metaphysical finalities. Genealogy seeks out discontinuities where others find continuous development."[11]

For those committed to the idea that religion somehow transcends history, practices, material conditions, and so on, Foucault's insistence on the highly contested nature of all epistemological claims and all essentialized categories of human knowledge is troubling to say the least. And so Asad's observations, grounded as they are in Foucault's penetrating analysis of modern Western social orders, make particularly compelling reading in light of the assumptions of Moran and many others in the field of religious education.

Asad's genealogy of religion begins with a critical examination of anthropologist Clifford Geertz's celebrated definition of religion as a cultural symbolic system. According to Geertz, a religion is a "system of symbols which act to establish powerful, pervasive, and long-lasting moods and motivations in men."[12] Religious symbols (objects, rituals, texts, etc.) function "by inducing in the worshipper a certain distinctive set of dispositions (tendencies, capacities, propensities, skills, habits, liabilities, proneness) which lend a chronic character to the flow of his activity and the quality of his experience."[13] For Geertz, the anthropological study of religion is a two-stage operation. The first stage consists in analyzing the system of meanings encoded in the symbols that constitute a "religion proper." The second stage is the attempt to relate this system to "social and psychological processes."

Asad's point is that this is a false and arbitrary division that allows Geertz to think it possible (and desirable) to propose essentialized, cross-cultural definitions of religion, symbol, belief, and so on. According to Asad, "Religious symbols—whether one thinks of them in terms of communication or cognition, of guiding action or of expressing emotion—cannot be understood independently of their historical relations with nonreligious symbols or of their articulations in and of social life, in which work and power are always crucial."[14] The functioning of religious symbols in Geertz's scheme—dependent as his scheme is on this two-stage design—is strikingly independent of context, discourse, and practice. The material conditions in which religious symbols are actually able to produce religious dispositions are not acknowledged or addressed; such conditions, in fact, are not recognized to be, as they surely are, *constitutive of* these so-called dispositions. In other words, there is a failure to see that moods, motivations, and dispositions cannot be established or induced independently of the forms of life in which they exist. As Asad asks:

> Can we, for example, predict the "distinctive" set of dispositions for a Christian worshiper in modern, industrial society? Alternatively, can we say of someone with a "distinctive" set of dispositions that he is or is not a Christian? The answer to both questions must surely be no. The reason, of course, is that it is not simply worship but social, political, and economic institutions in general within which individual biographies are lived out, that lend a stable character to the flow of a Christian's activity and the quality of her experience.[15]

Geertz's formula is too simplistic and reductive to account for the complex ways religion produces its effects. So Asad is, in effect, asking Foucault's famous question: how is it that (religious) power creates (religious) truth? To answer this question Asad looks not to the famed postmodern theorists of the academic elite but back in time to the early church's most influential theologian, St. Augustine, who "was quite clear that power, the effect of an entire network of motivated practices, assumes a religious form because of the end to which it is directed, for human events are the instruments of God. It was not the mind that moved spontaneously to religious truth, but power that created the conditions for experiencing that truth."[16] For Augustine, then, it was not mere symbols that generated dispositions in the Christian believer but power—"ranging all the way from laws (imperial and ecclesiastical) and other sanctions (hellfire, death, salvation, good repute, peace) to the disciplinary activities of social institutions (family, school, city, church) and of human bodies (fasting, prayer, obedience, penance)."[17]

Geertz's preoccupation with symbol, along with his positing of a symbolic system separate from practices, leads him to distinguish between "religious" and "secular" dispositions, and thus the essentializing of religion as a transhistorical, transcultural phenomenon is assumed to be inevitable. Moreover, Geertz's definition of religion turns out, interestingly enough, to be conspicuously *Protestant:* the stress on symbols, dispositions, moods, motivations, and so on implies a believing *individual* as the prime locus of religion and fails to pay sufficient attention to disciplinary practices and systems of institutional authority that are of prime importance in many non-Protestant traditions.

Asad then works backward to undertake a genealogical survey of Geertz's understanding of religion and to explain how such an understanding has found widespread acceptance in the culture, church, and academy of modern Western societies. He notes that it was the fragmenting of the unity and authority of the Roman Church and the religious wars of the seventeenth century that made possible systematic attempts at creating a universal definition of religion. The substance of these attempts came out of the advancement of something called Natural Religion—born from the shift in attention from God's words to God's works and a phenomenon believed to exist in all cultures. Nature became the real space of divine writing. As Norman Sykes has observed:

> For a time . . . the Word of God assumed a secondary position to his works as set forth in the created universe. For whereas the testimony of the latter was universal and ubiquitous, the evidence of Revelation was confined to sacred books written in dead languages, whose interpretation was not agreed [upon] even amongst professed Christians, and which related moreover to distant events which had occurred in remote times and in places far removed from the centres of learning and civilization.[18]

Part and parcel of the invention of natural religion was an emphasis on *personal belief;* it was now possible to conceive of religion as a set of propositions to be believed in, which could subsequently be compared to the beliefs of other religions and to the findings of natural science (also an invention of post-

Reformation western Europe). Perhaps no one defended this understanding of religion and religious belief more confidently than Immanuel Kant:

> There may certainly be different historical *confessions,* although these have nothing to do with religion itself but only with changes in the means used to further religion, and are thus the province of historical research. And there may be just as many religious *books* (the Zend-Avesta, the Vedas, the Koran, etc.). But there can only be *one religion* which is valid for all men and at all times. Thus the different confessions can scarcely be more than the vehicles of religion; these are fortuitous, and may vary with differences in time or place.[19]

Once such a view took hold, "the classification of historical confessions into lower and higher religions became an increasingly popular option for philosophers, theologians, missionaries, and anthropologists of the nineteenth and twentieth centuries."[20] That is to say, various religious traditions could be categorized (by members of the modern, enlightened "religious" establishment) through a kind of schematic taxonomy in which the privileging of certain "religious" forms and conventions and the disparaging of others was thought to be an exercise in objective science. Asad's compelling point, then, is that what has been taken by many to be self-evident—that religion is essentially a matter of mood-inducing symbols, that it has characteristics and purposes that are universal, and that it is distinct from any of its particular historical or cultural forms—is in fact a view that has a specifically *Christian* history. The result: "this effort of defining religion converges with the liberal demand in our time that it be kept quite separate from politics, law, and science—spaces in which varieties of power and reason articulate our distinctively modern life. This definition is at once part of a strategy (for secular liberals) of the confinement, and (for liberal Christians) of the defense of religion."[21] Yet there simply cannot be a universal definition of religion, not only because the elements that would constitute it are historically and culturally specific but because the definition itself would be a product of discursive processes.

The last point to be made from Asad's critique, before returning to the discussion of Moran's work, is that theorists who claim
universal applicability for their definitions of religion, faith,
belief, and the like are ignoring the historical, social, political,
and gendered specificity of these definitions. Put another way,
these theorists (be they educators, philosophers, theologians,
or others) presume to occupy a neutral Archimedean point,
a place from which they are able to see things "as they really
are." It is not necessarily, and usually not ever, an arrogant kind
of presumptiveness; most theorists, including Moran, are not
themselves willfully claiming an exclusive, privileged access to
reality. It is, rather, that because their scholarly endeavors derive
from the modern quest for the universal, they assume (however
unintentionally) modernity's own epistemological superiority.
They are, in effect, denying the value-laden, power-infused
character of all our seeing and knowing.

Getting Outside of Ourselves: The Fallacy of Perspective

Moran states that there are two aims of religious education:
"(1) to teach people to practice a religious way of life and (2)
to teach people to understand religion."[22] That these two objectives strike most readers of Harris and Moran's book as entirely
reasonable (what else would religious education be about, after
all?) makes articulating a critique of them all the more difficult.
That is, if we inhabit a world where "the religious" is taken to
be a self-evident category of human experience *and* the starting place for Christian education/catechesis, then it becomes
enormously challenging to question such claims while remaining intelligible to those whose categories and terms are being
disputed. Moran's and others' conceptions of religious education,
Christian education, faith, God, the church, and so forth are
built on the philosophical foundations of modernity—and a concomitant domesticated and democratized Christianity—which
a trinitarian, worship-centered theology of Christian catechesis
seeks to call into question.
    Let me explain. The account of Christian education I am
proposing assumes that "at the heart of catechesis we find, in
essence, a person, the person of Jesus of Nazareth, 'the only Son

from the Father . . . full of grace and truth.'"[23] This is the beginning and end of catechesis, and all efforts at making disciples
worthy of the name Christian—varied though such efforts may
be—turn on this simple yet profound truth. Moran proposes
that while it is good to train children, men, and women in the
practices of a particular faith tradition, it is equally important
to "compare" one's particular faith tradition to another one
and, even more significant, to "situate" one's tradition within
the broader context of religion *qua* religion. What I hope I have
already shown is that this is a feat that simply cannot be pulled
off. Moran thinks he is able to do this because he assumes that
it is possible to step outside of one's beliefs and convictions in
order to neutrally evaluate them. But it is not possible to evaluate one's beliefs, practices, and convictions in a nonprejudicial
way—this is the lie of modernity. If we are already situated, as
Moran rightly notes, then there is no "outside" from which to
make judgments or offer comparisons. Literary theorist and
critic Stanley Fish helps illumine this point when he says that

> critical self-consciousness . . . is the idea that you can in some
> way step back from, rise above, get to the side of your beliefs and
> convictions so that they will have less of a hold on you than they
> would had you not performed this distancing action, thereby
> enabling you to survey the field of possibilities relatively unen-
> cumbered by the beliefs and convictions whose hold has been
> relaxed. This seems to me to be *zany* because it simply assumes
> but never explains an ability to perform that distancing act, never
> pausing to identify that ability and to link the possession of that
> ability with the thesis that usually begins discussions that lead
> to this point—the thesis of the general historicity of all human
> efforts.[24]

It is a bind that Moran cannot escape: conceding (rightly) the
embodied, situated character of all theological discourse *along
with* insisting that such discourse be reflexive of its embodiment,
neutrally observant of its situatedness. Fish also helps us to see
the irony implicit in efforts like Moran's: in trying to assuage
any one religion's claims to universal truth (i.e., the perceived
tendency toward hegemony and a totalizing stance that would
silence or dismiss other truth claims), his own totalizing tendencies are revealed. That is, the very desire to engage in dialogue,

promote plurality, mitigate difference, and situate particular pedagogies within the wider realm of religious education betrays Moran's indebtedness to the imperialism constitutive of the modern project.

John Milbank, in an essay on dialogue between religious traditions, notes that "the terms of discourse which provide both the favored categories for encounter with other religions—*dialogue, pluralism,* and the like—together with the criteria for the acceptable limits of the pluralist embrace—social justice, liberation, and so forth—are themselves embedded in a wider Western discourse become globally dominant."[25] The very way that Moran conceives of and articulates the matter at hand—that the various kinds of religious education are but a part of a larger human project centered on transcendence or fulfillment or justice or equality or well-being—presupposes the highly specific rhetoric that undergirds liberal social orders, which, despite protestations to the contrary, is anything but neutral. When Moran says that "religious education has to do with the religious life of the human race and with bringing people within the influence of that life,"[26] not only does he proffer the muddiest of mission statements for the task of religious education, he continues to trade on a set of categories and assumptions that are laden with the imperialist rhetoric of liberalism.

Under the heading "Teaching to Understand Religion," Moran contends that "somewhere in each religion is the admission that, because religion is only relative, God may have other ways of salvation that are not evident to us. This admission is formulated from within the belief in the supreme importance of each respective religion. . . . No religion can proclaim itself as absolute; it is relative compared to God."[27] This is an extraordinary claim—alarming, even—but I suspect that most readers of Moran's book would not see it as such, so schooled have we all been in the modern myth that various religions are but differing (and ultimately nonconflictual) paths to a universal experience of the god who stands above all particularity and contingency. But in fact, in attempting to argue that the rival truth claims of particular religious traditions need not be seen as a problem (we all *can* just get along), Moran arrogantly assumes to speak for the world's religions in a way that can only be deemed totalizing, reductionist, and paternalistic. His arrogance is unintentional, of course, but it is only because the category of "religion" has been invented and sacralized that it becomes possible (and acceptable) to display such blithe confidence in one's ability to neutrally assess the religions of the world and make stunning theological pronouncements about and for them. Only when it has already been decided that what is really of "supreme importance" is not the content of any one religion's practices and convictions but a commitment to a vaguely defined, humanist religiosity can contempt for difference be masked as religious tolerance.

But even more important, Moran's project of attempting to transcend religion for the sake of (an empty) unity becomes itself a kind of religion. Lesslie Newbigin speaks directly to this impulse when he says that

> it is understandable that anyone faced with the clashing diversity of religious commitments should seek some basis for unity among them, or at least some agreed common framework. The difficulty is that we are dealing here with *ultimate* commitments, and the basis that I accept can only be *my* commitment. . . . It is very understandable that we should look for some point of view which would enable us to bring together these clashing commitments in a single framework. It is understandable, but we have to face the fact that it is impossible. The framework that I devise or discern is my ultimate commitment or else it cannot function in the way intended. As such a commitment, it must defend its claim to truth over against other claims to truth. I have no standpoint except that point where I stand. The claim that I have is simply the claim that mine is the standpoint from which it is possible to discern the truth that relativizes all truth. That claim is the expression of the ultimate commitment that is my real religion.[28]

Thus attempts, like Moran's, to broker agreement and cultivate unity from a place where one purports to see and understand unencumbered by religious convictions of any sort are already faith commitments of the deepest kind.

And despite the desire to "understand religion" (one of Moran's stated aims of religious education), there is no real encounter with the other, no substantive engagement with difference. Instead there is the presumption to speak *for* the other, which, good intentions notwithstanding, is the embodiment of the kind of Western arrogance that Moran finds so offensive. Fish's critique of liberalism is fitting for Moran's classically liberal project:

> Liberalism is a way not so much to avoid conflict (because liberalism is born out of the unhappy insight that conflict cannot be avoided) but to contain it, to manage it, and therefore to find some form of human association in which difference can be accommodated and persons can be allowed the practice and even cultivation of their points of view, but in which the machinery of the state will not prefer one point of view to another but will in fact produce structures that will ensure that contending points of view can coexist in the same space without coming to a final conflict.[29]

I suggest that Moran believes that something called "religious education" is meant to function as this kind of neutral "structure" that will mediate conflict between various religious pedagogies. The difficulty with such a view is that it wrongly assumes such neutrality is possible. To the contrary, "*any* structure put in place is *necessarily* one that favors some agendas, usually by acts of recognition or nonrecognition, at the expense of others."[30]

Splitting the Difference: Jews and Christians in Dialogue

In a book on Jewish-Christian relations, Moran argues that while Judaism and Christianity are distinctive religious traditions (the book's title is *Uniqueness*), thoughtful, ecumenically minded practitioners of each of these religions need to surrender some of their particular faith claims or redefine some of their cherished doctrines in order for genuine communication and mutual enhancement to take place. "The language of 'Christian faith' and 'Jewish faith' simply freezes conversation at the level of polite exchange and political toleration. Worse, Christian life and Jewish life are reified by these terms."[31]

Moran is concerned about ensuring that Christianity and Judaism "make sense" to "contemporary people"—not least to Christians and Jews themselves. For instance, the theological term *revelation* in both the Christian and Jewish lexicons needs to be defined and communicated in such a way that, first of all, it does not offend and, second, it does not contradict what reasonable, educated people already believe about the world, nature, science, and history. "The Christian or Jew who has been educated according to the criteria of modern historiography, critical inquiry, and methods of science cannot cavalierly announce that the modern world is simply wrong. . . . Revelation is the present, personal, and more than personal experience of all peoples."[32]

What I want to suggest, and will develop more fully later in response to the writings of Thomas Groome and Mary Boys, is that Christians (and Jews) live by stories that do in fact announce that the modern world is wrong. I am not talking about a fundamentalist resistance to or denial of the discoveries of science; I am saying that it simply is not possible to think of the Christian narrative or the Jewish narrative as only one point of view, a "unique" perspective on a world that exists in a different, "modern" way. As Milbank puts it: "There is no independently available 'real world' against which we must test our Christian [or Jewish] convictions, because these convictions are the most final, and at the same time the most basic, *seeing* of what the world is."[33]

To put it as simply as possible: Moran's basic assumption seems to be that there exists an open, neutral space where people can meet when they're not being religious. To think, as Moran does, that revelation in Jewish or Christian terms can be emptied of its content for the sake of something that all humans "experience" is to treat the words of Christian and Jewish doctrine as if they could be grasped and evaluated independently of how they are actually embodied, interpreted, performed, and given life in Christian and Jewish communities.

Two other examples. First, Moran suggests that for the sake of better Jewish-Christian relations, Christians need to distinguish between "Jesus" and "Christ." When Christians attempt to engage in fruitful conversation with Jews, "the casual interchanging of Jesus, Christ, and Jesus Christ is a severe obstacle."[34] The historical person of Jesus, the Jew from Nazareth, can function, it would seem, as a foot in the door for opening up dialogue between Jews and Christians; the designation *Christ,* as traditionally understood and confessed by most Christians, erects barriers of division that thwart the ecumenical enterprise. Moran is right to insist that "Jesus was uniquely rooted in the Palestinian Judaism of his time."[35] But what he fails to do is draw out the theological (and social, political, economic, and liturgical) implications of this often-overlooked claim; he makes no connection, for example, between the shape of Jesus' life as a first-century Palestinian Jew and the circumstances of his death at the hands of the Roman imperial authorities. That Jesus was Jewish is supposed to be enough to engage our Jewish friends, but to call Jesus the Christ "can lead to the most narrow-minded intolerance toward everyone who will not accept Jesus Christ."[36]

Using the term *Christ* can be acceptable as long as we mean by it that Christ is "the axis of the world, the relational reality that guarantees equal opportunity for all human beings, who are themselves representatives of nonhuman creation."[37] Such a statement might be a basic tenet of the kind of benign humanism Moran appears to champion, but as I will soon argue, it does nothing to further honest and respectful conversation between committed Christians and Jews. For Christians the life, death, and resurrection of Jesus Christ render their meaning *only* in particularity and contingency. The cross of Christ therefore can never be separate from a narration of Jesus' identity (or the identity of Christians, for that matter).

Moran reproduces modernity's severing of Christ from Jesus because such a separation is encoded in the logic of the modern anthropology of religion (remember Kant and Locke). Thus Moran's objections to the designation "Jesus Christ" are in effect soteriological ones: Jesus the Jew is admired for his radical politics and progressive social agenda, but Moran cannot bring himself to affirm the *salvific* power of Jesus' cross and resurrection. That is, Jesus, who points us to the cosmic, universal "Christ event," is able to act symbolically and metaphorically in human affairs, but not concretely and materially. On this view, Christian identity cannot be bound up with the identity of Jesus Christ but must be rooted in a general anthropology for which Jesus is the primary (but not necessarily the only) exemplar. Otherwise, Moran is convinced, Christians cannot speak productively and respectfully to Jews.

Second, and related, the word *resurrection* is drained of all coherent meaning when Moran states, "Whatever physical and psychological facts were the case in the experience of Jesus' disciples (an issue that the original documents can never resolve), the term resurrection indicates a breakthrough to unique personhood. . . . Resurrection is about living and dying and living, about doing your work the best you can and loving those around you."[38] This and the above pronouncements are breathtaking in their ignorance (or willful disregard) of basic Christian doctrine, their swaggering certitude, and their New-Agey hollowness. I do not say this to belittle Moran or his objectives; his desire to enhance understanding and communication between Christians and Jews is honorable. But what he fails to realize is that the quasitheological declarations he cavalierly puts forth in the admirable cause of interreligious dialogue are potentially *more* offensive to Jews (and to Christians), not less.

Conversations between religious traditions are of course possible, and identifying the commonalities and differences between Christianity and Judaism can be instructive and profitable, and indeed is necessary. But this is not because these traditions can be transcended and objectively assessed from some impartial, neutrally available reality. Rather, all justification, all argument, all evaluation necessarily occurs *within* a given tradition's own set of convictions, narratives, doctrines, and practices. In the case of Christianity and Judaism, such conversations often involve the painful working through of significant disagreements and misunderstandings. Nothing is gained by suggesting, as Moran does, that for the sake of conciliatory conversation each tradition's language must be depleted of its power and meaning, so that it becomes possible to say, for example, that "resurrection can only make sense to those who value and enjoy life."[39]

In contrast to Moran's approach, it is only by paying close attention to practices and narratives and to a community's use of language—the way it worships, the kind of world it speaks and sings and prays into being—that understanding between normative traditions can take place at all. It seems counterintuitive to suggest that the more one holds to one's own tradition's narratives, convictions, and practices, the better able one will be to engage the narratives, convictions, and practices of another. Such a stance seems unduly parochial, even supercilious, and thus objections like Moran's appear reasonable and understandable. But in fact, it is only when Christianity insists on the primacy of its speech that it can be genuinely, generously, and compassionately open to the other. As Rowan Williams puts it:

> Other stories and other confessions enrich the Christian's commitment: a prolonged sharing with a Jew, a Marxist, or a Buddhist will uncover facets of the human world which conventional Christian speech seems unaware of. The challenge then becomes . . . to manifest that such insights are essentially "at home" with the vision of Christ as the universal *logos*. If he can be found at the heart of another truthful, visionary and compassionate human project, the Easter gospel can indeed be seen to be catholic. . . . Where there is salvation, its name is Jesus; its grammar is the cross and resurrection.[40]

This is not, as Moran might fear, an arrogant insistence on Christianity's moral superiority, but is fundamentally a claim about *language*, about how the way we talk to another can be only *in* the language we speak. And yet it does assert a certain kind of linguistic preeminence: "Christian believers make the bold claim that no other language than that which speaks of the crucified and his resurrection can speak comprehensively of what it is to be 'saved,' to be whole as a human being before God."[41] It is a claim about the uniqueness of the Christian vision, the ecclesial project itself, and the conviction that "the Christian faith is not a world-view, a system of intellectual propositions whose mere acceptance thereby differentiates Christian from non-Christian."[42]

In regard to dialogue between Christians and Jews, it is only when Christians maintain their distinctiveness as worshipers of Christ, and Jews as followers of Torah (in all the rich particularity entailed by each of these confessional stances) that fruitful conversation will be possible. In other words, we should not empty theological terms like *revelation* and *resurrection* of their content or deny their historical and contemporary import. Rather, elucidating the fullness and complexity of their meaning within the context of a community's life and worship is the only hope for honest exchange.

This of course involves enormous risk: the risk of misunderstanding or misinterpreting, of falling back lazily onto hurtful stereotypes, of giving up when it gets too hard. But there are Jews and Christians who are committed to the difficult task of speaking frankly and respectfully and who recognize that the peculiar speech of Christians and of Jews must be maintained in all its oddness—not softened, weakened, or compromised so as not to slight or offend. Jewish philosopher Peter Ochs, whose efforts at engaging Jewish and Christian thinkers across a spectrum of philosophical and theological disciplines have been met with eagerness and appreciation, speaks convincingly and candidly about what is at stake when Jews wrestle seriously with particular truth claims of the Christian tradition:

> The Christian doctrines of the Incarnation and the Trinity present two main challenges to traditional Jewish study. One challenge is that the narrative of God's incarnation in one Jew belongs to a history that Jews do not share and cannot accept as part of their story. In this case, the Christian doctrine of the Incarnation appears comprehensible but simply wrong: the event did not occur. A second challenge is that the doctrine of God's having three identities appears incomprehensible: the Jewish biblical record does not speak of God in a way that allows us to characterize His nature as a relation among Father, Son, and Holy Spirit. From this perspective, Trinitarian doctrine, like the Kabbalah, appears incomprehensible and alien even before it appears wrong. The traditional Jewish response is therefore to walk away from any discussion of such things. For this third epoch of Judaism, however, Jews are called to do more than throw up our hands in the face of Christian doctrines; we must, instead, find a way to reason Jewishly about them.[43]

Ochs's recommendation, clearly, is not that Christians forsake their particular ways of talking about God and Jesus (or Jews theirs) in order for there to be dialogue and understanding. Nor does he suggest that Christians and Jews should retreat to a nebulous realm of generic, hollow "religious-speak" so as not to insult or demean one another. Rather, he says that "to render Christian beliefs about God comprehensible in Jewish terms, Jews need only identify these elemental beliefs and observe how Christian tradition retains and also reinterprets and extends them."[44]

From a Christian perspective, it is crucial to keep in mind that one of the great challenges for the church is to remember that the history of the Jews is essential to our own story as Christians. As Stanley Hauerwas has said: "Such remembering cannot be based on feeling guilty about the Holocaust, since guilt soon fades or becomes a substitute for honest appraisal. Rather, we must learn to remember with the Jews a history that certainly includes the Holocaust because we are learning that the Jews are our partners in discerning God's way in the world."[45]

Perspectives like those of Ochs and Hauerwas make it clear that it is only in the *performance* of Jewish or Christian "beliefs"—in how such convictions are brought to life in a community's ongoing telling of its story—that they can be evaluated by insiders and outsiders alike. Moran's position, wedded as it is to liberalism's proposition that there exists a generally available category called "religion" into which Christianity and Judaism can be neatly sorted and cataloged, treats beliefs as if they could be comprehended and interpreted independently of such performance and embodiment.

Summary

I have tried to problematize the term *religious education*, arguing against its use as a general category under which "Christian education" can be classified as an individual variety (as, by analogy, *species* is related to *genus*). I have maintained that "religious education" is a concept born of the particular history of knowledge and power that is a crucial component of the making of modernity. I have argued that Moran's basic premise—that "religious education can be seen as the attempt to bring into one conversation many religious languages"[46]—is fundamentally flawed in that it assumes it possible to neutrally assess the various religions of the world, while at the same time it bankrupts the theological vocabularies of these same religious traditions.

Thus to promote "religious education" in general, universal terms is to participate (however unwittingly) in the modern project of dissolving difference, of attempting to identify a common set of general, "religious" principles on which all "reasonable" people can agree. This set of principles, articulated in various ways from the dawn of the Enlightenment until now, includes freedom and justice as its hallmarks. To these themes we now turn.

2

FREEDOM AND JUSTICE FOR ALL

Religious Education as Modern Project

I am thoroughly convinced that Christianity can be and should
be an empowerment to the quest for human freedom.

Thomas Groome

Introduction

In the previous chapter I suggested that the way religious
education has been constructed as a discourse and discipline
betrays its indebtedness to liberalism—the philosophical and
theological traditions of the seventeenth and eighteenth centuries that deified reason and rationality, and that, it should also
be noted, produced the liberal Protestant traditions of the nineteenth and twentieth centuries, typifed by the work of thinkers
such as Paul Tillich and Reinhold Niebuhr. Such developments
are really of a piece, forming a single story line (what Ugandan
priest-philosopher Emmanuel Katongole calls the "liberal prot-

estant metanarrative") that created the necessity for thinking of religion as a problem to be managed: "Only when Christianity has ceased to be a 'fleshy embodiment' of specific practices and processes and becomes a set of beliefs (a 'gnosis') separable from practices, does one seek a way to draw moral (practical) implications from these beliefs, thus creating the question of the relation between practices (ethics) and beliefs (religion)."[1] Out of such a metanarrative emerged the tendency to substitute the particularities of a given faith for the generalities of a vaguely defined, universally available, humanist-oriented religiosity. For instance, to claim that God is Father, Son, and Holy Spirit might be problematic, but to say that God is good (or just or loving or kind) is sufficiently vague as to be offensive to no one.

Freedom and justice were similar themes that could be marshaled in support of a system that took as its highest goods the cultivation of individual liberty and the pursuit of happiness. Indeed, these ideals were deemed necessary for mitigating the conflicting ways that such inalienable rights might be exercised. For our purposes, it is enough to note that the liberal Protestant tradition that produced religious education also championed justice and freedom, loosening these concepts from their theological moorings and offering them in service of the project of promoting a stable social order and a responsible citizenry.

Religious Education as Spiritual Endeavor

Such a move is evident in the work of Thomas H. Groome, who, like Moran, has written what are deemed to be seminal texts in the field of religious education. Groome is widely thought to be the premier theorist of religious education today and is also known for his activism on behalf of various reform movements within the Roman Catholic Church. His 1980 work *Christian Religious Education: Sharing Our Story and Vision* is considered by many a mainstay of the seminary training of Christian educators. In it he sets out to explore the nature, purpose, and context of Christian religious education and to gesture toward an educational approach that he calls "shared praxis." This pedagogic theory is at the forefront of a book that came a decade later, *Sharing Faith: A Comprehensive Approach to Religious Education and Pastoral Ministry—The Way of Shared Praxis,* a mammoth tome with, as the subtitles suggest, an equally ambitious agenda. "Shared praxis" refers to a teaching/learning arrangement centered on group dialogue and undergirded by a "praxis-based" epistemology, a "relational, reflective, and experiential way of knowing in which by critical reflection and lived experience people discover and name their own story and vision and, in a Christian education context, the Story and Vision of the Christian community."[2] One of Groome's more recent books, *Educating for Life,* was also hailed by critics as a breakthrough endeavor in the practice of Christian pedagogy and as the crowning achievement of his life's work.

As one might expect, none of Groome's texts has received any substantive criticism from within the ranks of the discipline, and each continues to be admired by new generations of Christian educators. Spanning more than twenty years of his academic career, Groome's writings do not give evidence of any significant shifts in his thinking, though *Educating for Life* is a deliberate attempt not only to make his core themes and arguments more accessible to the laity of the church but also to impart, as the subtitle puts it, *A Spiritual Vision for Every Teacher and Parent.*

After a career of writing for educators, pastors, catechists, and other church leaders, Groome concludes that the "foundations" of a Catholic philosophy of education turn out, surprisingly (or perhaps not so surprisingly), to translate nicely into a *"humanitas* anthropology" that can inform the educative practices of all teachers and parents, regardless of their "religious" convictions and affiliations (or lack of them). Such an anthropology presupposes particular "attitudes and commitments" on the part of the teacher: an affirmation of persons (approaching learners with a "deep-down sentiment of positive esteem"), an anticipation of persons (being able "to see great possibilities in people"), and a love for persons (recognizing that "to educate well invites love from the soul of teacher and parent").[3]

The tenets of Catholicism are loosened from their theological, ecclesial, and liturgical moorings so that they might help to promote this humanizing education and contribute to the nurture of all people as spiritual beings. For example, after briefly explaining the Catholic Church's teaching on sacraments, particularly sacramentality as a theological category and the hermeneutical lens through which church and world are envisioned, Groome claims that "apart from its warrant in Christian theology, such a worldview [sacramental cosmology] can ring true to a person's own experience or find support in many other systems of faith or thought."[4] That is, a humanizing education can help all persons to see life as a gift and the world "as essentially 'good' for us."[5] When discussing Catholicism's "outlook that human nature is essentially social," Groome makes a similar point: "Apart from any theological warrant, the social sciences share a similar conviction. They describe the process of taking on human identity as socialization."[6] For Groome, much of Christian doctrine can be seen to be in congruity with the best insights of sociology, psychology and philosophy, thus giving the church's teaching the kind of critical purchase that can raise its estimation in the eyes of outsiders and skeptics and can serve to promote a *"spiritual vision of education that is humanizing,* a curriculum that educates *for life for all."*[7]

My treatment of Groome's work here is not exhaustive by any means; my intent, as with my critique of Moran's work, is to lay bare what I take to be its faulty suppositions and, by extension, its flawed prescriptions for educative practices in the church today. What I attempt to do is to trace the origins of his thought and the substance of his proposals to an agenda that can be seen to be fundamentally at odds with the aims of a doxological, trinitarian catechesis.

While Groom, like Moran, uses the term *religious education,* he writes from a more explicitly Christian perspective than does Moran. Like Moran, though, he couches his terms and definitions in now familiar language—with added accents of Paul Tillich: "Religious education focuses specific attention on empowering people in their quest for a transcendent and ultimate ground of being."[8] Groome expressly avoids using the term *Christian education* because of its "pejorative connotations" and "oppressive overtones," particularly for those persons whose religious training has taken place in the Sunday school tradition of American Protestantism. He prefers the term *Christian religious education* (the title of his most influential book) when discussing the educative activities of Christian communities: "By putting the adjective *Christian* before *religious education*, we Christians remind ourselves that we do not own the enterprise but are only one expression of it. Given our history of imperialism in the West, that is an important reminder. Then, the term *religious education* after the word *Christian* reminds us that the quest for the transcendent is far broader than our own community and tradition."[9] Groome's characterization mirrors that of Moran in the taken-for-granted quality of the assertion that the term *religious education* names a general activity that all "religious" people can name and recognize, even while they engage in it in specific and particular ways.

Indeed, Groome makes much of the dichotomy of universal and particular, insisting that there is no religion-in-general but that "religion finds expression in specific historical manifestations."[10] He quotes Roman Catholic theologian Richard McBrien: "There is literally no such thing as religion as such. There are specific religions which participate, to one degree or another, in the general definition of religion."[11] However, as was noted with Moran's work, such statements do not overcome the division of universal and particular; what they do, in fact, is reproduce it.

Groome also makes mention of the term *catechesis*, noting the attempts by Bernard Marthaler and John Westerhoff to propose a meaning broad and expansive enough to include the whole course of initiation and socialization, the entire process of Christian becoming. But for Groome, catechesis must always be subsumed under the larger enterprise of general religious education:

> Even if catechesis could be so broadly redefined [as Marthaler and Westerhoff suggest], there is a great disadvantage in doing so. It fails to name and thus severs the Christian education enterprise from its commonality with education and religious education. If this happens, then from what discipline does one draw to empower the activity? How does one do catechesis, or train other people to do it, or build programs to effect it? If we use the term *catechesis* to name the total enterprise of sponsoring people toward Christian faith, then it is difficult to know where to begin or how to prepare oneself to be a catechist. The word *catechesis* is such a "Church word" that the tendency will be (and often is) to draw upon only the "sacred sciences," and especially theology and scripture studies. If the same enterprise is called *Christian religious education*, however, then the word *Christian* calls for the activity to be informed by theology and scripture and studies. But

the name also points to another very obvious source—the science
of education (and thus to the many other sciences which inform
education) to draw from to empower the activity.[12]

In the critique that follows, I hope to show why the questions
Groome asks here are ill-conceived ones that betray his indebtedness to liberalism's invention of religion and his uncritical
embrace of "education" and "religious education" as generic
entities of which "Christian education" is a particular expression. I will call into question his claim that for the efforts of
Christian formation to be "empowered" one must necessarily
draw on the academic discipline of education. Without denying
the usefulness of insights from other arenas of human inquiry,
I will maintain that the proper training ground for "doing catechesis," for "training other people to do it," and for "building
programs in it" is not the university department of education
but (to borrow a phrase from Phillip Pfatteicher) the "school of
the church": the liturgical assembly of Christians gathered in
praise and worship of the Triune God.

Christian Education and the Kingdom of God

Much of what shapes the substance of Groome's work has
already been observed in relation to Moran's efforts: theories of
cognitive and faith development explicated by Jean Piaget, James
Fowler, and others are prized for their relevance for understanding and carrying out the task of Christian religious education;
the idea of faith as a human universal is accepted without reservation; religion is defined as the primal human quest for the
transcendent; Christian education is understood as one facet
of the general enterprise that is religious education. Groome is,
however, deliberately more attentive to theology and biblical
themes than Moran in his descriptions of what the education of
Christians should look like. The rubric under which he sketches
his pedagogical program is the kingdom of God (in his more
recent writings called the "reign of God"), which he defines as
"a symbol that represents the active presence of God in power
over, in, and at the *end* of history."[13] Drawing on insights from the
Hebrew Scriptures, Groome describes the kingdom of God as a

reign of justice and peace, wholeness and completion, happiness and freedom, fullness and plenty, the end to human suffering; it is the embodiment and the complete realization of God's will for God's people (Ps. 146:10; Isa. 25:6–8). "For the Israelities the Kingdom of God is already a reality in that it is Yahweh who rules all things and people. And yet the final completion of the Kingdom is still to come."[14] Noting the centrality of the kingdom of God in the preaching and teaching of Jesus, Groome highlights Jesus' self-identification with God's kingdom, Jesus' radicalizing of the law of the kingdom as love without limits, and the New Testament's insistence that the kingdom of God is a gift that comes only through the grace of God.

Building on these biblical images and insights, Groome then forges a definition of the kingdom of God that assumes the necessity of "reinterpret[ing] the symbol and its meaning for our lives in light of contemporary experience and consciousness."[15] What this means is that the church "will have to harness its ministry and whole way of being in the world toward helping to create social/political/economic structures that are capable of promoting the values of the Kingdom."[16] This, according to Groome, is what it means for the church to be a *political* entity. Arguing against those who contend that the church must be apolitical, that its role is to stay above the fray of the temporal and political, Groome warns, "If the Church makes a concerted attempt not to participate in the political realities and, claiming to be above them, takes a position of silence, it has by that very silence taken a political stance."[17]

Groome's account of the kingdom of God and the church's "political role" in the wider culture owes much to his interpretation of liberation theology. He in fact grounds a good deal of his project in the liberationists' stress on the kingdom of God and the concomitant call to justice and freedom from oppression. Liberation theologians, says Groome, "insist that Christian theology must arise out of a context of active participation in society on behalf of the values of God's kingdom."[18] Without delving into the complexities and subtleties of various liberation theologies that might nuance Groome's observation, it can be said that Groome indeed does share in the general liberationist stance that, as Daniel Bell puts it, "embrace[s] the modern vision of politics as statecraft . . . [and] assume[s] that the state [is] the pinnacle of political life and the fulcrum of social change."[19] That is, Groome, like many who work and write within the liberationist framework, takes for granted that the term *political* refers to the action and apparatus of the state as the principal agent in ordering the social, economic, and political realities that affect and shape its citizenry. *Politics* is thought to name the mechanism by which social change is possible, and thus Groome's call for Christians to be political is a summons for the church to shake off its long-standing complacency and abandon its privileged indifference, that it might fully immerse itself in the political processes that will promote Christian "values" and usher in the kingdom of God.

Groome is right, of course, to insist that the church by virtue of its very existence is political, but he errs in claiming that the church's "political role" is to promote the "values" of God's kingdom in service to the larger *polis* (which for Groome is the real—and only—politics). In naming something called "the political realities" in which the church must actively participate, Groome fundamentally misconstrues the nature of the church itself as *polis*. The church is not, as he would have it, the guardian of a set of moral values (love, justice, freedom), an agency that strives to encourage the adoption of these values by the larger culture, the wider society, or the state, so that the kingdom of God might be manifest in the "real" world. Rather, the church itself is a challenge to the primacy and legitimacy of the larger culture, the wider society, and the state; the church itself is called to be an alternative *polis* to the so-called real world. Indeed, from a Christian perspective it is the church as *polis* that *is* the "real world."

Similarly, Groome's call for a "public" theology also betrays his indebtedness to the modern project:

> Mainline North American churches are growing in awareness that they are to live a "public" faith, a faith that is socially and politically responsible rather than focused exclusively on sacral concerns. Christian faith demands that its claimants join the public discourse and the political struggle for a better world. This aspect of Christian faith was until recently identified exclusively with liberation communities and theologies, but now permeates the

"establishment" church. An emerging literature calls for a "public" theology and church and for a "public" religious education.[20]

Here it is clear that Groome's surrender to the discourse that undergirds modern, liberal social orders is total and unambiguous. There is, once again, the predictable summons for the church to abandon its parochialism—its "exclusively sacral concerns"—so that it might marshal its efforts toward the realization of its true end: to be "social and politically responsible" in the "struggle for a better world."

Groome never questions these distinctions between public and private, between sacral and political, nor does he challenge the logic that renders such categories sacrosanct, self-evident, and natural. That something called "the political" has set the agenda for the church's expression of its "faith" is accepted without reservation. But if, as I have already noted, there is no place that is not just another perspective—"there is no 'public' that is not just another province"[21]—then there can be nothing natural, nothing given, about Groome's concession to so-called political realities or his assessment of the role of the church in the world. This way of conceiving of politics as statecraft and of the church as a contributor to the political order will be taken up again when I examine the work of Mary Boys. But first we must look at Groome's deployment of the terms *freedom* and *justice* in his call for a more public theology and a more political church.

Freedom for and Freedom From

An integral part of Groome's understanding of the kingdom of God as foundational for Christian life and education is his notion of human freedom, which is really the core theme of his entire pedagogical project: "In effect, I am here proposing the language of freedom as the most comprehensive way of talking about the corporate consequence and condition of living with and for the values of the Kingdom of God . . . [that is,] Christian faith lived in response to the Kingdom of God has the consequence of human freedom."[22] Groome wants to articulate an account of human freedom that will be compatible with a wide range of philosophical, psychological, sociological, and theological traditions. First, he approvingly cites the three themes that dominate conventional construals of human freedom—the ability to act free from constraint (freedom of action), the capacity for self-determination (freedom of choice), and the ability to make free decisions (rational freedom)—as necessary for a comprehensive understanding of freedom in a Christian context. Second, he positions his claims about human freedom under the headings "freedom for" and "freedom from." We are free, according to Groome, *for* God, *for* others, and *for* ourselves, and we are free *from* sin—both personal and corporate. Moreover, to be free means to become free like God, though Groome does not spell out exactly what this understanding of freedom implies or entails. What he does say is that this freedom "is far from license or rugged individualism to do as one pleases, but [is] freedom *from* inner compulsion and external oppression, and freedom *for* becoming fully alive persons who fulfill their responsibilities for the well-being of self and others, for the personal and common good."[23]

Such freedom, made possible by Jesus the Liberator, is tripartite. It is spiritual, in that "we can transcend the mundane and passing to reach out for union with the ultimate Transcendent."[24] It is personal, meaning "the interior, psychological aspect of freedom" that allows for "an autonomy of will whose horizon is the Kingdom of God."[25] And it is social/political, in that Christ's dying and rising "is a means of grace to empower the human struggle with history for an ever-increasing degree of freedom from sin as it is embodied in the economic, political, and cultural arrangements of our world."[26] The implication of this for Christian religious education is that all educative efforts must, according to Groome, promote "human emancipation." As he says, "Whenever, wherever, and however we educate in the Christian faith tradition, that activity should empower the human quest for freedom."[27]

In taking on Groome's account of human freedom, we are back to a point made earlier about how difficult it is to question and critique such construals (of freedom, of justice, of religion . . .), given the power and pervasiveness of modern descriptors and how captive we all are to the philosophical and anthropological suppositions of liberalism. When Groome says that "both the impetus for and the consequence of people living in Christian faith is the wholeness of human freedom that is fullness of life for all, here and hereafter,"[28] who would disagree? This is a claim that in many ways is hard to argue against; no one, after all, is opposed to freedom, to "fullness of life for all." In the world we inhabit, Groome's definitions of Christian faith and human freedom do not need to be explained. However, without denying that the notion of freedom is integral to the gospel and to Christian faith, I suggest that Groome's way of putting the matter is troubling for at least two reasons—one christological, the other ecclesiological. First, Groome's account does not provide a thick enough description of what freedom actually means in relation to Christ and, more specifically, in relation to the historic Christian confession that God is triune. Second, Groome's formulation implicitly takes as its starting point the individual and separates Christian freedom from any substantive account of the church.

Let me clarify. Groome asserts that "our own efforts to live for God's reign are empowered by the grace of God, which, in the Christian covenant, is mediated through the historical event of Jesus the Christ."[29] But he does not flesh out in any meaningful way how the doctrine of God or the life, death, and resurrection of Jesus give substance and weight to his notion of freedom, or how Christian faith might in fact critique or subvert the distorted views of freedom we inherit and blindly accept from the culture. He simply begins by describing freedom as "fullness of life for all" and then proceeds to give (thin) theological justification for such a construal. It is not enough to say, as he does, that freedom must be exercised in community and that freedom entails responsibility to others, for human autonomy, rather than God, is still placed at the center of Christian faith and at the heart of efforts at education.

Moreover, Groome's notion of freedom as "freedom for" is never sufficiently developed; we are never told what such freedom looks like, how being free for another is materially, concretely enacted and embodied within the Christian community that supposedly gives it its meaning and coherence. What Groome does say is that:

freedom of action in our freedom for God and ourselves made
possible by Jesus Christ, is, in fact, a freedom for others. In this
sense, it is a "limited" freedom—limited in that we cannot act as
we please regardless of the consequences for other people. . . .
Freedom from a Christian perspective can never be understood
as "raw" freedom in the sense of an unbridled "individualistic"
freedom. Rather, it is a limited freedom that is actualized and
contained with within a "communalistic context."[30]

However, invoking the caveat that freedom is always exercised
in community does not do the work of giving shape and substance to Christian freedom as it relates to and is dependent on
Christ and the church, nor does it necessarily oppose the view
of freedom as autonomy. Groome may concede that Christian
freedom can never be construed as license, but he fails to connect
his account of freedom, finally, specifically, to the cross.

As Christians, we are not called to be free but to be holy; we
are not admonished to be self-determining but to allow ourselves
to be transformed into the likeness of Christ: "Our goal is to be
shaped into the entire *form* of the *incarnate,* the *crucified,* and the
risen one."[31] To say this is not to diminish the pressing concerns
that arise from the abusive and exploitive practices that have
served to subjugate persons and whole populations throughout
history and into the present time. Freedom from oppression
in its myriad forms *is* intrinsic to the gospel and its proclamation. But in the Christian lexicon the word *freedom* undergoes a
change in definition, a semantic shift of sorts, so that its meaning cannot be fully grasped or articulated within the linguistic
framework of the secular order in which the quest for human
autonomy leads not to freedom and human flourishing but to
the slavery of the self.

In naming politics as the realm in which we are called to
struggle to make all people free (and in assuming that it is the
church's task to encourage this process along with the promotion of "kingdom values"), Groome ignores the fact that the
realm of the political, as it is instantiated in modern, capitalist
social orders, encourages and produces the opposite effect. If,
as Groome affirms, freedom is understood as the ability to act
and decide unencumbered by outside pressure and coercion, and
even if true freedom can be exercised only in community, such

freedom is an illusion, a fiction, a fantasy. For the sphere of the political—connected as it is in the modern west to the market forces of consumer capitalism—does not exist to make us free but to cultivate a citizenry of seemingly autonomous persons whose desires are shaped (manipulated) to entrap us in the compulsion to consume, while believing the insidious lie that we are indeed free. Here we can return to the work of Foucault and his crucial insight that power is not (only) a repressive force that denies and subdues but a "productive network which runs through the whole social body."[32] It produces bodies, creates pleasures, forms and shapes desires. Political orders, and the apparatuses that support them, do not make us free (independent, distinct, singular) so much as they render us all alike. This is a truth with profound implications for the catechesis of the young, who in their desperate yearning for autonomy and independence—a desire sown and cultivated by a savvy media culture—could not be more alike, particularly in their enslavement to the culture of fashion and the industries of music, movies, and television.

This, I fear, is where Groome's account of freedom leads us: to an inability to fully grasp, critique, and, most important, resist a social order that continually utters in its political rhetoric, glossy ads, and television commercials that most pernicious lie—that we are free or that we can be free. This is not to say that Groome would condone the cultural and political manipulations that attempt to deceive us; it is to say that his account of Christian freedom does not possess the theological resources necessary to contest and oppose such machinations. Freedom (like justice) can mean many things, and not all of them are compatible with the gospel of Jesus Christ.

It is the lack of a christological focus for Groome's account of freedom that is most worrisome. As John Howard Yoder has put it:

> The ultimate and most profound reason to consider Christ— rather than democracy or justice, or equality of liberty—as the hope of the world, is not the negative observation, clear enough already, that hopes of this kind generally remain incomplete and disappointing, or that they can lead those who trust them to pride or brutality. The fundamental limitation of these hopes is found

in the fact that in their search for power and in the urgency with which they seek to guarantee justice they are still not powerful enough. They locate the greatest need of [hu]man[ity] in the wrong place. . . . Those for whom Jesus Christ is the hope of the world will for this reason not measure their contemporary social involvement by its efficacy for tomorrow nor by its success in providing work, or freedom, or food or in building new social structures, but by identifying with the Lord in whom they have placed their trust.[33]

Groome may not disagree with Yoder's claims; in fact, his reflections on human freedom are often couched in christocentric language: "In Christian faith, Jesus sets people free *from* sin."[34] Elsewhere, he says that through Jesus all of humanity is empowered to "say yes to life" and that "because the freedom that God makes possible in Jesus is not simply for souls later but is to begin with history, freedom as an intentional purpose should suffuse the whole enterprise of Christian faith education."[35] But such winsome declarations continue to beg important questions: What is the real nature of the kind of freedom Groome champions? How is his account of freedom dependent on the Christian doctrine of God and the nature of freedom in Christ? Is it possible that freedom for Groome, despite the overlay of theological terms and categories, remains underneath it all rooted in the modern formula of freedom as autonomy?[36]

Christian freedom is best construed, I suggest, not as the political prize that Groome encourages us to pursue but as *gift.* The self-giving of the Father to the Son (who himself reflects fully the Father's self-giving) and the pouring out of the Spirit enact and display the freedom-in-communion that *is* the very nature and being of God. This brings us to the trinitarian, ecclesiological focus of freedom that is lacking in Groome's account. Through Christ, persons are brought into a new kind of relationship—the *ekklesia* of God—through which we exist as participants in the very life of the Trinity. Our freedom, then, and our very identity are a function of our dependence on God and one another and our service to God and one another. And thus true freedom requires perfect obedience—a conformity to the patterns of Jesus' life as he lived it in obedience to his

Father's will. An obedience that, contra Groome, makes faith possible in the first place.

The word *obedience,* of course, is a red flag on the road to personal freedom and self-rule; to be truly free, we are often admonished, is to obey no one. Throughout the church's history, moreover, the term has often been used in support of practices that have degraded and humiliated women, the poor and powerless, the colonized and dispossessed; misappropriations of the term *obedience* have undergirded institutions that have sanctioned and promoted human enslavement in a host of guises. Nevertheless, the correction for such distortions is not to discard the word altogether but to discredit its corruptions and retrieve its rightful use in Christian discourse. Obedience, for the Christian, is not an act of passive resignation to the insufferable demands of another; it is a sharing in the cross of discipleship, through which we are transformed into the image of Christ and made to share in the eternal communion of Father, Son, and Holy Spirit, a communion that *is* perfect freedom. It is a tautology: true obedience for the Christian is true freedom. Thus Christian freedom finds its meaning most determinedly in the cross and resurrection, in cruciform living that has as its context the worshiping community gathered in eucharistic fellowship, embodying the forgiveness and reconciliation that the cross of Christ makes possible.

Perhaps the best way to highlight what I take to be the lack of theological substance and an uncritical alliance with the tenets of liberal philosophy in Groome's notion of freedom is to ask how he could make any sense of Bonhoeffer's powerful insight that "when Christ calls a person, he bids that one come and die."[37] For Bonhoeffer, the freedom that comes from true obedience and from answering the call to discipleship is not a fatalistic surrender to the forces of evil in the world, nor is it located in a longing for and attainment of Christian martyrdom. Rather, it is a quality of existence determined not by social and political processes designed to ensure self-actualization but by a call to share in the divine life of God, to suffer with and for another, and to participate in the restorative work of forgiveness and reconciliation.

Freedom for the Christian can never be realized within the sphere of politics construed as statecraft; rather, it is operative within the church as *polis*—the *ekklesia* of God, whose worship is itself an alternative to the politics of modernity in which we are made to exist as strangers to one another and as slaves to ourselves and our disordered desires. While Christians are always called to resist, denounce, and struggle against all forms of slavery and oppression that would diminish any person anywhere, we recognize that the hope of genuine and lasting freedom does not lie in the transformation of the political order but in the binding of ourselves to one another in love, mercy, and forgiveness, in obedience to the cross of Christ. As we will explore more fully in part 2 of this book, the church at worship—in its liturgy, its witness, and its work in the world—is the "political reality" in which such freedom finds its truest expression.

Christian Religious Education and the Cause of Justice

Just as Christian educators are to educate for freedom, they also, according to Groome, must educate for justice. But like his account of freedom, Groome's treatment of the term *justice* is betrayed by a weak ecclesiology and a hollow trinitarianism. He relies on cursory readings of ancient and medieval sources (the complex and important views of justice of Aristotle, Augustine, and Aquinas merit single-sentence summaries) and proffers a notion of justice that is derived from and supportive of a model of human relations that cannot help but perpetuate and legitimize *in*justice. That is, Groome's account of justice is, in the end, insufficiently radical for his own desired political ends.

Groome notes that from the beginning Christianity has had a strong tradition of social justice; its roots in the Jewish prophetic tradition reveal a God who demands justice and desires *shalom.* Jesus' compassion for the poor and suffering and the early church's activism on behalf of those in need are also upheld as examples of historic Christianity's devotion to justice and its enactment in the church and the world. But the biblical witness cannot, according to Groome, supply us with all we need to know about justice and how it is to be carried out in the world in which we live. "There is great passion in the biblical call to justice—it can light a fire in the tummy. It lacks, however, the precise and analytical categories needed for discerning, administering, and living the virtue of justice in everyday life. Such precision is more readily suggested by the philosophical tradition of the West."[38] Part of what Groome is referring to here is the tradition of Catholic social teaching that began in 1891 with Pope Leo XIII's encyclical *Rerum Novarum,* in which the church's theology of justice was injected (and, in Groome's estimation, invigorated) with terms and categories borrowed from the traditions of modern liberal philosophy. Though Groome neglects to mention it, this papal encyclical tradition drew not only on the tenets of liberal philosophy but also on the prior "social Catholicism" that developed in the mid- to late nineteenth century, which was itself a transmuting of earlier medieval teachings on the nature of justice.

For Groome, the papal encyclicals of this period (beginning with Leo XIII), and the philosophical traditions in which they are grounded, are a welcome advance of the church's mission in the world, concerned as they are with workers' rights, just living conditions, and the dignity of all people. Because these progressive teachings are rooted in natural law, they "can provide the basis of a *public* sense of justice."[39] And while Groome argues that Catholic Christians are in greater need than Protestants of reclaiming the *biblical* mandate as an inspiration for doing justice, he also contends that because the church's social teachings are cast in "philosophical language, with conviction reached through persuasion rather than biblical authority, [they] become accessible in the marketplace of society."[40]

Before moving on to Groome's treatment of Catholic social teaching and my own reflections on his views, a few points are worth noting. Groome does not say how and why it is that "philosophical language" can persuade the persons (consumers?) who populate the "marketplace of society," but one of the problematic implications of this claim is the assumption that "philosophical language" is a neutral tool that can be taken up to communicate the biblical/theological idea of justice in a way that is persuasive to the casual outside observer while leaving the biblical notion of justice unaltered. To the contrary, language is never neutral: to couch one's account of biblical justice primarily in philosophical terms and categories is fundamentally to alter it. For example, and as we will see in more detail later, to articulate an account of justice based on modernity's discourse of "rights" (even if such rights are deemed God-given) is to advance a meaning of justice in which a person's claim to fair and equal access to social and material goods is less about participation in a divinely ordered human community whose *telos* is love of God and love of neighbor and more about liberalism's construction of the *individual* as one who must compete for the limited resources available for social and economic advancement. Moreover, Groome's presumption that philosophical language is persuasive, while a reliance on Scripture invokes an authority that cannot be compelling, is itself revealing. In the end, Groome has opted for a "public" definition and display of justice that are merely propped up with biblical imagery and theological themes.

In summarizing the Catholic social teaching that began with *Rerum Novarum*, Groome favorably highlights five primary theses: First, there is the call to honor the sacredness, dignity, and priority of the person. "All of us have intrinsic dignity and every human life is sacred. In philosophical terms, a person's capacities for knowledge and self-reflection, for love and freedom, attest to a singular status."[41] Second is the belief that human dignity confers rights and responsibilities. "Human rights are claims to the spiritual and material goods that persons need to realize their dignity. Human responsibilities are duties that we have toward God, self, neighbor, and creation, precisely because of our status and capacities."[42] Third, humans are understood to be essentially social beings. "The society and state are fundamental extensions of this social nature of the person. . . . The *society* is all the collective relationships—political, economic, cultural, and legal—that structure the shared life of a populace at the local and national levels. The *state* is the aspect of a society that exercises political authority."[43] Fourth, justice demands care for the common good and the public order. "The 'common good' combines respect for every individual with care for the social well-being of the collective. . . . The 'public order' is a subfeature of the common good and refers to the state's responsibility to oversee public safety, public morality, and the tenets of legal justice for all."[44] Fifth and last, "justice is served both by subsidiarity and by societal agency. The principle of subsidiarity encourages addressing social needs at the lowest level effective, instead of expecting everything to be done at the macro level of the state. . . . The principle of societal agency reflects the state's responsibility to step in and provide whatever else is needed for personal and common good."[45]

In further defining the forms of justice that are mandated by these five tenets, Groome notes that distinctions were made in the social teachings between commutative justice (the demand for honesty and fairness in all human exchanges), distributive justice (which insists that all social goods be distributed equitably), and social justice (that which pertains to society's responsibility "to create structures that protect the dignity of all and allow each member to participate according to needs, talents, and choices").[46] After recounting the five basic tenets and the three forms of justice, Groome notes how biblical and theological convictions support these views of justice in at least three ways. First of all, returning to the theme of the kingdom of God, he argues that God's reign is a "profoundly social as well as spiritual symbol . . . requiring commitment to justice and peace as well as to personal holiness of life."[47] Second, recalling the liberationist stress on solidarity with those who suffer, Groome insists that "people of faith should make an 'option for the poor.'"[48] And finally the pursuit of justice also requires an active commitment to *peace;* justice and peace are, under this rubric, symbiotic.

Justice, Love, and the Common Good

Groome's definition of justice, dependent as it is on a favorable reading of the modern papal encyclical tradition and on the liberationists' call to take seriously the plight of the world's poor and oppressed, is appealing to many because of its seemingly radical nature—the church is roused from listlessness and called to active engagement in social and political processes that promote freedom, equality, and the dignity of all people. Seeking justice is construed as an urgent matter of political activism. For those who have been disappointed by the church's lack of political awareness and involvement, Groome's summons to action is welcomed as a way to recover Christianity's relevance and legitimacy in an ever more secular order.

Yet while there is much right in the appeals to the intrinsic dignity of all people and the claim that justice and human rights are connected, the problem with Groome's schema is that it concedes too much ground to liberalism's conception of justice and pays too little attention to earlier theological construals of justice, which are in fact far more radical in their implications for human flourishing and well-being than the modern liberal view. Because Groome begins with Leo XIII and not with Aquinas, his understanding of justice is influenced more by the principle of fair distribution of goods in the liberal economy than by a vision of a human community whose aim is the divine ordering of shared life in holy pursuit of the common good. This is not to suggest that the social encyclicals Groome relies on are devoid of theological reasoning and argument for their conception of justice, but it is to say that one must recognize in them what Daniel Bell describes as "the gradual and subtle move away from justice as the principle of a community's solidarity, in a robust sense of the common good, to justice as a fundamentally distributive force that secures rights in societies distinguished by the absence of anything but the thinnest of conceptions of the common good."[49]

Groome's enumeration of the qualities of justice, following the logic of the encyclical tradition and liberation theology, takes as its operative context the temporal order of the secular state. The language of rights is detached from a theological vision that presupposes one's participation in a community mirroring the divine order of the Trinity, and is wedded instead to liberalism's view of human relations as essentially self-interested and contract based. Bell describes this changing pattern of human relations that marks the shift from the medieval to the modern:

> In the course of making the case for social justice, social Catholics eventually adopted the modern discourse of rights. They essentially embraced the conclusions of modern social contract theorists, namely that society was rightly understood as constituted by a conglomeration of rights and duties adhering to individuals over against the whole. The medieval vision . . . had construed rights in terms of the divine ordering of the human

community as that order was spelled out in a series of divine, natural, and human laws. As such, right was fundamentally a matter of consent to or participation in the divine order and the individual was understood as possessed by Christ and a recipient of all the good that one is, has, and does. In the newer tradition, God's right established discrete rights possessed originally by individuals—by virtue of their creation in the image of God and endowment with a certain dignity—and then derivatively of communities. According to this conception, the individual occupies the central position as right is associated with a human power to control and dispose of temporal things. Individuals, in other words, became essentially proprietors.[50]

As was noted earlier, Groome describes the social nature of the human person as having its fundamental expression within the society (political, economic, cultural, legal relationships) and the state (the arena in which political authority is exercised). Thus his conception of the common good is based on the arrangements of liberal social orders, in which the securing of rights and equal access to material goods are meant to function as the prime guarantors of justice. The role of the church in all of this—in helping to create a just society—is to instill in the wider culture the values of the kingdom of God (values that can be articulated in "philosophical" terms so as to make them more amenable to a skeptical or indifferent "public"): to promote dignity and the sacredness of human life and to foster respect for the rights of all persons. But Groome's plan ultimately is insufficiently radical for his own ends. As Bell points out, "The formation of just persons involves a great deal more than consciousness raising on the issue of human rights. . . . The formation of just persons is not primarily a matter of getting their values right; it is a matter of redirecting desire."[51]

Groome's conception of justice, in other words, is not up to the task of actualizing justice in any meaningful way; it lacks a rigorous accounting of how justice is specifically, materially, concretely embodied in human communities so that *injustice* can be recognized, confronted, resisted, and rooted out. It fails, finally, to be sufficiently theological, to recognize Christianity itself "as a fully material reality—that is a social-economic-political formation—in its own right,"[52] a reality that contains within it the resources necessary to form persons capable of resisting the forces that perpetuate injustice. For Groome, Christianity and the kingdom of God remain merely "symbolic," understood as an assortment of values detached from the lived commitments of Christian women and men and offered in service to the real *polis,* the state: that "aspect of a society that exercises political authority" and the only arena in which meaningful justice can be realized.

Moreover, Groome's notion of the common good, like that of the social encyclicals, is sustained fundamentally by the narrative of modernity's story of the self—a narrative designed, ipso facto, to keep us strangers to one another. That is, where Aquinas understood the common good as a shared love of God and neighbor in pursuit of holy living, its modern version is reduced to little more than a cluster of individual rights. Justice therefore is no longer thought to be the virtue that grants unity to the pursuit of the common good but is, rather, "the facilitator and enabler of the pursuit of private goods."[53] Thus when Groome situates justice within the realm of the "public order," where it "is served both by subsidiarity and by societal agency," he has cast his lot with a conception of human relations and the common good that colludes with rather than contests the market-driven practices that distort the Christian vision of the common good. As Bell points out:

> Justice that is primarily distributive rather than unitive essentially becomes simply the regulator of conflict; it becomes a matter of maintaining the peace between the multiple private goods that compete for society's resources. This peace, however, is a fragile peace that does not so much resemble genuine harmony as it does a temporary cessation of strife, a tenuous balance of power that could at any moment issue in renewed conflict and violence.[54]

Groome's own linking of peace with justice hangs together by the thinnest of accounts of peace—the "fragile peace" that Bell speaks of—and cannot make sense of another of Bonhoeffer's crucial insights: "The peace of Jesus is the cross."[55] Much more than simply the absence of conflict, genuine peace, as Bonhoeffer well knew, assumes the practices and disciplines of Christian community. Peace is not a "value" promoted by the church in service to political strategies intent on minimizing strife in a hostile world; rather, Christ's peace is a sword of division, sundering the ties between son and father, daughter and mother, and wielded by the one who *is* the new life that the cross makes possible for all the world. Peace, for those concerned about justice, is the *ekklesia* of God, instantiated as an alternative to politics-as-conflict-management.

Finally, to do justice in this world is, as Rowan Williams's reading of Augustine reminds us, to do justice to God. "Our task is truthfully to reflect back to God what God is, to mirror God's glory—not because God without us is ignorant, but because we have already begun to see what we are when we look toward God. The vision of God is the cornerstone of justice: when we know ourselves to be before God, we know ourselves to be the object of a costly and careful attention, searching out the whole of our truth, accepting it, and engaging with it."[56] In such knowledge we recognize that we must give to others what is given to us: truth sustained by grace. But more than that, says Williams, Augustine considered justice in society unthinkable apart from "returning God's attentive, loving gaze in silence and praise. A society that doesn't understand contemplation won't understand justice, because it will have forgotten how to look *selflessly* at what is other."[57] Therefore anything that Christians say about justice must begin not, as Groome would have it, with human dignity or individual rights or the public order or societal agency, but with the church's doctrine of God—the God "whose very life is 'justice,' in the sense that Father, Son, and Holy Spirit reflect back to each other perfectly and fully the reality that each one is—'give glory' to each other."[58]

Summary

Groome appears to strive for a theologically centered account of Christian education—he says things like "obedience to God's will is of the substance of Christian faith."[59] Yet it is clear that the rules that regulate his speech are at odds with a trinitarian grammar, which insists that terms such as *freedom* and *justice* are not transparent and self-justifying but must be evaluated in light of the church's faith in Jesus the Son, whose life, "perfectly reflecting the self-giving of the Father, is shown in the pouring out of the Spirit."[60] The freedom that Jesus makes possible is not a benevolent sanctioning of all our wants and wishes. Rather, the cross of Christ is the nexus at which freedom becomes possible by God's own gifts of forgiveness and restoration. The manifestation of this freedom in Christian community bears witness (partially, imperfectly) to the freedom to love and serve another that is the very nature of the Triune God. It is only after we have identified the heart of the Christian faith as life in communion with God—who lives in eternal freedom and love—that it becomes possible to talk about something called "human freedom." And even then, the commonplace terms invoked to describe what it means to be free often ring hollow, trite, even false.

The way Groome understands the meaning of justice for the practice of Christian education reveals his own complicity with the modern, liberal view that assumes that "justice" is a self-evident category of human experience, available to anyone apart from the norms, traditions, and practices that would give it shape and substance and definition: "The divine edict of justice requires education for personal and social transformation. Beyond the context of explicitly Catholic education, all Christians who teach anywhere—school, home, or program—in whatever capacity, are required by their faith to educate for justice, albeit without imposing their religious language on participants."[61] Insofar as Groome believes it possible for Christians to "educate for justice" without speaking and teaching, embodying and inhabiting Christian language and discourse, he has misconstrued the very nature and purpose of Christian formation and proposed a model of Christian education fundamentally at odds with a trinitarian, doxological catechesis.

3

Faith and the Public Good

Religious Education as Responsible Citizenship

It is the work of religious education to lead people outside the confines of their narrow experience, to broaden their horizons and deepen their capacities to feel and act.

Mary Boys

Introduction

The work of Mary Boys, a Roman Catholic and a member for three decades of the Sisters of the Holy Names, centers on three prominent themes: the relationship of biblical scholarship to practices of Christian pedagogy, the educational implications of Jewish-Christian dialogue, and a concern for how the church can educate Christians as "responsible citizens" who will contribute to the transforming of the world. While I will make mention of the first theme, as dealt with in her early book *Biblical Interpretation in Religious Education,* I will focus primarily on the other two areas of interest that have dominated Boys's work in more recent years: Jewish-Christian relations and the need to educate for a responsible citizenry.

The Bible and Religious Education

In her first book, *Biblical Interpretation in Religious Education,* Boys sought to explore the ways the scholarly enterprise of biblical interpretation and the appropriation of the Bible as Scripture by ordinary Christian women and men can be mutually informing. She takes as her test case the failed experiment of *Heilsgeschichte* as a leitmotif in the catechetical movement of Catholicism in the early 1960s. *Heilsgeschichte,* meaning "salvation history," refers to a hermeneutical principle first articulated in nineteenth-century German Protestantism and further refined in the twentieth century by prominent biblical theologians Gerhard von Rad and Oscar Cullmann. Developed against the broad background of reaction to the Enlightenment, *Heilsgeschichte* conceived of the Bible as an account of divine salvation worked out in human history. Proponents of this view assumed that God is revealed in history (as opposed to "nature") and that such revelation is progressive—moving through successive, historical stages. The progressive nature of God's revelation in human history can be seen, for example, in the way the New Testament fulfills and completes the Old Testament. As Cullmann put it, salvation history is the "hermeneutical key" that links all the biblical texts together.

After briefly tracing the development of *Heilsgeschichte* within European and American Protestantism, Boys examines its appropriation in the "kerygmatic renewal" movement of Roman Catholic catechetics. Kerygmatic theology, deriving from the Greek word for "proclamation," emphasized the vitality of the early church's preaching of the gospel. Through the work of Josef A. Jungmann and Johannes Hofinger, kerygma and salvation history in the Catholic context were intertwined: "religious teaching must lead the faithful to a vital understanding of the content of faith itself, that they may interiorly grasp it, and thus grow to spiritual maturity and proper independence in religious life. . . . What is needed is not a knowledge of the 'many' but of 'the one'—the unity that lies behind the many, the all-embracing salvific plan of God."[1]

Boys then traces the decline of *Heilsgeschichte* as a hermeneutical principle in Catholic religious education. The theological concerns that contributed to this decline centered on several areas: a faulty deployment of the concept of "revelation" (Boys notes Gabriel Moran's criticism of the term's parochialism within the *Heilsgeschichte* schema); the devaluing of the Old Testament and the implicit denigration of Judaism that emerged from the progressivist view of revelation; a "christocentrism" that was too allied with cultural predominance and insensitive to Christianity's relationship to Judaism; and an ecclesiology that was insufficiently eschatological. Yet of more significance than the theological objections raised to *Heilsgeschichte,* Boys concludes, were the cultural and educational changes of the 1960s. The technological advances of the age—crystallized for the culture in the landing of humans on the moon—redefined the nature of human progress while bringing about an intense focus on human growth. "The 'Space Age' coexisted with the 'Age of Therapy.' Terms such as 'human potential,' 'freedom,' and 'relevance' typified an introspective, even narcissistic, turn in the culture. . . . For many this was also an 'Age of Crisis,' when moral and spiritual questions called for a revolution in thought and action."[2] Educational theory and practice were undergoing their own cataclysmic shifts, with much attention being paid to the reform of science education and to the development of behavioral objectives and competency-based teacher education. Boys notes that many observers "called attention to the political nature of education, criticized the way in which schooling in the Western world tended to maintain the status quo, and suggested that more critical eyes be focused on education from a sociological and philosophical vantage point."[3] Catholic religious education in the 1960s, as it broke from the model that wedded kerygma and *Heilsgeschichte,* mirrored the cultural and secular educational trends of the era: an affinity for the social scientific approach emphasizing the empirical and behavioral, movement toward an experiential catechetics, and an attempt to work deliberately from a nonkerygmatic foundation (Boys notes that at the forefront of this effort was the work of Gabriel Moran and Thomas Groome).

Having traced the rapid ascent and equally rapid decline of *Heilsgeschichte* as a leitmotif in Catholic catechetics, Boys then offers several suggestions for articulating a proper relationship between religious education and contemporary biblical scholarship. First, she defines religious education as "the making accessible of the traditions of religious communities and the making manifest of the intrinsic connection between tradition and transformation."[4] Like Moran and Groome, Boys assumes that the words *religion* and *religious* name readily identifiable practices and attributes of communities and individuals, though she intends that these terms exert their meaning within the particular context of American Catholic education and catechesis. Central to the task of making traditions accessible and of manifesting the link between tradition and transformation is sustained, systematic attention to and engagement with modern biblical criticism. Boys is concerned that because nineteenth-century American Catholicism was entrenched in anti-intellectualism and was slow to embrace the emerging discipline of higher biblical criticism, it has lagged in the much-needed effort to "facilitate the development of a faith which encompasses a critical sense."[5] If religious education is fundamentally about teaching traditions and showing how traditions are transformative, then the tools of biblical criticism, she suggests, offer unique and valuable insight into the process by which the traditions of Judaism and Christianity have been remembered, preserved, and enacted. For example, "form and redaction criticism," argues Boys, "provide a perspective on the malleability and vitality of traditions and a view of the various interests which catalyzed the preservation and adaptation of traditions."[6] Boys's basic point is this: because historical critical methods have revolutionized the study of the Bible and because Catholic doctrine and practice historically have fostered only a superficial understanding of Scripture, it "is imperative that biblical criticism more adequately permeate the life of the church."[7]

She does not, however, advocate the church's wholesale surrender of the Bible to the "experts." Boys rightly notes that the Scriptures are not the exclusive preserve of the guild of biblical scholars and that the insights of scholars and critics must be offered in service to the church and its ministry. Moreover, she notes the dangers that the "professionalization" of biblical studies has presented for faithful scriptural interpretation. And yet one wonders if Boys is too uncritically allied to biblical criticism as the saving hope for religious education and to a view of Scripture that instinctively assumes the superiority of modern modes of interpretation. For instance, in commenting on the work of Hans Frei, whose *Eclipse of Biblical Narrative* was fairly recent when Boys's own book was published, she contends that Frei's "implicit call for a return to modes of interpretation from the 'precritical' era appears highly questionable."[8] Implicit in Boys's own proposal is a casual dismissal of centuries of biblical interpretation within the church and the unexamined assumption that precritical exegesis is superseded by advances in form, textual, historical, and redaction criticism simply because the former is "old" and the latter "new."

Perhaps more important, though, is that Boys appears committed to a view of Scripture and of education that conceives of the Bible as a book to be "understood" in its original context rather than a set of narratives to be embodied and inhabited in the present by the particular communities for whom they are authoritative. "Biblical criticism," she contends, "serves to correct oversimplifications that, especially when hardened into ideologies, have done untold harm."[9] It is true that biblical criticism can illuminate scriptural texts in ways that are important for engendering faithful practice. For example, social and historical analyses of the roles of women in early Christianity have shed light on passages in the Pauline and deutero-Pauline writings that admonish against female leadership and women's authority in the church. When we attend to the texts' social setting, the cultural prejudices of the time, the political pressures on the early church, and other biblical texts that speak favorably of the work of women in ministry, the harsh directives in the epistles lose their force as literal prohibitions for our own time and place. When the Pauline and deutero-Pauline writings are placed in the larger context of biblical Christianity and baptismal vocation, the New Testament witness can be interpreted as consistent with, indeed supportive of, the exercise of ordained leadership by women.

But an undue emphasis on the "original meaning of a passage" can obscure the truth that the biblical witness is multistranded and polyvalent and that scriptural interpretation is always open-ended. Despite Boys's insistence on paying attention to the *history* of biblical texts, she is, I suggest, insufficiently historical in her approach to Scripture and its interpretation. Because the Bible exists always amid temporal, cultural, and social change, that is, *within history,* the church's engagement with it and interpretation of it is continually in flux. Nicholas Lash speaks to this reality when he argues that the church's interpretation of Scripture is best thought of as *performance*—as rendering, bearing witness to the truth of the Bible in ways in which the "meaning" of a given text is never definitively captured but is always sought and constructed as it is lived out.[10] (An idea which, interestingly, was in its beginning stages in the later work of Hans Frei.) Since each new performance is a new event in the history of the meaning of the text, "there is no such thing as an interpretation that is 'final' and 'definitive' in the sense of bringing that history to an end."[11] Moreover, the authority of scriptural "performance" does not derive from a correspondence to the latest research published in the *Journal of Biblical Literature,* though biblical criticism has a secondary role to play in helping the community to reflect critically on the intricacies of texts and their meaning(s) for the community's life together.

Where Boys proposes that "biblical criticism offers a paradigm for theological reflection in the church,"[12] I suggest, following Lash and others, that the community engaged in the work of interpretation (perhaps with the aid of the biblical scholar) must itself be paradigmatic. Of course, communities may be poor performers of Scripture; that is, they may fail—sometimes miserably—in their attempt to be truthful witnesses of the Scriptures. Discernment about what constitutes a poor performance of Scripture is not always easy to come by, but as Lash suggests, "the quality of our *humanity* will be the criterion of the adequacy of the performance."[13] When communities do fail, it is not because they have employed an inadequate interpretive theory or a faulty hermeneutical strategy. Rather, failure is the result of a refusal to allow the biblical text to exert its own critical judgment on the lives of Christians and of the church's inability to cultivate the kind of character in community that would make our readings and performances of Scripture a witness against the principalities and powers of the world.

In fairness to Boys, the themes of "performance" and "embodiment" did not dominate the biblical studies literature in the late 1970s in the way that they do today. But it is still true, I think, that she does not appreciate that while she has deconstructed *Heilsgeschichte* and its interpretive failures, she has unwittingly reproduced what was most problematic about it to begin with: the assumption that proper biblical interpretation rests on securing the proper "hermeneutical key" to unlock the text's meaning. Boys might be able to talk now about keys rather than a single key and about meanings rather than a single meaning, but she has still surrendered to the critics' implicit claim of the necessity of "interpretation theory"—a theory that can provide "a basis for religious educators to develop alternatives to a proclamatory mode of education."[14]

For Christians (and for Jews, one could argue), interpreting the Bible is a lifelong process of learning to embody its narrative vision—of becoming, as Stephen E. Fowl and L. Gregory Jones have suggested, "wise readers of scripture."[15] Such a process, moreover, requires nothing less than the moral formation and transformation of those who seek to embody it. And so, paradoxically, faithful, discerning communities of accountability are both the prerequisite and the end goal of biblical interpretation. Because scriptural interpretation occurs in particular communities in particular times and places, and because the biblical witness itself is multistranded and diverse, "no particular community of believers can be sure of what a faithful interpretation of Scripture will entail in any specific situation until it actually engages in the hard process of conversation, argument, discussion, prayer and practice."[16]

The faithful performance of Scripture does not begin or end with the critic's proclamation. And thus to lay out a plan, as Boys attempts to do, in which biblical critics and religious educators are to collaborate to make Christians more biblically literate is, at the very minimum, to locate the community's work of biblical interpretation and its ultimate purpose in the wrong place; it is to misidentify the primary locus for faithful scriptural embodiment. For what is curiously absent from Boys's proposal—and it is curious because Boys herself is Roman Catholic, steeped in the historic liturgy of that tradition—is any discussion of the *context* out of which scriptural interpretation and embodiment emerge and thrive: the church at worship. The liturgy is the site at which the biblical texts exert their normative claims on the lives of Christians. The telling and retelling of the biblical stories in all of their depth and breadth, complexity and ambiguity, take place in the liturgical assembly gathered weekly for worship to pray, sing, and preach these texts into being. The appointed Scripture readings

mark the seasons of the church year as counter to the culture's
ordering of time; they shape the church's liturgy as a whole and,
by extension, shape those who hear, read, pray, proclaim, and
sing them. To isolate the Scriptures from their liturgical context
is fundamentally to misuse them. While Boys's proposals do not
explicitly endorse this disjuncture, her description of the "problem"
(that biblical criticism is insufficiently attended to in the local
church) does not help to overcome such a division.

"Has God Only One Blessing?" Judaism in Christian Terms

In examining the writings of Mary Boys that have emerged
from her participation in dialogues and colloquia within and
across Jewish and Christian communities, it is clear that what
I have identified as the latter two themes of her work are really
of a piece, for it is her view "that serious and sustained involvement in ecumenical/interreligious education is crucial for the
transformation of the world. . . . Religiously committed men and
women come to the public forum with powerful and necessary
tools for the transformation of the world. They bring the sacred
into the public realm."[17] She also insists on the necessity of Jewish-
Christian dialogue for helping Christians to do the hard work
of identifying and rooting out anti-Judaism and anti-Semitism
in their myriad forms and for overcoming historic Christianity's
"supersessionism," which, while overtly rejected by many mainline
churches, is still deeply ingrained (and thus covertly operative) in
the "conventional account of Christian origins" familiar to most
Christians.

Such an account is summed up in all-too-familiar propositional
statements that distort the biblical witness and the nature of Jewish theology and identity: that the God of the Old Testament is a
God of wrath and the God of the New Testament is a God of love;
that the Jews rejected Jesus as their Messiah because they were
waiting for a royal, glorious Messiah and could not recognize Jesus
as the Anointed One; that the hypocritical Pharisees show how
legalistic Judaism had become by Jesus' day; and that because the
Jews were unfaithful to their covenant with God, their covenant
has ended and Christians are now the people of God.[18] Boys notes,
"Although the conventional account is told with varying degrees

of depth and sophistication, it is powerful and pervasive. It offers a dramatic contrast of the loving Christ against legalistic Jews. It also provides an orderly picture of the beginnings of Christianity, a clear rationale for the church's displacement of the Jewish people, and an unequivocal warrant for Christian identity."[19] And so Boys seeks to challenge Christians to reflect critically on the conception of Judaism implicit in the church's understanding of itself, in its readings of New Testament passages that deal specifically with Jews and Jewish practice, and in the basic tenets of the Christian faith.

To that end she embarks on a genealogical survey of sorts to trace the roots of the many forms that Christian anti-Judaism has assumed through the centuries. Her commitment to delving into the specifics of Jewish and Christian faith, practice, and language stands in stark contrast to Moran's attempt to neutralize the particular convictions of Christians and Jews for the sake of a common "religious" experience. I will suggest later that Boys, in fact, does pursue Jewish-Christian dialogue as a modern project much in the same vein as Moran and Groom, but she is able at least to grant more integrity to the beliefs and practices of Judaism and Christianity and to resist the impulse to smooth over the dissonances of these two traditions.

Boys is at her best when examining Jewish-Christian relations in particular historical contexts and drawing out the nuances that make facile reductions of the complex historic relationship between Judaism and Christianity unconvincing and irresponsible. She notes, for example, that the shift from rival to enemy in the church's estimation of Jews, for example, must be seen to be derived from a confluence of forces beyond the merely theological. "A theological substratum was virtually always operative in anti-Jewish outbreaks, but economic, political, and social factors must be taken into consideration as well."[20] While both Christianity and Judaism have in successive eras undergone various changes in polity and practice, and their relationship to each other has borne the marks of these shifts, the issue of supersessionism—the idea that the Christian church has displaced Israel as the favored people of God because of the Jews' rejection of Jesus—remains the enduring problem to be addressed.

In looking at some of the New Testament texts that bear on this issue of the relationship between church and Israel, *ekklesia* and

synagogue, Boys rightly notes that the anti-Jewish polemics in
the Gospels must be evaluated in light of the historical contexts
out of which they emerged. She insists that a plain reading of the
texts—a reading that she identifies with a literalist, fundamentalist
approach to the Bible—must be rejected. In challenging an approach that takes these texts at face value, "an educational task is
implicit. . . . It is no small matter to educate Christians to a more
complex reading. In effect, we are inviting people to a reading
that seems to contradict the apparent meaning of the text—and
this with a text that is a (indeed for many *the*) precious artifact of
their faith."[21] To this end, Boys proposes a close reading of how
the Pharisees are depicted in the Gospel narratives. Her aim is to
compare the portrait of the Pharisees that emerges from these
New Testament writings with what recent biblical scholarship
has discovered about pharisaic Judaism in the Second Temple
period. (I should also note here that Boys prefers the term *Second
Testament* to *New Testament*.)

However, such a narrowly focused examination of the texts,
while perhaps helpful in fleshing out the complex reality of the
Judaism of Jesus' day, is in danger of failing to grasp the larger
theological agenda underlying these writings. For even if the portrait of the Pharisees in the Gospel witness is caricature, such an
exaggeration needs to be seen against the backdrop of the late-
first-century struggle for proprietary claim of Israel's biblical and
theological legacy. That is, the New Testament's portrayal of the
Pharisees cannot be isolated from the bitter, even hostile argument
over which group—Jewish Christians or pharisaic Jews—could lay
claim to rightful ownership of Israel's heritage. As Richard Hays
points out, "The polemics in these texts must be set within the
original context of *intra-Jewish* debate and conflict."[22]

These are, in effect, family squabbles, yet they are deadly serious ones. Boys, however, does not take as her starting point the
internal theological arguments about Torah and messiahship.
Instead, in looking at Matthew's Gospel, she states: "The harsh
denunciation of the Pharisees in Matthew 23 must be read in the
context of the literature of its day, in which it was commonplace
to use slanderous language about one's opponents."[23] For Boys,
the issue is understanding particular linguistic conventions so that
the anti-Jewish polemics of the Gospels can be situated within the
larger literary traditions of the ancient world. But such a reading

begs important questions internal to these texts themselves: *Why* the slanderous language? What is at stake in these intra-Jewish debates and conflicts? To say, as Boys does, that scurrilous language was a hallmark of Greco-Roman literature hardly explains its use. Boys's point is that a contextual reading of these anti-Jewish polemics reveals them to be untrustworthy accounts of first-century Judaism. "In short," she insists, "the Second Testament's portrait of the Pharisees is unreliable as history."[24] The Gospels' portrayal of the Pharisees as hypocritical legalists is inaccurate, and the church's subsequent embrace of such a view is, according to Boys, unwarranted. The Pharisees, she maintains, "did not hate grace, repentance, and forgiveness, nor did they think of ordinary people as sinners 'without hope in God's sight.' Rather, Pharisees were committed to drawing upon Torah for wisdom about everyday life, and this translated into an interest in law. . . . That interest, however does not mean they were self-righteous legalists absorbed by trivia and externals."[25]

But such a defense of the Pharisees hardly seems to be the point here, for the Gospel narratives are not concerned to give an accurate account of first-century Judaism; that is not their nature as *Gospels*. As Hays notes regarding the Gospel of Matthew, "It is a foundational document that claims for the community of Jesus' followers the exclusive possession of Israel's Scripture and tradition, against the counterclaims of the pharisaic movement. The figure of Jesus in Matthew becomes the one authentic and definitive interpreter of the Torah. Those who oppose him (and his disciples) can only be hypocrites and 'blind guides' (23:24)."[26] There is no way to get around or smooth over the "chilling narrative detail" in Matthew's ascribing "responsibility for the death of Jesus to the whole Jewish people *and to their descendants* [Matt. 27:24–25]."[27] Similarly, John's Gospel reflects the "Johannine community's frustrated and angry response to Jewish interlocutors who have refused to 'continue' in accepting the community's extraordinary claims about Jesus."[28] The most important hermeneutical question about these texts, then, is not how they have misinterpreted the Judaism of Jesus' day (though this is an interesting question) but how we ought to read them within what Hays calls "a wider canonical frame of reference" which assumes God's enduring faithfulness to Israel.

Boys's claim that these polemics employ textual strategies common in the literary tradition of ancient Greco-Roman rhetoric does not help us to see and interpret these writings as *Scripture* and as texts that support rather than deny Christianity's rootedness in the Judaism of Jesus' and Paul's day. In other words, if these New Testament writings need to be deconstructed, it should not be done primarily with the help of redaction criticism or in the same way linguistic analysis is applied to ancient rhetorical texts, but rather with the aid of the Old Testament. The "original intentions" of the authors of Matthew's and John's Gospels—intentions that indeed can be construed as anti-Jewish—are not of primary concern. As Hays puts it:

> If Jesus dies, as John's Gospel has it, as the Passover Lamb, then surely the result of his death is to lead Israel again and finally out of bondage. Even if some fail or refuse to claim the protection of his blood on their doorposts, the deepest purpose of his death must be to rescue Israel. Or again, if, as Matthew has it, the cup at the Last Supper is Jesus' "blood of the covenant, which is poured out for many for the forgiveness of sins" (Matt. 26:28), then what ironic soteriological resonance is triggered when all the Jewish people cry, "His blood be on us and our children"? Surely Jesus' death reaffirms rather than negates God's forgiveness and covenant love for Israel?[29]

While Boys is silent on the apostle Paul's discussion of Israel and his understanding of the status of the Jews in light of Jesus, Hays insists that "the theological position taken by Paul in Romans 9–11 ought to be judged determinative for Christian attitudes and actions toward the Jewish people, and that the other New Testament writings must be either interpreted or critiqued within this Pauline framework."[30] This passage is the working out in Paul's theology of God's election of Israel, the mystery of Israel's unbelief, and the conviction that "all Israel will be saved" (Rom. 11:26). For Paul, "God has not just selected a faithful remnant from among the Jewish people; rather, he has created a new community that embraces Gentiles *along with* the Jewish remnant. . . . [This] remnant must be understood not just as the lucky ones who are saved for their own sake; rather, they remain as a sign and witness of God's abiding faithfulness to the people Israel, a proof that God has not abandoned his people."[31] Such a view allows the Pauline writings to read and interpret the Gospel texts on Jews and Judaism, and in the process the church-Israel question is put within the framework of the larger scriptural story, in which God's fidelity to the covenant with Israel is unshakable. Supersessionism and other forms of anti-Judaism are biblically, theologically, and morally indefensible *not* because critical scholarship has shown that the first-century Pharisees were falsely vilified in the Gospel narratives but because Christian identity cannot be narrated, understood, or displayed apart from the story of God's continuing faithfulness to Israel. Thus the Christian church supersedes nothing and no one.

While Boys is concerned to combat the literalist readings of the Gospels that have sanctioned anti-Judaism through the centuries, her primary passion is for helping to foster the kinds of encounters that bring Jews and Christians together in conversation, and for imagining ways that the church might "re-educate" *Ecclesia* for a new relationship with *Synagoga*. "What will enable us to break the hold of the conventional account so that we might embrace a new 'story line' capable of situating us in right relationship with Jews and the God whose Name is holy for both communities?"[32] This question is important and urgent, yet Boys's first recourse in attempting to answer it is, again, to go outside the communal practices of either Judaism or Christianity to seek the counsel of the experts: "If we are to have room in the inn for a God who works among us in ways no less mysterious than our ancestors in faith, then we must be faithful to the new insights from scholars and others who have (and are) engaged in a deep level with Jews and Judaism."[33]

Boys has concluded, erroneously, that the New Testament Scriptures cannot be a resource for implementing better relations between Christians and Jews. She insists also that the supersessionist cast of much of the church's liturgy needs to be addressed and emended: "Reworking lectionaries and, in particular, educating teachers and preachers with deeper knowledge of the literal level—the historical and literary contexts of texts—would contribute to a more adequate 'composition of place' of Jesus of Nazareth."[34] Moreover, the "christocentrism" of the church's worship needs to be called into question, since "the liturgy's nearly exclusive emphasis on redemption in Christ may implicitly lead Christians to censor radical questions."[35]

While it is true that ongoing work is necessary to combat subtle and not-so-subtle forms of anti-Judaism in the church and its worship, I suggest that Boys's efforts at fostering Jewish-Christian understanding are much closer to those of Moran (with all the attendant problems in his approach already outlined) than a cursory reading of her argument might suggest. That is, even though Boys insists on the integrity of Jewish and Christian beliefs and practices, the position she herself assumes in assessing these traditions (more subtly than Moran but no less certainly) is that nebulous view from nowhere, the perspective beyond all perspectives that attempts to evaluate the Bible or the liturgy as if one were not already shaped profoundly by Scripture and by the church's worship. This is not to say that Boys as a lifelong Catholic and member of a religious order does not recognize that she has been formed by Christian discourse and practice, but rather that she thinks it possible to engage in dialogue with Jews and in critique of Christian theology in ways that can be theologically neutral.

Consider these musings by Boys: "Let me acknowledge here that I, like most Christians involved in Jewish-Christian dialogue, have many questions about the meaning of the Christ that are not readily resolved. What does it mean for us today, for instance, to claim that Jesus is the Son of God through whom we are saved? What does it mean for us to proclaim that Jesus is the Messiah, the agent of God's justice and reconciliation, when the world remains so broken and divided?"[36] Such questions, I suggest, betray not only a defeated Christology but a resignation from a discourse and set of practices that make Jewish-Christian dialogue intelligible and possible in the first place. That is, the very naming of the "problem" that exists between Christians and Jews presupposes the claim that Jesus is Lord. Boys puts forth a model of Jewish-Christian relations that seems to assume that the best we can hope for is not to hurt each other's feelings anymore. But ridding the church of supersessionism through educational methods derived from historical research, *without* maintaining the fundamental theological and biblical connections between Israel and the church, will have the effect of widening rather than bridging the gap between Christianity and Judaism.

The larger issue behind all of this is the shift in thinking that conceives of Judaism and Christianity as "religions" to be believed in rather than the church and Israel as communities of people embodying particular narratives and practices and bound together by a common history and heritage. Thus, in relation to the notions of covenant and promise, longing and expectation, George Lindbeck has noted that "fulfillment is no longer conceptualized in terms of the biblical narratives of God keeping and confirming promises and prophecies to persons and groups, but in terms of the impersonal patterns of evolutionary progress according to which one religion provides the conditions for the emergence of a better and higher one. Fulfillment now applies to religions, not peoples."[37]

One of the gains of understanding the church as Israel in nonsupersessionist terms is that Christians are now free to hear God speak not only through the Old Testament but also through postbiblical Jews. "The Jews remain," Lindbeck argues, "God's chosen people and are thus a primary source for Christian understandings of God's intentions."[38] To regard contemporary Jews thus is to engage Jewish theology and practice in specific, sometimes risky ways, not in general, neutral, "safe" terms. For instance, Lindbeck suggests that Christians have much to learn from "the talmudic practice of juxtaposing contrary opinions as authoritative instead of blandly harmonizing or brutally rejecting one or another as Christians have usually done."[39] Yet I think the element of danger must always remain present. If we want the conversations between Jews and Christians to result in more than cultural enrichment for each of these communities, then we must recognize that "any serious dialogue between Jews and Christians will remain tense and risky, especially in light of the painful history that lies behind us."[40]

For Boys such dialogue is rooted less in the conviction that the church is Israel and stems more from the question "What sort of education and formation in faith enables persons to participate intelligently in a religiously pluralistic society?"[41] Taking a cue from this word *pluralism*, perhaps one of the most fruitful outcomes of Jewish-Christian encounters that could be hoped for is a mutual stance of resistance against a "pervasive pluralistic consumerism destructive of all enduring traditions and communities."[42] That the church and Israel are both minority cultures within the vast network of dehumanizing technologies known as capitalism might offer the most compelling reason for engagement and collaboration.

Repairing the World

As mentioned earlier, one of the underlying rationales for Boys's efforts in Jewish-Christian dialogue is the hope that religiously committed men and women will "come to the public forum with powerful and necessary tools for transformation of the world."[43] Jews and Christians, as they encounter each other's traditions and learn to break down the walls of division, also bring these traditions and the skills honed in dialogue to bear on "public life" in order that the sacred might be made visible in the realm of the secular and that social change might be possible. Boys links such efforts to the vocation of religious educators, who "are called to design and enact educational processes in such a way that people (1) realize the world is in need of repair; (2) believe that something can be done to repair it; (3) form a community of persons who sustain each other in the work of repairing."[44] There is a clear resonance here with the work of Thomas Groome, who, as noted in the previous chapter, envisions the work of Christian religious education to be helping the church to help society in creating and maintaining "social/political/economic structures that are capable of promoting the values of the Kingdom."[45]

That it is the task of the church to infuse the secular realm with sacred values is an unquestioned given in the work of both Boys and Groome. Whereas "the kingdom of God" functions as a guiding trope for Groome's project, Boys names the metaphor of the body of Christ and the liturgy of the Eucharist as "two vital resources for education for the repair of the world."[46] The implication of the first is that "any religious education in the Christian tradition is grounded in community,"[47] though such a truism is never connected in a direct way to Boys's claim about transforming the world. She gives more attention to liturgy and the Eucharist, suggesting that liturgy invites worshipers to involvement in the work of repairing the world. By breaking through the individualism that dominates the culture, the liturgy teaches us to care about others "as members of one body."[48] The Eucharist, moreover, exerts its power ethically and eschatologically: the holy meal calls us to solidarity with the poor and suffering and enjoins our participation in working toward that time when all will feast together at the heavenly banquet.

The educator's role, then, becomes *translation* (my description of Boys's ideas here, not hers): how to communicate, how to interpret, the ethical and eschatological dimensions of Christian faith and practice so as to compel and persuade the wider secular public that social change—the repair of the world—is not only possible but urgently necessary. While the liturgy in general and the Eucharist in particular offer a vision for what the "repair of the world" might look like (community, wholeness, well-being, freedom, etc.), it is still necessary, according to Boys, for the church to engage the world on the world's terms if Christians want to be taken seriously as full partners in the work of justice and meaningful social change. "Engagement in social analysis, says Boys, is an enactment of one's belief that something *can* done to repair the world. It also tempers one's idealism with the discipline of secular warrant and public reason—the only way disciples can make their case to the citizenry at large."[49]

The "Public Church": Citizenship and Discipleship

Boys takes up Martin Marty's idea of the "public church" as "a family of apostolic churches with Jesus Christ at the center, churches which are especially sensitive to the *res publica*, the public order that surrounds and includes people of faith."[50] According to Boys, a public church, like the public theology called for by Groome, serves the vital function of bringing humanity to a new stage of faith (echoes of Fowler here), a faith in which, as Marty puts it, "the God of prey is left behind and people can affirm what they believe without pouncing on others."[51] Within such a scheme, the central question of the educational enterprise is "How is it possible in a pluralistic society to educate people in the traditions of their own community of faith while simultaneously preparing them to participate in the shaping of the *res publica*?"[52] How can the church recover as one of its primary tasks the fostering of co-operation with those in the political realm who seek to cultivate responsible citizenship and to promote agendas of "justice, equity, and harmony"?[53]

Once again, all of this may strike us as not only apt but admirable; what, one might ask, could be problematic about helping to advance such obvious good in the world? Who is not in favor of justice, equity, and harmony? But such questions betray the subtle ways in which many who claim to speak as Christians unwittingly adopt the categories of modernity and assume the necessity (and superiority) of those categories for describing, explaining, and interpreting both the world and the church. Why, for example, is it assumed that the "political realm" is an empirical, incontestable given? When Boys says that "it is the responsibility of the religious educator, among others, to evangelize in such a manner as to engage civic concerns,"[54] why is it taken for granted that the "civic" constitutes an arena of action into which "religious" concerns must be translated? The answer to these questions lies, again, in the unquestioning alliance with the liberal orthodoxy that emerged from "the West's definition of itself"[55]—an orthodoxy whose tenets include the privatization of religion and the regarding of the public realm as a natural, inevitable given.[56]

Emmanuel Katongole helps us to see what is wrong with this way of characterizing the church's relationship to the political realm, the social order, the wider "public":

> Since there is no way to transcend or escape the particular, "public" can never be understood as a topologically higher plane of engagement with others, managed by some "conversational restraint" by which one is bound to agree in advance to say nothing at all about fundamental disagreements. Nor is "public" an invocation of a philosophical attitude (Categorical, Universalization, etc.) which one adopts by stripping one's reasons and arguments of any particular associations. "Public," just like universality, is a name of a *direction* rather than a *terminus*, a mission rather than a clear picture of the goal. "Public" is the very *process* by which one allows the practices of a particular tradition or polity to act as a critic as well as be enriched by coming into contact with different peoples and histories.[57]

Katongole's way of conceiving of "public," particularly the notion of "public" as a process, means that the church's engagement with the wider social order takes the shape of *witness*, of giving embodied, material form to the practices and convictions that order the lives of Christians. Such a view does not concede the primacy of the "public" (and its discourse) for legitimizing this witness. As Katongole goes on to say, "The crucial question is how to be a 'living' tradition, i.e., a community suffused with a normative creative tension and sufficient openness to allow such contact with the other."[58]

The issue then is not whether the church should engage the wider public (the question is not "public or not public?" but "what sort of public?").[59] Rather, Christians must ask questions like these: What language do we speak? What grammar orders our speech? What sort of power do we invoke? What vision animates our encounter with the other and the witness we seek to make to the other? How is the church itself a *polis*—an alternative ordering of power and human relations that counters the notion of politics as statecraft? These questions have enormous implications for catechesis, for they remind us that to live as faithful disciples of the one who binds us to the very mystery of God means that we will be called to resist and to lay bare modernity's illusions and self-deceptions. Its language will not be our language, its grammar not our grammar, its power not our power, its vision not our vision, its politics not our politics.

Boys, like Groome and Moran, remains caught up in modernity's false vision of the world that purports to be "realism"; she, like they, has surrendered the gospel's politics of witness—of the cross and of risk—to a politics that takes as its greatest good the cultivation of the free, responsible self. This is no more evident than in her approving quotation of sociologist John Coleman, who says that "churches must regain a sense of their public role as corporate citizens. They can uniquely create forums for a moral culture of politics and economic life. They can provide shared 'neutral space' where politics can be pursued beyond mere naked interest."[60]

It is difficult to know where to begin in challenging a statement such as this, laden is it with the kind of logic I am suggesting is deserving of serious critique. For Coleman, Boys, Groome, Moran, and many others who speak and write within the field of religious education, it is simply assumed that "the religious" is a mindset or disposition or orientation that, when functioning at its best, contributes positively (e.g., advances human rights, promotes freedom, justice, and equality) to a more determinative, more elemental reality understood as "politics" or "culture" or "the secular" or "the public." The value of the church, from such a perspective, lies in its capacity to promote the "moral culture of politics and economic life"—to enhance responsible, ethical citizenship in the public realm. Since Christianity is understood to be connected somehow to "morality" (a term whose definition, like that of "religion," is simply assumed to be self-evident), churches are deemed specially qualified to enter moral debates in the public arena, in service to the advancement of the public good (which also is never clearly defined).[61] Politics and economics are taken for granted as entities whose origins, histories, and practices require no narration, no explanation.

The suggestion that churches can provide a neutral space exposes not only Coleman's mistaken assumption that neutrality is possible but also the more profound error that the Christian church exists to be in service to the greater public and the politics it pursues. In framing her position around Coleman's claims, Boys contends that "educators in the church . . . have something to gain from the public sphere precisely because the demands of citizenship enhance discipleship"[62] and that "to teach another the obligations of citizenship suggests practice in 'translating' religious meanings into secular terminology."[63]

In contrast to all this, I am suggesting that Christians live by a narrative that we take to be a counterstory, *the* counterstory to "the way things are." Again, as John Milbank has noted, "it is impossible to think of our Christian narrative as only 'our point of view,' our perspective on a world that really exists in a different, 'secular' way. There is no independently available 'real world' against which we must test our Christian convictions, because these convictions are the most final, and at the same time the most basic, *seeing* of what the world is."[64] It might be objected that such a view arrogantly assumes to position the gospel as metanarrative—as a story that subsumes all other stories. The reply to such an objection is, I'm afraid, equally audacious: it could not be otherwise.

But what must not be lost on those who are offended by such a bold assertion is the truth that *all* claims to speak about reality are already, by their very existence, metanarratives: all-encompassing stories about what is real and what is true. There can be no escape into a realm that is not already some other realm. Moran, Groome, and Boys all write about religious education from within the metanarrative of modern liberalism, but since one of the components of the story of modern liberalism is its putative objectivity and impartiality, they fail to see that "religion" and "religious education" are already ideologically laden "structures" (in Stanley Fish's terms) that do not and cannot afford one a neutral perspective on *particular* religious traditions or their respective pedagogies.

They also remain caught in the trap of thinking that "the religious"—vaguely defined as having to do with "the sacred"—is only one aspect of "the social" or "the civic," and that to be religious is to strive to advance an agenda of justice, equity, and harmony established not by theological reflection on the nature of God and Christian community, but by the social order itself (specifically, the social order conceived of as promoter and defender of freedom, justice, and responsible citizenship). The existence and legitimacy of this order are never called into question.

Again, as Milbank reminds us, "the Christian grasp of reality *right from the start* is utterly at variance with anything the world supposes to be 'realistic.' This is why it is so absurd deliberately to import the world's realism into the sphere of Christian ethics as if, when it came to the practical crunch, we could set our entire religious vision to one side. In Christian terms, it is the world that will never understand the world aright."[65]

Summary

In chapter one it was noted that Gabriel Moran's vision of the task of religious education involves many religious languages brought together into one conversation. While there are particular faith-centered educational endeavors (like Christian education or Jewish education), *religious education,* for Moran, names the enterprise that "situates" the pedagogical practices of various religious traditions into a wider theoretical construct and into "the worldwide conversation of today"—a conversation whose ultimate purpose is to help persons "understand religion" in the hope of fostering more "tolerance, understanding, and peace in the world." Similarly, in examining the work of Thomas Groome in chapter two, we saw that "Christian religious education" is deemed to be but one expression of the attempt to empower persons in their quest for transcendence and for the "ultimate ground of being"—a quest that is assumed to be primal and universal. In more specific terms, to do Christian religious education from Groome's perspective is to educate Christians in the ways of freedom and justice so that the church might fulfill its appointed task of helping to create a more just and equitable world.

The work of Mary Boys, I suggest, fits readily within this same trajectory, charting the same course as the work of Moran and Groome. Her treatment of Jewish-Christian relations is more nuanced than Moran's—Boys does not rush, as he does, to empty theological convictions of their content for the sake of meaningful "conversation," but she does, like Moran, assume that neutrality is possible. With Groome, Boys insists that the work of Christian education involves "translating" Christian themes and ideas into secular terminology in order that the church might contribute to the transformation of the social order and the repair of the world.

I have noted how difficult it is to contest such construals of Christian/religious education, how hard it is to argue against projects and proposals so resolutely committed to the esteemed values of peace, tolerance, understanding, harmony, justice, and freedom. But what I hope that I have demonstrated is that the projects of Moran, Groome, and Boys are, finally, insufficiently radical for their own desired political ends, for they have not recognized that they remain caught up in and indebted to the very modern, liberal, capitalist order that their work strives to overcome.

In contrast, I have suggested, Christian discourse promulgates its own epistemology and advances its own vision of what is real and what is true; it instantiates itself, startlingly perhaps for many of us, as the true politics. And in such knowing and seeing, and within the *polis* of the *ekklesia*, we are transformed as our lives bear witness to the truth and love of the Triune God, whose life is our life.

PART TWO

PEDAGOGY
WITHOUT
APOLOGY

4

WORSHIP AND CATECHESIS

Knowledge, Desire,
and Christian Formation

The knowing person can never quite catch up with how he or she knows; in achieving knowledge he or she is always already beholden to assumptions, antecedent interests and tacit procedures which are not themselves known—if to be known means to be fully available for inspection and certification by consciousness.

Joseph Dunne

Now desire, not Greek "knowledge," mediates to us reality.

John Milbank

Introduction

How do we know what we know?

In answering such a question, our first impulse might be to say that to know is to be *taught*—to engage in a process of *learning.* Commonly in the modern industrialized West such teaching and learning occur within the structured environment of a classroom, with various pedagogical tools and techniques at the disposal of the teacher. To be schooled in such a way is to participate in the transfer of educational content from teacher to pupil. We often speak of this way of knowing/learning as the "educational process," by which learners—through the skill of the teacher and their own receptivity to the didactic methods at hand—acquire knowledge, master concepts, accumulate data, absorb information, and so on. Understood this way, knowledge is conceived of as a kind of repository of neutral facts, and the mastery of these facts constitutes the process and the ultimate goal of coming to know.

This "objectivist" view of knowledge and learning, which is deeply embedded in current educational practices (despite numerous challenges to it), is rooted, of course, in the larger philosophical project of modernity: the quest for truth and autonomy and the concomitant privileging of a self-transparent reason. While the philosophy born of this pursuit was a "flight from authority"—from tradition, history, community—it was also a "flight to objectivity." As Descartes himself proclaimed,

> I concluded that I was a substance whose whole essence and nature consists only in thinking, and which, that it may exist, has need of no place, nor is dependent on any material thing; so that "I," that is to say, the mind by which I am what I am, is wholly distinct from the body and is even more known than the latter, and is such, that although the latter were not, it would still continue to be all that it is.[1]

This flight to objectivity required, as Descartes made clear, the devaluing of historical contingency, the material world, and bodily existence. Susan Bordo has suggested that Descartes's entire epistemological project marks a "retreat from the medieval world of connectedness and interdependence—of organic unity—into the modern, clinical universe of purity, clarity, and objectivity."[2] "The Cartesian knower," Bordo points out, "being without a body, not only has 'no need of any place' but actually *is* 'no place.' He therefore cannot 'grasp' the universe—which would demand a place 'outside' the whole. But, assured of his own transparency, he can relate with absolute neutrality to the objects he surveys, unfettered by the perspectival nature of embodied vision. He has become, quite literally, *objective.*"[3]

While Bordo's (and others') critiques of Enlightenment epistemology reveal the flawed and fatal character of this way of knowing/learning, our contemporary pedagogical practices continue to be lured by technique, preoccupied with method, and seduced by the false promises of objectivity. As educator Parker J. Palmer observes, "There are plenty of pedagogical experiments around these days, many proposals for innovative and engaging ways to teach and learn, but most of them deal only with techniques. They leave the underlying epistemology unexamined and unchanged; they are not well grounded in an alternative theory about the nature of knowing."[4] Indebted as such experiments and proposals are to the scientific method and the rationalism of Enlightenment thought, they purport neutrality in rationale and motivation and assume an instrumentalist logic by which particular methods and techniques can be "applied" within and across a variety of settings and contexts; indeed, any such model of learning is regarded (approvingly) as context free.

When the mastery of data is the primary goal of learning and what it means to know, then the process or practice by which that putative mastery occurs is not connected to nor dependent upon any particular social, cultural, or linguistic context for its intelligibility. Such a model is designed to meet with equal success no matter where or when it is employed. As Joseph Dunne points out, under this view everything essential in teaching can be disembedded from the contexts and traditions that would provide coherence; it is assumed, moreover, that knowledge resides in a knower/learner who is detachable from "contexts and engagements in which she is already inescapably taken up."[5]

Knowledge and Conversion

Our sensibilities about the "educational process" continue to be shaped by these highly questionable claims of efficiency and neutrality. (My earlier critique of Gabriel Moran's work was meant to demonstrate, among other things, how subtly such claims operate in the discourse of contemporary religious educators.) What is suppressed or denied in the uncritical embrace of objectivism is the truth that such pedagogy is, in the end, a "strategy for avoiding our own conversion."[6] If, on the most basic level, the knowledge that Christians aspire to is, as it was for Augustine, knowledge of God and knowledge of self, then such knowledge will not, cannot, leave us unchanged. Like Augustine, we will come to know that the self is disclosed only in and through the doxological—the praise and adoration of God.

Although Augustine writes almost nothing about worship—about the doxological per se—cult is, in fact, decisive for creating coherence and context for his treatment of various theological themes, ideas, and doctrines. The modern tendency to read *The Confessions* as the interior monologue of an overly self-conscious intellectual is to miss entirely the radical ecclesiology, the presupposition of Christian community, that situate Augustine's prayer to God. *The Confessions* is, in a peculiar way, a very *liturgical* book. Not only is it Augustine's prayer to God, but it also unfolds his dawning "knowledge" of the very nature of humans as doxological: "Yet these humans, due part of your creation as they are, still do long to praise you. You arouse us so that praising you may bring us joy, because you have made us and drawn us to yourself, and our heart is unquiet until it rests in you."[7] For Augustine, praise and knowledge are inextricably bound together, neither one prior to the other, neither explainable apart from the other:

> Grant me to know and understand, Lord, which comes first: to call upon you or to praise you? To know you or to call upon you? Must we know you before we can call upon you? Anyone who invokes what is still unknown may be making a mistake. Or should you be invoked first, so that we may then come to know you? But how can people call upon someone in whom they do not yet believe? And how can they believe without a preacher? But scripture tells us that those who seek the Lord will praise him, for as they seek they find him, and on finding him they will praise him. Let me seek you, then, Lord, even while I am calling upon you, and call upon you even as I believe in you; for to us you have indeed been preached. My faith calls upon you, Lord, this faith which is your gift to me, which you have breathed into me through the humanity of your Son and the ministry of your preacher.[8]

As Patricia Hampl, in her preface to *The Confessions,* observes: "Augustine's longing to know is not merely intellectual. He must know as one knows through love—by being known. *Deus, noverim te, noverim me,* he prays. God, let me know You and know myself."[9] To know is to praise and to praise is to know.

As long as our own understanding of what it means to know and learn remains wedded to the modern fiction of the cool, clinically detached observer and to a view of the end of knowledge as the technical mastery of information, we fail to recognize (as Augustine surely was able to) that to learn, to know, is to be *transformed*—it is to implicate ourselves, our very bodies, in the actions and practices of learning and coming to know. Maria Boulding reminds us, for example, how baptism would have been a powerfully transformative act for Augustine. His own understanding of it would have involved much more than an intellectual or analytical grasp of its meaning, for the sacrament was, in Augustine's time, "a harrowing adult initiation experience, a true cult act signaling a changed life, not to be confused with the mild christening ceremonies of our own time."[10] What Augustine would have "known" from and about his own baptism could not have been separated from the act itself; *who* he was could not be narrated apart from those formative events that were constitutive of his very identity. Knowledge and (liturgical) action were (and are) fundamentally linked.

"There are settings," Dunne notes, "in which people invariably not only know but act; where their knowledge is intimately connected with ways of conducting themselves, relating with others, getting things done."[11] Farmer, poet, and essayist Wendell Berry makes a similar point when describing the ecology of practices that constituted life on family farms in the early part of the twentieth century. Commenting on the educational import of such practices, he observes: "An important source of instruction and pleasure to a child growing up on a farm was participation in the family economy. Children learned about the adult world by participating in it in a small way, by doing a little work and making a little money—a much more effective, because pleasurable, and a much cheaper method than the present one of requiring the adult world to be learned in the abstract in school."[12] Berry's observations should not be interpreted as one man's wistful longing to return to an uncomplicated past but as a critical judgment against our current culture's failure to know what it means to properly form the young and our inability to see that all real knowing "arises within a prior establishment and comportment in the world, and is carried forward through practices that are themselves densely embodied, linguistic, and historical."[13]

Such practices, whether they be those associated with farming or worship, intend our transformation—not only in the sense that our minds are changed or our intellects conditioned (though this is certainly important), but in the deeper, Augustinian sense that we are *constituted differently*. That is to say, knowledge's integral connection to action, doing, practice, habit, and ritual means that what we know cannot be separated from who we are or, within the confessional, eschatological language of the church, who we hope to be.

Thus my original question, "How do we know what we know?" should now be recognized as deeply indebted to the Cartesianism under scrutiny here and to the objectivist view of knowledge that deserves dismantling. In other words, a doxological, liturgical, eucharistic account of knowledge—as I am attempting to develop—assumes that we can never be at any distance from the knowledge we need. All knowledge, as Stanley Fish points out, is situational—"already known or dwelt in; it cannot be handed over in the forms of rules or maxims or theories."[14] Perspective or critical distance—what objectivism demands and proponents of method rigorously pursue—is impossible and pointless, a hopeless fiction. This was the point made in chapter 1 in regard to Moran's claim that one of the primary goals of religious education is to "understand religion"—to "situate" one's particular faith tradition within the broader context of religion *qua* religion. Such a distancing act, I suggested, is a trick that cannot be pulled off. There is no way to "step back from, rise above, get to the side of your beliefs and convictions so that they will have less of a hold on you than they would had you not performed this distancing action."[15] Perspective, to reiterate the point, is a fallacy: there can be "no transition from 'knowing that' to 'knowing how.'"[16] Thus in thinking about knowledge and worship, we find ourselves making the move from epistemology to ontology. I will not be suggesting that it is the Eucharist that answers the question "How do we know what we know?" (for this is an unanswerable—and undesirable—question) but simply that the Eucharist gives us God.

Such a construal of what it means to know and learn has broad implications for worship and catechesis. In recent years there have been attempts to "integrate" Christian education and worship/liturgy—to join together what has been, in the minds of many, too long divided. But much of the work in this area has assumed an understanding of Christian education that is deeply indebted to modern social-scientific accounts of self, knowledge, human consciousness, moral development, stages of faith, and so on.[17] They have, in other words, shared many of the same problematic assumptions that were observed and assessed in the work of Moran, Groome, and Boys. These endeavors have been predicated on a kind of disciplinary divide that trades on the categories of modern social theory (in its various guises) but is highly questionable within a thoroughgoing Christian narration of identity and selfhood. Other, related attempts at "connecting" education and worship have often been technical, instrumentalist, and/or utilitarian in approach—that is, education by, with, or through the liturgy. As John Westerhoff points out, "Some religious educators have made the serious mistake of speaking of teaching *by* or *with* the liturgy, thereby reducing the liturgy to a didactic act. To *use* the liturgy is to do it violence."[18]

In contrast, to admit the integral connection between knowledge and action, between learning and bodily practice, is to recognize that Christians worship is the site at which our formation and education are initiated and completed (insofar as they can ever be complete). What we *do*, how we *act*, in the liturgical assembly shapes us in particular and powerful ways and is both formative of identity and catechetical in the most basic sense. Such a view rejects the categorical distinctions that create the false need for a bridge between "education" and "worship." It also challenges modern (Cartesian) accounts of the self and knowledge and assumes instead that "human subjectivity is not a self-contained 'given,' anterior to its performance, but that its subsequent performances are just as much involved in the constitution of its identity."[19] In other words, where contemporary approaches to catechesis usually assume the priority of a singular, stable human subject in whom the implementation of method and technique will result in something called "education," a liturgically driven, doxologically shaped theology of catechesis does not take as its starting point "the individual." There is no fixed and stable self, no completed being, prior to its doxological performance.

To be even more specific (and to take the discussion in a direction that will be explored more fully later), we can say that it is in eucharistic worship that we *know* most fully—not in the sense that we intellectually grasp the sacramental *mysterion* but in the sense that we are constituted as a people who abide in the truth of God's own trinitarian life. In this way the liturgy fulfills its catechetical function "not as exposition apart from faith, but as a performative *act* of faith."[20] Thus catechesis is inseparable from doxology.

Knowledge and Worship

The "knowledge" imparted in worship is not simply cognitive—it is not the mere grasping of data by the intellect—but is material and corporeal; it is a knowledge that can be known only in the doing of it. It is, at heart, bodily and performative. We are habituated to and in the knowledge of the Christian faith by the ritual performance that is worship, so that a deep unity between doctrine and practice is taken for granted (again, the notion that "education" and "worship" are categorically separate realms is rejected). For example, when we share the peace of Christ in the eucharistic liturgy, the gestures, postures, and movements that constitute this act are a kind of performative knowledge. This is one of the settings in which, as Dunne suggests, our knowledge is integrally connected to ways of conducting ourselves. The act of sharing the peace of Christ is not merely symbolic; it is not expressive or representative of something else, but actually discloses, embodies the real. We may call it a sign, but it is a full sign—one that contains already within it (albeit imperfectly) that which it signifies.

Understood this way, the ritual signs and gestures of corporate worship *produce* certain kinds of knowledge, or one might say that bodies are produced that *know differently*. As M. Therese Lysaught argues, "For the Church to fulfill its call to discipleship, to be active in the world concretely and materially, the Body of Christ must literally be embodied. . . . Discipleship—that is, authentic, lived Christianity—requires the production of Christian bodies."[21] In sharing the peace, we extend our bodies toward one another, embrace one another, gesturing our willingness to risk living in peace with one another; we are not simply offering a pious morning greeting, but are in fact making a radical political claim—materially, bodily—about the nature of Christian community and life within the body of Christ. We are learning, *in the doing* of this act at each Communion celebration, what it means to claim the name *Christian*—to know that this is who we are and what is required of us before we approach the Communion table. Liturgical practices like sharing the peace (or kneeling or genuflecting) are not mere displays of ritualized behavior; rather they are acts that function to produce particular kinds of people. Therefore, to reflect on the catechetical power of worship is not to explain how it should affect or influence behavior or attitudes, or what the practices of worship "teach" in a didactic way, but rather how it is that worship produces those who worship and how worship itself creates for those who worship an alternative ontology, a countercommunity, another way of being in the world.

Further, the economy of words and gestures in ritual speech serves to form and catechize in ways that formal discourse about this practice cannot. Indeed, any formalized instruction about the practices of sharing the peace would be meaningless if detached from the context of a worshiping community. Any formalized teaching about *any* particular practice or doctrine must concede the primacy of worship for shaping persons to be able in the first place to receive and understand such doctrinal instruction. Worship catechizes, and worship is the matrix and milieu from which all other catechesis can take place.

Knowledge and Difference

It is, however, more complicated than that. For what can it mean, to continue with one of the examples above, to share the peace of Christ in a world at war? Formation and catechesis always occur within the context of alternative construals of the real and the good. Worship takes place in specific cultural, social, linguistic, political, and economic settings that have everything to do with what we understand worship to signify and accomplish, with the kind of "knowledge" we garner from it. Therefore, we must understand worship "within a semantic framework whereby the significance of an action is dependent upon its place and relationship within a context of all other ways of acting; what it echoes, what it inverts, what it alludes to, what it denies."[22] This is not unlike the notion that the sharing of the eucharistic meal is an economic act that locates, defines, and judges all other economies. The worshiping community gathered in table fellowship constitutes an alternative vision of reality ("inverting" and "denying" in Catherine Bell's sense), giving embodied, material form to an alternative way of being in the world. Therefore, one might ask how it is that worship establishes and manipulates its own differentiation and purposes *in the very doing of the act* within the context of other ways of acting. How is it that authentic Christian worship offers a kind of privileged contrast, a narrative-knowledge that is counter to the ubiquitous and deeply seductive myth of the unencumbered modern subject within the capitalist-driven, consumer-oriented, media-saturated cultures of the industrialized West?

How, in other words, is worship—particularly the table fellowship of the Eucharist—an act of *resistance* that forms and transforms those who worship? How does worship teach and catechize worshipers in countervailing ways, establishing a "privileged contrast," and how does such catechesis create a community of worshipers who *know differently*, who are constituted contrarily to the dominant ways of thinking, acting, and being in the world? These questions will be taken up in more depth in a later chapter, but I can at least say now that Christian worship can be understood to explicate Jonathan Z. Smith's critical observation that ritual is, above all, the assertion of difference.[23] Thus the eucharistic celebration is not fundamentally *display* but the *production* of, in Bell's terms, "ritualized agents": those whose knowledge is bound up in the communal actions they undertake. It is, again to echo Augustine, the linking of knowledge with the conversion of the self.

Knowledge and Communion

The Eucharist is not the act of a preexisting church. As Orthodox theologian John Zizioulas argues, "It is an event *constitutive*
of the being of the Church, enabling the Church to *be.*"[24] The
source of such being is God's very self: "The life of the eucharist
is the life of God Himself. . . . It is the life of *communion* with
God, such as exists within the Trinity and is actualized within
the members of the eucharistic community. *Knowledge and communion are identical.*"[25]
To know is to abide in the truth of God's own trinitarian
existence. This knowledge is unavailable apart from the eucharistic fellowship that calls into being this reality. Again, with
Augustine (or, as Zizioulas might suggest, Irenaeus, Ignatius,
and Gregory), knowledge comes in and through the doxological. If catechesis is concerned with seeking to know and learn
the truth of the Christian faith, then it is fair to say—as radical
as it may seem—that the eucharistic worship of the gathered
community is the locus of truth, for

> the Word of God does not dwell in the human mind as rational
> knowledge or in the human soul as a mystical inner experience,
> but as communion within a community. And it is most important
> to note that in this way of understanding Christ as truth, Christ
> himself becomes revealed as truth not *in* a community, but *as* a
> community. So truth is not just something "expressed" or "heard,"
> a propositional or logical truth; but something which *is,* i.e. an
> ontological truth: the community itself becoming the truth.[26]

Such an account of truth, community, and knowledge cannot help but seem strange, even imperialistic, within most of
the social and cultural settings in which the church at worship
currently finds itself. Indeed, inasmuch as the church in many
places has sought to join the market by packaging and promoting the gospel as a commodity available for consumption by an
increasingly discriminating "shopping public," the notion of the
Eucharist as an alternative politics, a countertruth, is unintel-
ligible. But it is precisely in "the community itself becoming the
truth" that the worshiping body is formed as a counterculture,
a contrast society.[27]

It is the liturgy in its entirety (the prayer, praise, and proclamation that surround the Eucharist) that calls into being this alternative community. As Walter Brueggemann has suggested, "Sunday morning is the practice of a counter life through counter speech."[28] In preaching, for example, the sermon finds its significance in its situatedness within the liturgy itself, not as "the individualistic, virtuoso performance with which so many Protestants are familiar."[29] The sermon should embody and articulate what is expressed in the "gathering of the congregation, songs of praise and doxology, recitations of God's mighty acts, reminiscences of Jesus, the celebration of the sacraments, and a blessing and sending of the people into the world."[30] All of this works to produce "persons who have an instinctive knowledge . . . embedded in their bodies [and] in their sense of reality."[31]

This means that the knowledge that comes through the worship of God is ultimately a kind of counterknowledge to the ways the real and the good are instantiated in the wider culture, affording the possibility of resistance to what Christians might take to be false and harmful construals of what is real and what is good. This "practical knowledge" reconfigures and reimagines the order of power in the world such that normalized power relations are called into question and the order of power (and desire) is brought under the scrutiny of the community itself becoming the truth. The imagined world of the liturgy that is called into being by our acts of speech to, for, and about God is not only an alternative reality or a counterculture (that is, it is not alternative in the sense of consumer choice); rather, this vision of the real proclaims dissatisfaction with the existing order, with "the way things are." The language of the liturgy (verbal and bodily) signifies differently, creating a new set of possibilities for human existence; it puts the world under judgment—not condemnation but judgment. To partake of the Eucharist is to enact judgment against a world at war with itself; it is to recognize the subversive nature of this act of communing at Christ's table. The sign and that which it signifies cannot be separated; the Eucharist not only points to the gospel story but is itself its incarnated proclamation. To know this gospel story—to learn it, to be shaped by it—is not merely to hear and assent to it but to embody it, to give it living, material form and substance.

Knowledge and the Triune God

John Westerhoff has said that the purpose of catechesis, the goal of Christian education, is to help the church learn to live by the story that has called it into existence. This story, as I have already said, is not simply one interesting tale among many; rather, it is our fundamental way of seeing the world, of orienting ourselves in the world, and of knowing who we are (and who we are not). And yet this story can neither be told nor understood apart from participation in the community created by the story: the body of Christ. It is life within the body of Christ that situates and makes meaningful the story we seek to make our own. As followers of Jesus Christ, we participate not only in his teaching but also in his body. From a catechetical perspective, there is no "knowledge" of Jesus (of God, the church, the gospel) apart from communion with the Father and Son through the power of the Holy Spirit. As Bonhoeffer says: "It is wrong to assume that on the one hand there is a word, or a truth, and on the other hand there is a community, existing as two separate entities, and that it would then be the task of the preacher to take this word, to manipulate and enliven it, in order to bring it within and apply it to the community. Rather, the Word moves along this path of its own accord."[32] Catechesis does not begin, therefore, with theory or method, doctrine or dogma, but with the body of Christ already formed by the Word.

The heart of this story is the church's identification of God as triune: "God is the Father who raised the crucified Jew Jesus from the dead and poured out their common Spirit upon all flesh."[33] The doctrine of the Trinity is foundational for the identity of Christians and for the ongoing shaping of Christian community, and yet our grasp of what such a doctrine means is not merely a mental operation of giving intellectual assent to the church's historic claim that God exists as one *ousia* and three *hypostases*. The *truth* of this doctrine, in other words, is not available to us outside of our own participation in the forms of life that bear witness to God as Trinity—and such participation is at the heart of the church's catechetical enterprise.

Pedagogically speaking, this means that we cannot stand outside the story in order to learn it, to know it. To learn the story is already to be caught up in the ever-unfolding drama of God's redemptive purposes—purposes accomplished through the people Israel, through the life, death, and resurrection of Jesus of Nazareth, and through the ongoing mission and ministry of the church in the world. Thus we have no perspective on this story—at least not in the sense that Moran and others speak of "situating" our story within a larger "religious" framework. This narrative identification of the Triune God, as Bruce Marshall puts it, "organizes a comprehensive view of all things, and especially of human nature, history, and destiny."[34] We learn to say that God is triune by learning to live within the pattern of trinitarian relations that are at the heart of the church's creeds, Scriptures, prayers, and sacraments.

Catechesis historically has been about the reshaping of identity and the transformation of the self into the likeness of Christ. The catechumenate of the early church was an endeavor in such transformation, an attempt at an intentional, ongoing, communally centered, liturgically driven transformation of persons so that they might become icons of the risen Christ (image = εικονα). It was (and is) recognized, however, that this transforming work is accomplished not by the catechist, nor by the priest, nor by the catechumen herself, but by the power of God through the Holy Spirit:

> This conforming of human beings to the crucified and risen Christ is a unitary action of the whole Trinity, and indeed seems to realize the most interior and primal purposes of the triune God. The Father has eternally and effectively willed—predestined—our conformity to his Son (cf. Rom. 8:29; Eph. 1:5), who by accepting incarnation and the death from which the Father raises him, constitutes that original form of which we are intended images. The Spirit is the agent who, poured out from the Father by the risen Son and dwelling in us, immediately joins us to Christ and makes us his icons (see Rom. 8:9–11, 14).[35]

Therefore, catechesis was (and is) the process of making new converts *available to* the working of the Holy Spirit, which means habituating them over time in the practices of Christian community, namely eucharistic worship. It was also taken for granted in the early church that catechesis was a *performative* endeavor, not merely an exercise in dispensing doctrine, though catechetical efforts at their worst would come to emphasize the didactic over the performative, the instructional over the liturgical.

Worship, as I have said, catechizes, and worship is the matrix and milieu in and from which all other catechesis must take place. And because the church's worship of the Triune God is the beginning point of all catechetical efforts, the ways we deploy common pedagogical terms—words like *knowledge, self, intellect, subjectivity,* and so on—stand in stark contrast to their appropriation in secular educational settings. That is, as worshipers of the Triune God, we *know* differently. As Catherine Pickstock aptly puts it:

> This performance of faith, which does not operate according to the worshipping subject's full command of his action, but, rather, his submission to a *narrative* mode of knowledge which disallows the isolation of empirical or intellectual essences, subordinates that which the worshipper knows and does to that that which passes through him, beyond his analytic grasp. This *willing* subordination to the surprise of what arrives *alone* genuinely liberates him from the de-constitutive assumptions of autonomy, epistemological certainty, and self-presence of secular existence. By committing himself actively to becoming the conduit of the event of the Trinity, that is, by confessing his faith, the worshipper's subjectivity is enacted and fulfilled.[36]

Our knowing, then, has less to do with our ability to offer a rational account of what and how we know, less to do with achieving mastery over that which we seek to understand, and much more to do with *being known,* with participating in the very life of God in and through the practices that constitute the church's worship of Father, Son, and Holy Spirit. And because we believe that the story we are learning to live by is the story of God's gift of God's very self to us, we understand that our knowledge of this God is also a gift; we cannot know how we know. With Augustine, we must say: *Nisi credideritis, non intelligitis* (unless you will have believed, you will not understand). As Teresa of Ávila would put it a few centuries later:

> The faculties rejoice without knowing how they rejoice; the soul is enkindled in love without understanding how it loves; it knows that it is rejoicing in the object of its love, yet it does not know how it is rejoicing in it. It is well aware that this is not a joy which can be attained by the understanding; the will embraces it, without

understanding how; but, in so far as it can understand anything, it perceives that this is a blessing which could not be gained by the merits of all the trials suffered on earth put together. It is a gift of the Lord of earth and heaven, who gives it like the God he is.[37]

And Teresa reminds us that the God who is at the center of our life—who is the living mystery we seek to communicate—is not a God first postulated as ultimate transcendence or divine power, standing above all "religious" expression (in short, the god of modern theism), but is a God first prayed to, a God first worshiped, a God revealed to us as a community of persons—Father, Son, and Holy Spirit.

The self-disclosure of this God, which is the heart of the story we seek to live by, is, we believe, the truth of the world and of ourselves. Yet "there is no neutral standpoint, no place that is not some particular place, from which competing truth claims can be tested and compared."[38] And so to impart this truth—to do catechesis—is to be less concerned with *verification* (with attempts to explain, deduce, prove, validate, and so on) and more concerned with *manifestation*, that is, with living truthfully, showing forth, bearing witness to the love of the Triune God.[39] "The believing community," as Rowan Williams notes, "*manifests* the risen Christ: it does not simply talk about him, or even 'celebrate' him. It is the place where he is shown."[40]

Catechesis, then—our coming to know who and whose we are—is inseparable from doxology, the worship of Christ, the praise and adoration of Father, Son, and Holy Spirit. It is in worship, in the eucharistic assembly of Christ's body the church, that we are incorporated into the divine economy and given the gift of our very selves so that we might become the gift of Christ's body to and for the world. We are not and we know not apart from this communion. Where the modern subject is understood as a self-contained "essence," subsisting prior to all relationality and narrativity, the liturgical subject, the Christian self, is posited only *as* relationality. This is true for God, who exists only in relationship as a community of Persons, and it is true for us, those whose lives bear witness to the freedom and love that is God.

Catechesis—our learning to be followers of the Incarnated One—depends upon the crucial recognition that the Christ event, the story we tell of ourselves and of the world, is inseparable and unknowable apart from participation in the divine life of God. And of utmost importance from a catechetical standpoint: our access to this truth is through the eucharistic fellowship that is the very life of God. All pedagogies, all attempts at Christian formation must recognize this—that truth and communion are identified. That is, true knowledge is not a knowledge of the essence of things but of how they are conjoined to the communion event that is God's very self.[41] In a very real way, there is, for Christians and for the practices of Christian catechesis, nothing outside the liturgy.

Knowledge and Discipleship

> Discipleship is not limited to what you can comprehend—it must transcend all comprehension. Plunge into the deep waters beyond your own comprehension [Christ says], and I will help you to comprehend even as I do. Bewilderment is the true comprehension. Not to know where you are going is the true knowledge.
>
> Martin Luther,
> quoted in Dietrich Bonhoeffer's
> *The Cost of Discipleship*

To say that Christian education begins with the worship of the Triune God—and not with understanding religion (Moran) or with freedom and justice (Groome) or with cultivating responsible citizenship (Boys)—is to recognize that our coming to "know" this God requires nothing less than our moral transformation. Central to catechesis, then, is discipleship: the journey toward holiness that would lead us to "the mystery hidden for ages in God who created all things . . . that [we] may have the power to comprehend, with all the saints, what is the breadth and length and height and depth, and to know the love of Christ that surpasses knowledge, so that [we] may be filled with all the fullness of God" (Eph. 3:9, 18–19). Catechesis names the practices that foster and advance Christian discipleship, the journey toward holiness that is the calling of every Christian—the pilgrimage from baptism till death, the ongoing transformation of the self and the Christian community, the lifelong process of conversion, of learning again and again what it means to follow Jesus, to be the body of Christ in and for the world.

Discipleship is "nothing other than being bound to Jesus Christ alone."[42] Its prerequisite is obedience, its shape is cruciform, its *telos* is holiness. We learn what obedience is by obeying—not by first "understanding" what it means to follow Jesus but simply by following him, obeying the call to become disciples. Such obedience leads us necessarily to the cross, which is "that suffering which comes from our allegiance to Jesus Christ alone."[43] Through the cross we are born anew to a life of holiness, which is not our own moral achievement; it is not the accomplishment of an overly pious individual but is instead the gift of Christ's own righteousness bestowed on his body, the church.

Holiness is a "political" virtue before it is a personal attribute; that is, holiness names that quality of existence in the community of Christ's body as it seeks to bear witness to the holiness of God and to make known the setting apart of the church from the world so that the world might be brought into the fellowship of Christ and the church. "Sanctification apart from the visible church-community," warns Bonhoeffer, "is mere self-proclaimed holiness."[44]

To cultivate discipleship, to enjoin cruciform obedience so that the call to holiness is answered, is once again to subvert commonplace assumptions about knowledge and truth. The truth of God is not a thing to be grasped but a way of life to be embodied. Christian discipleship is this embodiment—the concrete, material, bodily enactment of faith and obedience that leads us beyond all human knowing to that place where we are transformed into the image of Christ, that we might be "imitators of God" (Eph. 5:1).

Knowledge and Desire

For Augustine, the only sure knowledge is that of desire: the natural, human longing that, when rightly ordered, finds its fulfillment, its *telos,* in the sociality of God—the community of Persons: Father, Son, and Holy Spirit. "I am clasped in a union from which no satiety can tear me away. This is what I love, when I love my God."[45]

Desire, as Daniel Bell points out, is not characterized by lack, deficiency, or privation; it is not constituted by absence. Following Bernard of Clairvaux, Bell writes: "Human desire is nothing less than a mirror of the positive, creative desire of God. Hence this desire is more accurately described as a presence, not a void or absence. . . . Desire [is] synonymous with love, understood as a positive, productive, self-giving force. As an expression of charity, desire is not so much an acquisitive drive, characteristic of a lack, but a generosity and donation expressed in the many forms of charity."[46]

Knowledge, we can say, is now desire shaped toward its true end—such that one might say that "false" knowledge is simply the "short-fall of an inadequate desire."[47] Knowledge, desire, and love, finally, collapse into each other. Knowledge is participation, not mere contemplation; it is *ontos*, not simply *epistēmē*. As participation, it is enacted in and through the corporate life of the church, initiated in baptism and sustained through time by the sharing of Christ's body and blood in the fellowship of believers in Christian community. Knowledge as/in communion is never a knowledge outside the embodied practices of eucharistic fellowship, a fellowship of love and desire that is the very life of God.

This knowledge is not, as has already been said, a knowledge whose truth or validity rests on procedures or criteria that are independently available. Rather, such knowing is tied integrally to our *desire of the other*—the desire to enter more deeply into relationship with God and with other persons. "Desire," as Milbank notes, "shapes truth beyond the imminent implications of any logical order, so rendering the Christian *logos* a continuous product as well as a process of 'art.'"[48] Knowledge and truth are never finally achieved but are continually sought within communities whose desire is ordered toward participation in the life of the Triune God, who seek to love as God loves. To know rightly is to desire God; to desire God is to have the knowledge we need.

Summary

That much of what constitutes educative efforts in Christian communities today is bland, feeble, and ineffectual is a sign of the failure to take seriously the catechetical nature and power of the worshiping assembly, the body of Christ gathered in eucharistic fellowship, becoming the truth in a world captivated by falsehood and deception. Modern catechesis, multiform though it is, has generally assumed the "objectivist" model of learning and viewed Christian "knowledge" as context free, disembedded from the liturgy and life of the worshiping community. It has presumed the priority of the individual and the autonomous self and, in regard to Christian formation, has understood the liturgy to be at best supplemental, at worst superfluous.

This makes all the more urgent the need to pay more serious attention to preparation for and reflection on the church's worship. Such preparation and reflection are, ultimately, the core of Christian discipleship and the heart of extraliturgical formation and education. The forms of such preparation and reflection cannot be known and delineated a priori; they emerge out of particular worshiping communities' engagement with Scripture, tradition, cultural and political contexts, social and economic exigencies, and so on. The least that can be said is that the forms these practices take must assume that catechesis is a lifelong process of conversion—not a program for instilling rationalist book-knowledge in the young.

Given that the church in the modern West has, for the most part, been inept at the "assertion of difference" (Jonathan Z. Smith) that is the mark of authentic worship and witness, the kinds of catechesis undertaken needs to explore critically this momentous failure, to discern the ways we have been shaped by discourses antithetical to the gospel and the peaceable communion made possible by the Eucharist.

Finally, to argue that worship is the site at which our formation as Christians is initiated and completed is to say that the overall character of the Christian life—both inside and outside the church's worship—is liturgical, that we are liturgical beings, persons whose purpose and vocation are first and foremost to offer praise to God, to recognize the giftedness of our very existence, to envision, inhabit, and negotiate the world doxologically. What we know and how we know are bound up together in doxology, in the rightful ordering of desire that leads us to the truth of God's own life and love for us.

5

ENTRANCE

What We Bring with Us to Worship

I was glad when they said to me, "Let us go to the house of the LORD!"

Psalm 122:1

When worshipers who have ingested the religion of consumerism bring it unnamed and unrecognized into the place of worship, we have a radical conflict between two claims of ultimacy.

Michael Warren

God Bless America.

Irving Berlin

Introduction

It is the nature of human existence that bodies can be in only one place at a time. We know that to enter one space is to leave

117

another behind. When we enter into worship, we leave behind the places and spaces previously inhabited; we occupy new terrain. Yet we do, of course, bring much with us from those other places and spaces: assumptions and habits, convictions and dispositions, prejudices and politics.

It is the task of those concerned with catechesis to discern what enters with us into the liturgical assembly: How does our social and cultural formation affect the catechesis that occurs in worship? How are the ways in which we are formed and shaped by the wider culture subsumed into the very ways in which we worship?

When we enter into worship we greet one another in the name of Christ:

> The grace of our Lord Jesus Christ, the love of God, and the communion of the Holy Spirit be with you all.
> *And also with you.* [1]

Or perhaps,

> The grace of the Lord Jesus Christ be with you.
> *And also with you.*
> The risen Christ is with us.
> *Praise the Lord!* [2]

Like an overture to a symphony, the words of greeting introduce the themes to come. They also reveal the character of worship as participatory rather than passive. During the entrance we sing a hymn in which we express to God our praise and adoration but which also *impresses* us, that is, it "norms and constitutes us as Christian people." [3] We offer an opening prayer or collect, such as

> Almighty and everlasting God, who in the Paschal mystery established the new covenant of reconciliation: Grant that all who have been reborn into the fellowship of Christ's Body may show forth in their lives what they profess by their faith through Jesus Christ our Lord, who lives and reigns with you and the Holy Spirit, one God, for ever and ever. Amen. [4]

In these speech-acts of entrance into worship we are led into the language of Christian liturgy; we are instructed, so to speak, in its grammar and lexicon, its rhythms and cadences. This language calls us out of ourselves and our preoccupations, habituates us in the church's vernacular, and binds us through time and space to other Christians who give voice to the same or similar greetings, hymns, and prayers.

Yet we always bring with us into worship fluency in other tongues, familiarity with the languages of other powers and discourses that would name and claim us. It is not always easy to recognize what we bring with us to worship—much of it is subtle and unspoken, rooted in the broader cultural socialization each of us undergoes as a citizen of the wider world, a socialization that often goes unreflected and uncommented upon. But what we bring with us to worship has everything to do with how we worship and how we are shaped by the worship we offer. And so the task of the catechist is to name those powers that come into the sanctuary space with us, to acknowledge their implications for shaping worshipers, to evaluate them in light of the gospel and its witness, and—probably most important—to offer when necessary effective means of resistance to them.[5]

In order to flesh out this discussion of entrance into worship—of what we bring with us when we gather for prayer and praise and what is at stake in terms of our formation as Christian disciples—I will focus on two of the "powers" that often enter the sanctuary space with those who come to worship. Within the context of North Atlantic Christianity, especially, not only do these powers enter into our worship, they often *pervade* it: consumerism and nationalism.

Consumerism, as I use the term here, names the set of ideas and practices that promote the facile, conspicuous, and excessive consumption of goods and services. Consumerism relies on a complex, systematic web of practices and beliefs through which persons are socialized from a very early age to expect the immediate satisfaction of all desire—physical and emotional, material and psychological. Not only does consumerism foster the longing to acquire and accumulate temporal goods in ever-increasing amounts (and the experiences of pleasure associated with this acquisition and accumulation), it creates and manipulates such desire. Many if not most Westerners defend consumerism as necessary for a thriving and robust economy (an unquestioned good in a consumer-capitalist order). As practiced by most inhabitants of the industrialized West, consumerism enjoins a lack of critical awareness of its deleterious effects on individuals and the communities in which they live. That is, it is simply assumed to be the way things are. While we may be guiltily aware that we have too much "stuff," most Westerners remain ignorant (perhaps willfully so) of the subversive power of marketing strategies—aimed at our ever-increasing consumption of products, services, and experiences—to manipulate human desire, thwart imagination and creativity, and destroy genuine community.

Consumerism emerged from the industrialist-technicist-capitalist ideology that continues to sustain it and is driven by the vast technologies of media and advertising. And it will be my argument here that consumerism is deeply embedded (though sometimes subtle in its application and effects) in the worship practices of much of Western Christendom.

By *nationalism* I mean the commonly held, though not often voiced or articulated, view of the nation-state as an entity predicated on the inclusion of some groups and the exclusion of others (often by force or violence) and as that entity that affords each person his or her primary sense of identity and belonging. Nationalism, dependent as it is on the maintaining of boundaries (real and imagined), encourages fear and distrust of the other—the outsider, the one who transgresses the real or imagined boundaries—which cannot help but be at odds with the gospel's call to hospitality toward the stranger and the foreigner. Moreover, nationalism by definition demands an allegiance that subsumes all other allegiances. For Christians, whose fidelity to the God of Jesus Christ is also called to be singular and all-encompassing, such a demand is deeply problematic.

Related to nationalism, and significant for my argument here, is patriotism, which is defined simply as love for and devotion to one's country. In the post-9/11 context of American Christianity, a kind of hyper-patriotism has taken hold and continues to be evident in the worship of Christian communities across the theological and liturgical spectra. Liberals and conservatives, Protestants and Catholics, high-church and low-church Christians gather to proclaim loyalty to Christ and the church while at the same time (and without any sense of irony or betrayal) extolling and blessing the actions and attitudes of the nation-state. The response by most Christians to the events of September 11,

2001, revealed, at best, a deep confusion about the relationship between church and nation, piety and patriotism, and, at worst, a willingness to abandon the gospel's call to peaceableness—a willingness that serves (unintentionally, of course) to mock and belittle the church's historic confession that Jesus, not Caesar, is Lord.

The notion of the church as *polis* has been surrendered (if it had ever been rightly understood in the American context at all) to a view of the nation-state as the true politics. As was noted in chapter 2's discussion of the work of Thomas Groome, the church has been and continues to be understood primarily as a social agency, albeit a "spiritual" one, in service to the greater good of the "real" *polis*—the American democratic social order. Worship in many Christian communities since 9/11 has been constituted, I suggest, more by prayers for the preservation of the republic than by the plea that all nations, including our own, perhaps especially our own, might be redeemed and transformed.

That these two cultural forces—consumerism and nationalism/ patriotism—are mutually informing and mutually sustaining is, of course, a given. (Americans were admonished, after all, in the immediate aftermath of the September terrorist attacks, to demonstrate their nationalistic pride and patriotism fervor by, of all things, shopping.) I will, however, treat each of them—consumerism and nationalism—in turn, recognizing all the while their utter entanglement.

Consumerism, Narcissism, and the Therapeutic Sensibility

All of us, actors and spectators alike, live surrounded by mirrors.

Christopher Lasch

When the movie *The Truman Show* was released in 1998, sophisticated film critics and ordinary moviegoers alike wrung their hands over what they took to be the movie's prescient message: the age of Big Brother, gloomily foretold by George Orwell and others, has at last arrived. Privacy on any level was deemed to be a thing of the past. No area of our lives, from the familial to the financial, is immune from the scrutiny of the Ominous Other; we are all under surveillance of some kind. In the film, Jim Carrey's Truman Burbank is the main character in the world's longest-running television drama (thirty years and counting). Truman's entire life, his every move—from birth through childhood and adolescence, into adulthood, marriage, and career—has been fodder for the ogling masses, the millions of fans who have literally grown up watching him grow up. The catch, of course, is that all of this is unbeknownst to Truman—the only "true man"—who is not in on the joke. Truman thinks his life is real, authentically his. Everyone else knows the "truth": Truman, the poor fool, is a prisoner, a pawn in the hands of the master manipulator and TV producer (a redundancy, one could argue) named, none too subtly, Christof.

But the lesson of *The Truman Show* is not that we are all continually being watched; rather it is that all of us are continually watching others. The captive of TV is not the unsuspecting Truman; it is the knowing audience. It is we—the spectators who can't turn away, can't turn it off—who devour everything set before us and are left unsatiated, still hungry and wanting more. (But we are not, it turns out, *unhappy* prisoners. As Christof intones at one point in the film: "If we are trapped it is only because we love our cell.")

That the mass media have imprisoned us is not news, of course; they simply continue, with increasing skill and subtlety, to exploit our weaknesses and encourage our baser instincts and tendencies. Writing several decades ago, social critic and historian Christopher Lasch argued that Americans are overwhelmed by an annihilating boredom. Like animals whose instincts have withered in captivity, we now lack the capacity to feel, to imagine, to create and sustain meaningful community. We yearn for purpose and vigor in our bland, brand-name world. We seek life-changing experiences, looking for love, alas, in all the wrong places.

Such desire is not lost on the advertisers who continually assault our senses and insult our intellects. Car commercials, for example, are not mere fact sheets comparing various modes of transportation (how boring would that be?) but are instead sleek and sensual attempts to sell an experience, an image—a portrait of *you* scaling a mountainside in your all-terrain vehicle, *you alone* in your monster SUV (carpooling just isn't fashionable), the *new you* who will be smarter, sexier, and infinitely more interesting if you will only buy the latest model. What is being pitched in these ads is not a chunk of metal, an engine, and four wheels but power and prestige, glamour and allure—so much so that the car itself is often absent from the ad. The automobile is incidental; what you are being sold is a new vision of yourself—a vision dependent on cultivating the envy and admiration of those around you.

Which goes to show that consumerism is as much about marketing and selling experiences of pleasure and novelty as it is about the consumption of tangible, temporal goods. And which also goes to show how cultural narcissism is different from the rugged individualism of an earlier era. While individualism presumes a certain stoic isolation, narcissism is predicated on the necessity of an admiring audience. The narcissist sees "his 'grandiose self' reflected in the attention of others, or by attaching himself to those who radiate celebrity, power, and charisma."[6]

The television phenomenon *Survivor*—promoted as a test par excellence of the rugged individual—is in fact a classic illustration of the culture of narcissism in which the victory (and ultimate sense of self) of the "winner" is dependent on the voyeuristic gaze of an anonymous audience. What *The Truman Show* revealed with insight and nuance is now writ large on this television genre, known (in a most laughable contradiction in terms) as "reality TV." But there is no irony here, and certainly no subtlety. The "characters" in productions like *Survivor, The Mole, Fear Factor,* and *The Bachelor* (and countless others) are not unsuspecting stooges, victims of cunning and conspiracy beyond their control (no matter how dull-witted they may actually be). Instead, they are savvy opportunists who attempt to parlay their fifteen minutes of fame into lifelong stardom. And the loyal viewers of these shows are not disinterested observers. True voyeurs, we see ourselves connected to, implicated in, the spectacle we behold. Genuine narcissists, we regard the shows' contestants and the contestants' experiences as extensions of ourselves and our own lives.

"Reality TV"—and television in general—provides a set of shared experiences, a cultural prism through which the real is interpreted and assessed. But it is a trick, two-way mirror, because just as a *Survivor* cast member sees her grandiose self reflected in the attention and admiration of an adoring audience, so too the faithful fan finds his own life caught up in and mediated by the cult of pseudo-celebrity. And the image of each, like that reflected in a funhouse looking glass, is a perversely distorted one. Existence in a media-saturated culture—this hall of mirrors we all inhabit—becomes a most vicarious endeavor, for our illusions are so powerful and persuasive that we (think we can) live in them. Entertainment, as now seems painfully evident, has trumped life itself.[7]

But for all the ocular metaphors at work here, the gaze—for both the admirer and the admired—is finally an inward one. We want to feel good, we deserve to feel good, and we are intensely preoccupied with ourselves toward that end. "The contemporary climate," says Lasch, "is therapeutic, not religious."[8] What people hunger for today is not salvation but the feeling of personal well-being. (How could it be otherwise in a country whose founding document establishes the basic right of the pursuit of *happiness*?) Our culture's obsession with self-fulfillment is evident in car commercials and reality TV but is perhaps best displayed in that icon of popular culture who has most enthusiastically embraced the therapeutic sensibility: Oprah.

Several years ago, talk-show host Oprah Winfrey underwent her own conversion experience, disavowing sleaze and sensationalism and promising to devote her show—and herself—to the uplifting and inspiring. She has been widely praised for distancing herself from trash talkers such as Jerry Springer, Jenny Jones, and Ricki Lake, for bringing dignity back to daytime television, and for helping people to "find the power within" in order to live more fulfilling, satisfying, and meaningful lives. And since our therapeutic culture trains us to believe that we need "experts" to guide us on the journey into ourselves, there has been no end to the parade of personalities whose expertise Oprah has enlisted on behalf of the self-seeking masses. (In another interesting twist on the cult of celebrity in a narcissistic age, these so-called experts are now famous for being famous—not for their academic credentials or their clinical successes but for being Oprah's friends.)

But in the end the differences between Oprah Winfrey and Jerry Springer are only a matter of degree. Springer's shameless displays of assorted human miseries (the representatives of which are almost always young, uneducated, and poor) and Oprah's angst-ridden suburban housewives trying to find themselves have equally, and understandably, mistaken self-absorption for self-examination. They are victims of and yet co-conspirators in their own public humiliation. They have been duped into thinking that the embarrassing spectacle of daytime talk TV is breakthrough psychotherapy, when in fact the cliché-ridden pop psychology liberally dispensed by the pseudo-experts only aggravates the condition it is meant to cure. So in the culture of narcissism, where the possibilities for genuine self-knowledge are thwarted at every turn, where we live surrounded by mirrors, we discover again and again, as Truman did, that the joke is on us.

Church, Consumerism, and the Loss of Embodiment

As movies like *The Truman Show* and TV fare like *Oprah* and the so-called reality shows have made clear, the media have created the illusion that we are all connected, that we somehow know each other, and that we are deeply concerned about each other. This is the false intimacy that television, especially, invents and then exploits for its own commercial gain. An example: Not long ago the world witnessed the tragic loss of the *Columbia* space shuttle and its crew of seven astronauts. I say "the world" because the explosion of the *Columbia* was a global media event captured on television in real time and played out (repeatedly) on TV screens everywhere. Television audiences were "introduced" to the men and women aboard the spacecraft; we learned intimate details of their lives and were told of their dreams and aspirations, hopes and passions, professional accomplishments, and numerous deeds of virtue and heroism. We grieved publicly, gathering solemnly around our television sets, through which the images of the space shuttle and its crew took on an "echo of sacrality."[9] (The somber theme music and ominous-sounding program titles—a broadcasting tactic begun in earnest with network and cable coverage of the 1991 Gulf War—contributed to the heightened drama and sense of the sacred.) As viewers, we were made to feel as if we knew these persons who, by all accounts, were indeed remarkable human beings.

But of course we did not know the astronauts, and we do not—isolated in our own homes, seated comfortably in front of our TV sets—know each other. Our grieving for the crew of the *Columbia* was not really public or communal; it was private and disconnected, isolated and disembodied.

If anything does bind us together as a people in a media-driven, consumer-capitalist social order, it is that we watch the shows and consume the products whose advertising dollars line the pockets of television executives. Global consumerism ensures that the ties that bind us are the ones created by trans-national corporations whose goods fill our homes and whose product names are household words: Mickey Mouse, Nike, Big Mac. Children and youth, particularly, are the target audience for many such products. The marketing strategies that have brought about the cultural shift from mass consumption to the segmenting of the consumer public into niche markets have become increasingly difficult to resist. Anyone with young children recognizes, for example, the seductive power of the Disney corporation's merchandizing tie-ins to its movies and can attest to the difficulty in trying to defy such an omnipresent, increasingly manipulative force. As Susan Willis and her colleagues have pointed out, Disney teaches our (very young) children how to be consumers and how to recognize the obsolescence of last year's product.[10] Disney and other like-minded media conglomerates commodify play and leisure and seduce us into thinking that what matters most in the experiences we so desperately seek is novelty and innovation.[11]

The pressing question for those concerned about catechesis and Christian formation, then, is how we can help people faithfully to hear and manifest the gospel in church communities where our shared experiences are the ones provided by TV shows and commercials, Hollywood movies, media-narrated tragedies, celebrity gossip, and pop-culture trivia. If we sense that we have been deceived by the false intimacy the media create and exploit, and if we acknowledge that consumerism has become that which binds us together as a people, how do we reckon with the truth that we in the church have become, for all intents and purposes, a society of strangers? That when we enter into worship we bring a numbing passivity born of media bombardment and image overkill, a self-preoccupation created and nurtured by an increasingly therapeutic, individualistic, and narcissistic culture, and the not-so-tacit assumption that worship is but another attractively packaged commodity to be consumed by a savvy, discriminating, church-shopping public?

Neal Gabler has observed that because television has become "the primary means through which people appropriate the world, it promulgates an epistemology in which all information, whatever the source, is forced to become entertainment."[12] The church, I suggest, and particularly the church at worship, promulgates its own alternative epistemology: it offers and embodies another way of knowing, seeing, being in the world. When we enter into worship we participate in a "subversive reimagining of reality"[13] where passivity is rejected and the active participation of the community gathered together—the "work of the people"—is preeminent; where God, and not ourselves or our emotional or psychological needs, is the center of our worship, the object of our desire and devotion; and where worship is understood not as something we consume for our own benefit or gratification but as what we offer because of God's own graciousness and generosity to us. When we enter into worship we come into, as Walter Brueggemann has memorably put it, a "liturgy of abundance."[14] While consumerism is premised on the "myth of scarcity" (there is not enough to go around, so we grab what we can when we can), the church's liturgy assumes an economy of plenty, where bread is taken, blessed, broken, and given, where we find ourselves the undeserving recipients of God's extravagant goodness.

And yet in worshiping communities across Western Christendom, worshipers behave more and more like spectators, passively absorbing stimuli, much as we sit quiescently in front of TV, movie, and computer screens. Even in those churches where the congregations are not quite so passive—where there is movement, gesture, and interaction—what is often most highly prized is the entertainment value of such an "experience"—how it makes us *feel*, what it does for *us*. Does it uplift, inspire, move, console? We often assume mistakenly that the purpose of worship, our reason for entering into the liturgical assembly, is to "have our spiritual needs met" or "to get something out of it" that might sustain us through a long and difficult week ahead. But such sentiments are born of a preoccupation with the therapeutic and an obsession with our own well-being, and of the privatization of worship that assumes that the liturgy is useful only insofar as it advances our personal, private encounter with God—an encounter whose real purpose, ultimately, is to make us feel better about ourselves. But as Philip Pfatteicher bitingly suggests:

> In such a system, the liturgy is no longer the public work that its etymology implies but a series of private, personal experiences of intimacy and relationship. (I supplied once in a congregation where members after the service thanked me for "sharing" their service.) Liturgy is "worship experiences" in a place where the service begins not with the entrance hymn or "The grace of our Lord Jesus Christ" or "In the name of the Father, and of the Son, and of the Holy Spirit" but with a hearty "Good morning!" and its echo by the congregation, often repeated until its vigor and volume satisfy the presiding social director. Imagination and creativity seem, however, to be failing us; why is it that no one, as far as I know, has followed the benediction and dismissal with a hearty "Have a nice day!" (on feast days one may shout "Have a great day!")? The response would probably be "Take care."[15]

As I have already noted, we live in a culture that trains us to be obsessed with our feelings, with emotion and desire, with the "inner self." In such an ethos, the church is increasingly tempted to give in to the false notion that authentic worship requires that we conjure the correct emotional response. But the worship of God is not, of course, dependent on how we feel. Christian worship that is rooted in the historic forms of Word and Table—worship that recognizes that the Word challenges and provokes as much as it comforts and consoles, and that seeks to keep the sacraments central to the church's common life—is repetitive, predictable, ritualistic, and methodical. We say the same things over and over; we do the same things over and over.

The church historically has believed that such habituation is necessary for the formation of faithful disciples: humans are forgetful, but rhythm and ritual and repetition ward off such mindlessness. Living as we do in a culture that values melodrama, excess, and—above all else—novelty, we have come to disdain the repetitive and predictable, the ritualistic and methodical. What we want—what we are trained to desire and to expect—is spontaneity and spectacle. We want to feel good. But feelings, we also know, can be fickle. The acts of praise we offer in worship, the gestures, songs, our speech to, for, and about God—all of these "may or may not be accompanied by 'appropriate feelings'; what matters is that they are done."[16] That which we do repeatedly has the power to shape us, even if we are not engaged in it every second—even if we cannot summon feelings appropriate to the moment, whatever they might be. Worship, we must remember, is our gift to God, not to ourselves.

It is this notion of *gift* that a consumerist framework cannot make sense of. Consumerism, and the marketing, merchandising, and advertising strategies that sustain it, is predicated on an economy of self-interested exchange, not on the gratuitous self-giving that characterizes God's nature and the nature of Christian worship: God's gift of God's self to us and the offering of ourselves wholly in response to such generosity. As Catherine Pickstock has noted, the "liturgy is at once a gift *from* God and a sacrifice *to* God, a reciprocal exchange which shatters all ordinary positions of agency and reception."[17]

Our formation as consumers must therefore be met with a catechesis of doxology: The ways in which we are malformed and misshapen by a consumeristic culture of excess must be acknowledged, named, and confronted. Where consumerism promotes radical individualism and self-sufficiency, the liturgy presumes our creatureliness—our utter dependence on God and one another—and creatureliness presumes gratitude, the praise and thanksgiving that are at the heart of the church's worship. "Worship," notes Barbara Brown Taylor, "is how the people of God practice their reliance on their Lord."[18] Where consumerism trains and encourages appetites that can never be satiated, the liturgy reminds us that desire rightly ordered finds its true *telos* in the God at the center of our devotion.

Confronting the idolatries that consumerism enjoins means we have to begin to say more, to speak more directly and more often—from the pulpit, from the teacher's lectern, to Christians of all ages and stations—about the ways the church is held captive to distorted visions and narratives of self, community, and world. However, tired (and tiring) rants against materialism are not what are called for. Rather, Christians need to develop deeper, richer, more theologically engaged critiques of culture that communicate in compelling ways the distinction between our being creatures of a just and loving God and our being thoughtless, careless, compulsive consumers.

Here the twofold nature of Christian catechesis comes to the fore: Worship is the primary means of our formation as Christians, and yet extraliturgical catechesis is always necessary in order to counter false construals of the true and the good, to make evident that consumerism's shaping of the self is profoundly at odds with how we are formed as persons and communities by the worship of Father, Son, and Holy Spirit.

For example, when congregations are encouraged to reflect intently over a period of time on the participatory nature of the historic liturgy, they can be guided toward a more critical attentiveness to how it is that consumerism fosters the troubling passivity in worship I have talked about—the lack of engaged, communal participation, the assumption that we come to worship always to "get" something: personal fulfillment, comfort, chastisement, moral support, and so on. Practicing participation in the liturgical assembly week after week *and* engaging in sustained reflection on that communal, participatory practice (in conversations carried on in Sunday school, in Bible study groups, and in other intimate settings) can generate the critical awareness that our worship and our discipleship are often—almost always—compromised by the consumerist ethos that influences all of our human interactions. When we engage in such intentional catechesis we can come to recognize, as Michael Warren describes it, how the "material structures" of our lives have already formed us—our consciousness, our mentality, our biases, our priorities, our spirit—before we cross the threshold of liturgical space.[19] Such serious, sustained reflection can lead worshipers to recognize that when we enter into worship we are to come not as private individuals ready to consume or to take but as the gathered body prepared to give and to offer ourselves. And in our giving and offering we are, paradoxically, given back the gift of ourselves as those privileged to share in the life of God.

Groups of Christians might also reflect on their own practices of consumption within the wider culture, taking serious account of their consumeristic habits and the implications of such habits for faithful Christian living. But such an endeavor should be more than an exercise in lamenting the conspicuous consumption that characterizes modern life; rather, it must reckon seriously with the material conditions of consumerism—and the forms of social and political power that help to create them—which render us unable even to name and describe the problem. Situating this kind of catechesis within the language and practice of the liturgy (as opposed to treating it abstractly as simply an interesting modern dilemma) can give persons the linguistic and practical skills for identifying and resisting the cultural forces that make consumerism and the narcissistic, therapeutic culture associated with it appear to be natural and inevitable.

Moreover, rooting such efforts in the community's worship, and not just in individual, private opinions about overconsumption, can help to cultivate the trust and accountability necessary for this kind of risky venture to succeed. For instance, the conflicts and disagreements that arise when Christians begin to confront their consumeristic, narcissistic patterns and habits need to be located in the practice of peaceable unity that the Eucharist itself is. Differences need not be destructive when we remember that we sing together, confess our sin together, commune at Christ's table together—that our common life is rooted not in shared interests or a general like-mindedness but in the unity of Christ made possible by the work of the Holy Spirit, a unity that allows us to speak the truth in love about ourselves to one another. The discernment that becomes possible when we risk opening ourselves up to such corporate scrutiny and accountability is a "seeing with new eyes" that shapes our work and witness in the world.

Christians, in effect, must be trained to *see what is going on*—to become critical readers of culture and wise interpreters of the world around us, to be attentive to the times in which we live: "Do you have eyes, and fail to see? Do you have ears, and fail to hear?" (Mark 8:18). We must learn and we must teach others to cultivate an acute mindfulness, keener eyesight and sharper hearing, for we are shaped most profoundly, as Warren has suggested, by that which we pay attention to: "The only decisive counterforce to the cultural pressures of our time may be the power of whole communities struggling together toward an appropriate spirituality characterized by a transformed way of paying attention. These communities will be formed with the collaboration of liturgists and catechists."[20] We must also, in courageous and imaginative ways, encourage and put into practice tangible acts of resistance to the enslavement that consumerism seeks to keep all of us in—from local covenant communities who aspire together to defy the estrangement and isolation that consumerism fosters to small accountability groups agreeing to hold each other responsible for, say, how they spend their leisure time and what, if anything, they watch on television.

And yet to counter the consumerism, individualism, and narcissism of the wider culture is not, from a liturgical, catechetical point of view, to regard "the world" with contempt or derision. The liturgy is not a refuge from the "real world out there"; it is not "sacred" while the secular order is "profane," "spiritual" while the other is "material." Rather, a "liturgy of abundance" recognizes the world as a sacrament of the divine presence of God. In our fallenness it becomes impossible to see the world as sacramental; in the liturgy, however, we are able to expose secularism (in whatever ideological form it takes) for what it truly is: a "negation of worship."[21] *The Rule of Saint Benedict*, alluded to in the prologue of this book, can be read, I suggested, as one attempt at confronting this brokenness—a deliberate refusal to divide world and sacrament, work and worship, life and liturgy. So to be intentional about challenging the false gods of the world that would name and claim us—to do catechesis—is not to denigrate the world or to dismiss it out of hand but to learn to see it rightly, to be habituated into the kinds of practices that will enable us gratefully to enjoy it (praise, prayer, rest, recreation), and to learn, ultimately, how to love it. The challenge is, as Bonhoeffer put it, to live in the world without losing ourselves in it.[22]

Finally, the ecclesial community gathered together for worship is a *bodily* fellowship. While this may seem an obvious point, it is worth noting how consumerism fosters a loss of embodiment and what the implications of such a loss are for Christian worship and catechesis. A media-driven, consumer-capitalist economy, particularly one in which "virtual reality" has become the phantom locus for many who would congregate at the altar of conspicuous consumption, is predicated on the ability—the necessity, even—of escaping the body in technologically mediated ways. For example, the disembodiment that cyberspace produces and celebrates makes the other—whether persons, objects, or

information—"present to us on our screens only as manipu-
lable and consumable pixels."[23] Consumerism, as the quest for
unlimited enjoyment of virtual realities—whether mediated via
the Internet or through the purchase of a new car—configures
human relationships in ways that allow us too easily to disavow
what it means to be embodied creatures who require human
community and connectedness.

Indeed, from an ecclesial, liturgical perspective, the church's
very existence is constituted and sustained by the Persons-in-
relationship whom we name the Trinity. The church gathered
for worship and for work in the world is composed of bodies
that act, toil, worship, and suffer "in community with Jesus."[24]
That is, we are a bodily community because "the body of Jesus
Christ can only be a visible body, or else it is not a body at all."[25]
In worship we do bodily things: we eat and drink, we bow and
kneel, we embrace, we speak and sing, we are washed. Worship
requires our bodily presence and the engagement of our bodies in the actions and gestures that make the liturgy what it is.
And as our bodies are habituated into the practices that would
shape us as cruciform followers of Christ, we become *signs* to
and for the world: physical markers, flesh-and-blood exemplars
of Jesus' own earthly, historical, bodily ministry. We bear witness to the one who took on a human body for the sake of the
world, whose own body was broken for a broken humanity. We
enact Christ's love for the world—in bodily, material, tangible
ways—that the world might come to know its worldliness, its
estrangement from a good and loving Creator who wills its return and restoration.

Consumerism, by contrast, prizes the absent body, creating
false communities or, rather, collections of discrete individuals
(consumers) united only by their desire for and consumption
of the products being pitched via media whose very form and
structure ensure that persons remain isolated and detached
from one another. The gadgets and gizmos that now define our
technological age are marketed in ways that seduce us into
thinking that we can be *more* connected to friends and family,
when in fact such efforts encourage an unprecedented alienation
and anonymity in all our human dealings.[26] Insofar as we bring
with us into worship the dispositions and habits created and
nurtured by a consumerist social order and the loss of embodi-

ment constitutive of it, we risk thwarting the physical, material, bodily engagement that animates the worshiping community as the very body of Christ.

Nationalism and Christianity

> He is the image of the invisible God, the firstborn of all creation; for in him all things in heaven and on earth were created, things visible and invisible, whether thrones or dominions or rulers or powers—all things have been created through him and for him. He himself is before all things, and in him all things hold together. He is the head of the body, the church; he is the beginning, the firstborn from the dead, so that he might come to have first place in everything. For in him all the fullness of God was pleased to dwell, and through him God was pleased to reconcile to himself all things, whether on earth or in heaven, by making peace through the blood of his cross.
>
> Colossians 1:15–20

When we enter into the worship of the Triune God, we give witness to the truth that we are citizens of a commonwealth wider than that of the nation of our birth. We are, as members of the body of Christ, Christians without borders. We claim allegiance not to any earthly power or principality but to the Lord of the universe. Worship, as I have noted repeatedly in these pages, is the offering of praise and thanksgiving exclusively to this one, the one who reigns sovereign over all.

But if we enter into worship nowadays as savvy consumers, we also come with nationalism too easily wedded to our Christian convictions and our ideas about true and proper worship. This has always been the case, certainly, for Christians who live in the United States. Evangelicalism, for example, found fertile ground to grow on in the eighteenth and nineteenth centuries precisely because its individualistic impulses could be readily allied to the frontier spirit's championing of independence and self-expression—"values" that Americans (and outside observers) would come to define and admire as the nation's very heart and soul.

The coupling of Christianity and nationalism began, of course, centuries earlier with the conversion of the Roman emperor Constantine and the subsequent alliance forged between church and empire. But in the peculiar and paradoxical expression of such a union in the American context, the highly esteemed doctrine of "separation of church and state" has actually promoted the moral identification of Christianity and nationalism. As John Howard Yoder notes,

> once the separation of church and state is seen as theologically desirable, a society where this separation is achieved is not a pagan society but a nation structured according to the will of God. For nearly two centuries, in fact, the language of American public discourse was not only religious, not only Christian, but specifically Protestant. Moral identification of church with nation remains despite institutional separation. In fact, forms of institutional interlocking develop which partly deny the story of separation (chaplaincies, tax exemptions).[27]

Nationalism and its problematic link to Christianity and to Christian worship therefore are nothing new. There have been, of course, Christians through the centuries and into the present day who have raised questions about the propriety of such an alliance, who have warned of the dangers of the church's easy and eager sellout to the aims of the republic, whose very lives, lived out in alternative Christian communities, have been witnesses against a compromised and tainted Christianity and a falsely pious and unthinking patriotism. Examples include the desert fathers and mothers of early monasticism, and, in our own time, Dorothy Day's Catholic Worker movement and Clarence Jordan's Koinonia Farm. However, the voices of these dissident Christians and the counterwitness their communities have offered have been, on the one hand, ignored or dismissed and, on the other, ridiculed or vilified. For the facile identification of Christianity and nationalism in successive generations of American churchgoers has rendered such dissent unfathomable.

Nationalism in the years since World War II has come to be linked ever more closely with consumer capitalism. Citizenship in the modern Western nation-state is predicated less (if at all) on the cultivation of a virtuous populace and more on ensuring access to the market and the (endless) creation of capital. Lizabeth Cohen, in a book titled *A Consumers' Republic*, argues that in the current phase of cultural, social, and economic development, inhabitants of the United States are best described as citizen-consumers, for the market has now become the template for the citizen's relationship with the state. As she writes:

> Whereas from the 1930s to as late as the 1970s, to refer to the consumer interest was also to appeal to some larger public good beyond the individual's self-interest, the ubiquitous invocation of the consumer today—as patient, as parent, as social security recipient—often means satisfying the private interest of the paying customer, the combined consumer/citizen/taxpayer/voter whose greatest concern is, "Am I getting my money's worth?"[28]

Mass consumption has become the machinery, the driving force, of not only the American economy but of politics and culture as well.[29] Shopping malls, designed more and more to resemble the "old-fashioned," pedestrian-friendly neighborhoods they helped to destroy, are the new town squares—the places where citizen-consumers gather to engage in their primary civic duty: shopping. In such activities the soullessness of the American enterprise is revealed, for in a nation like the United States, which now exists primarily to undergird the market, the utter emptiness of the secular is laid bare, even as the secular state attempts to ground its sovereignty in the very will of God.[30]

Insofar as American Christianity historically has assumed that American democracy comes closer than any other ordering of social relations to manifesting the kingdom of God on earth, it has betrayed its distinctive witness of the church as a politics in its own right. And it has, more recently, played into the hands of a consumeristic, jingoistic nationalism, the pious rhetoric of which masks the violence and injustice upon which nationalism and the nation-state itself depend. That is, if the only thing sustaining the modern secular state is the market system, then the collusion of church and state represents not just a benign sellout by the church to the consumer culture (tragic and lamentable in itself) but something more corrupt and sinister. As Milbank puts it:

The modern secular state rests on no substantive values. It lacks full legitimacy even of the sort that Saint Paul ascribed to the "powers that be," because it exists mainly to uphold the market system, which is an ordering of substantively anarchic (and therefore not divinely appointed in Saint Paul's sense) competition between wills to power—the idol of "liberty," which we are supposed to worship. This liberty is dubious, since it is impossible to choose at all unless one is swayed one way or another by an influence: hence a supposedly "pure" free choice will only be a cover for the operation of hidden and uniform influences. People who fondly imagine themselves the subjects of their "own" choices entirely will, in reality, be the most manipulated subjects and the most incapable of being influenced by goodness and beauty. . . . Pure liberty is pure power—whose other name is evil.[31]

If one of the definitions of nationalism is that the nation-state affords persons their primary sense of identity and belonging *and* if the modern Western church, particularly the church in America, has articulated no real disagreement with such a view, indeed has been wholly complicit with it, then it is fair to say that the church has surrendered its central claim that Jesus is Lord to the nation's demand for unquestioned allegiance to free-market capitalism. On the surface, this may seem an outrageous claim. Churches continue, one could argue, in their worship, in their efforts at formation and discipleship, to confess the lordship of Christ and to proclaim the good news of the gospel. Yet the more complicated reality is that the church in the West has failed quite spectacularly to understand and teach—and therefore to embody in a meaningful way—the radical implications of such a confession and proclamation: those who confess Jesus as Lord will find themselves in profound conflict with any and all other appeals for loyalty and fidelity, especially those that would claim for a nation the sovereignty and power that alone belong to God.

"O Say Can You See": Nationalism, Worship, and Christian Formation

It was fitting that Oprah Winfrey presided over the interfaith service at Yankee Stadium, staged in the immediate aftermath

of September 11 and billed as "A Prayer for America." As mentioned earlier, Winfrey, more than any other figure in American
popular culture, has come to personify the culture of narcissism.
(In saying this I do not mean to suggest that Winfrey is an inher-
ently selfish person—quite the opposite, in fact, seems true. She
is famously magnanimous and philanthropic, and there is every
reason to believe that these are genuine qualities of her character.
But Winfrey has become iconic of the culture of narcissism partly
because her immense fame and popularity have created a kind
of voyeuristic, vicarious fascination with wealth and celebrity
that instills an obsessive self-regard in her admirers, and partly
because she does promote a therapeutic "spirituality" of inward-
ness and interiority that leads to the same thing.)

The event in Yankee Stadium, part Hollywood extravaganza
and part patriotic pep rally, revealed the troubling fact that even
as Americans gathered to mourn the loss of three thousand men,
women, and children, we could not help feeling most sorry for
ourselves. The woundedness felt by many in those early days after
the terrorist attacks was soon transformed into a defensiveness
that came dangerously close to suggesting, in subtle and not
so subtle ways, that because we are Americans our suffering is
somehow greater than the suffering of others in other times and
places. This obsession with "America" (and with our *feelings* as
Americans) was evident, if not pervasive, in churches across the
nation: in flag-draped sanctuaries; in the invoking of God's blessing on America alone ("God bless Afghanistan" was not often
uttered, nor even was God's blessing invoked on other "friendly"
countries who lost citizens in the attack); in the substitution
of patriotic anthems of America's past for the church's historic
hymns; in somber military processionals carried out in worship
spaces; in saying the pledge of allegiance prior to or in place of
reciting one of the creeds; in pious and sentimental sermons
designed to suggest, implicitly or explicitly, that being a good
American is synonymous with being a good Christian.

These were formative events in worshiping communities
across the United States. And while the broader issue of the
church's capitulation to the state and to nationalistic piety is, as
we have noted, a longstanding one, it was crystallized in a most
pressing way in the wake of 9/11. That is, while some Christians
have been insisting for a long time that, literally and metaphori-

cally, the American flag does not belong in the worship space, the matter was urgently real when it became clear that for many if not most American Christians the proud displays of American flags beside pulpits, on altars, and elsewhere in the sanctuary signified no betrayal of the church's singular symbol of loyalty and authority—the cross—and no capitulation to the imperial powers of the nation-state.

The challenges for Christian catechesis, we can see, are enormous: the challenge of discerning how to help Christians understand themselves as distinct from (though profoundly influenced by) nation, state, and tribe; of rediscovering and then enacting the distinctiveness of Christian community over and against a consumerist, nationalist, pseudo-Christian cultural piety; of grounding the ongoing formation of Christian disciples in the church's historic worship of the Triune God. Yet while the challenges are daunting, they are the ones that are now set before us; ignoring these difficulties has been one of the most serious failures of Christian catechesis in the contemporary church.

That there are no formulaic solutions, no programmatic answers to this complex crisis is not grounds for idleness, finger-pointing, and hand-wringing. Addressing these challenges requires, I suggest, a threefold strategy, which, while intimated in previous discussion, will be fleshed out as the remaining chapters unfold: first, raising awareness (in a variety of ways, liturgical and extraliturgical) that worship itself is the primary locus of Christian formation; second, implementing alternative visions of education and catechesis—not necessarily newer ones but better ones; and three, seriously reckoning with (not merely complaining about) the limitations and failures of current models of Christian education.

Because modern catechesis has been predicated almost exclusively on the paradigm of classroom education, it has fostered very little critical reflection on worship and its connections to formation—except for the kind of criticism that assumes worship is mostly a matter of taste and that worshipers' opinions should be solicited on everything from hymn choices to preaching styles.[32] Sunday school, as we will see in the next chapter, has not so much prepared children, women, and men for worship as it has competed with it. The church for the most part has failed to engage in the kinds of intensive, holistic, worship-driven efforts at Christian formation that matter most—that can confront the idolatries enjoined by consumerism, nationalism, and other powers that vie for our loyalty and allegiance. To assume that the principal solution to this dilemma is simply better Sunday school curricula or a deeper grasp of the stages of faith development is to remain caught up in the tangle of misconceptions that created the problem in the first place.

I mentioned earlier the value of nurturing small groups of Christians who agree to live out their Christian faith in intentional ways that make them accountable to one another—groups that reflect on, for instance, how they spend their time, money, and attention. Such communities within the larger worshiping body can give practical, tangible expression to the prayers, proclamation, creeds, hymns, and sacraments they share in corporate worship. At their best, these communities are about the work of overcoming the false dichotomy between worship and work, liturgy and life. They give incarnate form to what catechesis is at its core: lifelong learning and growth in discipleship—not merely the intellectual mastery of disembodied moral values. Their fundamental premise is that the "work" of worship (liturgy: work of the people) is continuous with Christian discipleship lived out in and for the wider world.

Such discipleship has at its heart a spirit of doxology—the presumption that a life lived after the pattern of Jesus is a life offered in service to God for the purpose of God's praise and glory (1 Cor. 10:31). Doxologically informed discipleship can confront the consumerist impulse or the tendency toward narcissism or blind patriotism, because worship trains us to be, above all else, persons of praise—persons whose identity is rooted in the exalted and exalting language of worship and its attendant practices, not in the dulling discourses of mass consumption, self-serving individualism, and unthinking nationalism. It is possible, then, to form and nurture Christians—to do catechesis—in ways that enact resistance to consumerism and nationalism because worship teaches us that our lives are gifts. Therefore our "selves" do not exist as slaves to the market economy, nor to serve the interests of the nation-state. Rather, our subjectivity is enacted when we commit ourselves to becoming conduits of the love, justice, and fellowship that is the trinitarian life of God, when we worship God so that we might then go forth to give visible, tangible expression to the triune relations of Father, Son, and Holy Spirit in the world around us.[33]

What we know about God and ourselves cannot be known except through *performance:* the living out of our giftedness, in joy and gratitude, in worship and beyond. The dissemination of this knowledge is not therefore a function of classroom instruction but is the actual scattering, dispersal, diffusion of the love of God toward the neighbor, the stranger, the other. To know is to love as we are loved. Doxological catechesis strives to shape and nurture disciples whose knowledge is, first and last, a knowledge of love and action.

None of this is new. In the fifth century Augustine admonished catechumens to "be what you see, and receive what you are. . . . If you receive worthily, you are what you have received."[34] In the Eucharist we become what we consume: the body of Christ, blessed, broken, and given for the world. We are to be the love of Christ incarnate in the world. The Eucharist (like the whole of the liturgy) does not simply mediate theological ideas or communicate moral truths to live by; it enacts an alternative epistemology, a different way of knowing. And we know and are known as we participate in, perform, and give life to the story that transcends all stories.

There is, however, a place and even an urgent need for the more didactic forms of catechesis and formation. The practice of teaching from catechisms, long derided for producing a pedagogy characterized by uninspired, unimaginative preachiness, might fruitfully be recovered as a means not only of communicating the central tenets of Christianity but of reconnecting belief and action, doctrine and practice. The concise question-and-answer format of a catechism need not preclude the possibility of deeper engagement and a more serious, ongoing encounter with the substance of the Christian faith. Indeed, good catechetical questions and their answers invite more questions and answers; their value lies in their inexhaustibility and their capacity to urge us to examine more rigorously the content of our convictions and the intersection of faith and practice.

Because we read catechisms (and all texts) out of the material conditions of our daily existence, we always bring our particular circumstances to bear on our understanding of the subject matter. The interface between the doctrinal content of a catechism and lived discipleship in a consumerist, nationalist ethos offers rich possibilities for meaningful inquiry and transformed living. For instance, what might be the consequences if a community of Christians intent on confronting the corruptions of consumerism and nationalism were to explore in conversation and daily living over a period of several weeks or months this single question from the catechism of *The Book of Common Prayer*?

> Q. What is prayer of oblation?
> A. Oblation is an offering of ourselves, our lives and labors, in union with Christ, for the purposes of God.[35]

Summary

This chapter began with the assertion that consumerism and nationalism are forces that not only enter into Christian worship but also often pervade it. In ways that are sometimes subtle, sometimes blatantly overt, our gathering together in the name of Jesus Christ to worship the Triune God is frequently determined more by consumeristic impulses and our allegiance to the nation than by a singular loyalty to the God who sustains us and calls us into worship and fellowship with the Trinity and one another. It is the task of catechesis to recognize that what we bring with us when we enter into worship is of great significance for how we worship and how we are shaped and formed by the worship we offer.

Once we enter into worship, we enact the story of salvation in song and speech, prayer, silence, bodily postures, signs, and gestures. Through the proclamation of the Word and our response to it we are shaped as disciples of Jesus Christ and are called to embody discipleship in the wider world.

6

PROCLAMATION AND RESPONSE

The Formative Power of Word and Water

We proclaim Christ crucified . . .

> 1 Corinthians 1:23

Drawing on nothing fancier than the poetry of [one's] own life, let [the preacher] use words and images that help make the surface of our lives transparent to the truth that lies deep within them, which is the wordless truth of who we are and who God is and the Gospel of our meeting.

> Frederick Buechner

Will you by your prayers and witness help this child to grow into the full stature of Christ?
  I will, with God's help.

> *The Book of Common Prayer*

Introduction

Proclamation presumes speech. When we enter into worship we speak and hear a different language, a sometimes difficult language—the language of prayer and praise, of judgment and hope—in all its nuance and complexity; a language rooted not in contemporary experience but in Scripture and the traditions of the church's historic worship and witness; a language that may shift over time (altering, for instance, gender-exclusive nouns and pronouns or reworking ancient idioms lost on modern ears) but that is never an entirely new creation since it rests on older, authoritative images and insights; a language valued not because it is old but because it bears the weight of the accumulated experience of the church catholic. Liturgy is, in one sense, this interplay of language and tradition, memory and imagination, in which the collected knowledge of a given practice—Christian worship—is transmitted as it is enacted in time and space. Transmission, however, is more than the static transferral of words and ideas from the past to the present; transmission presumes engagement, an active interfacing, which may mean (and often does mean) modification, adjustment, or correction. The proclamation of the Word in worship is a part of this work of communicating the traditions of the past: language binds us to history, but it also provides us with the parameters for negotiating the present and imagining the future.[1]

Earlier I noted how the worship in the church of my childhood was centered almost exclusively on the proclamation of the Word. For many churches in the evangelical tradition, like my own, preaching was (is) the highlight, the hallmark, the centerpiece of the Sunday morning service—so much so that many of my fellow church members would not have said that they were "going to worship" but that they were "going to preaching." As was also pointed out in the prologue, the liturgical renewal movement of the mid- to late twentieth century made significant strides in "decentering" the proclamation of the Word—which is not to say that efforts at liturgical reform sought to minimize the importance of preaching but, rather, that they were attempts to situate the sermon within the liturgy as a whole.

This chapter's focus is twofold: to examine how proclamation of the Word is formative of character and community, and how it is that our various responses to the Word are also (per)formative acts that shape and nurture Christian identity through time. The concern here is not so much with the "how to's" of preaching as with how it is that the proclamation of the Word shapes the work and witness of communities and persons—how it educates, how it catechizes them into particular habits and virtues, how it calls forth responses that lead to deeper theological reflection on and engagement with the world.

There are several ways in which congregants, within the worship service, respond to the proclamation of the Word: by reciting one of the church's historic creeds in affirmation of what has been proclaimed; by offering gifts (both monetary ones and the gifts of bread and wine—with the understanding that all such oblations are also signs of the offering we make of ourselves in response to the Word and in service to God and neighbor); by celebrating the sacrament of baptism, in which persons are initiated into Christ's body the church, granted new life, and given a new identity and vocation within the communion of saints. In the latter part of this chapter we will look most closely at this last response, baptism, exploring the catechetical nature of the rite itself and the pressing need for more rigorous pre- and post-baptismal catechesis in the lives of the newly initiated.

Preaching as Formation: Shaping Character and Community

Theologian Marva Dawn maintains that "sermons should shape hearers by bringing the transforming Word to nurture the development of their character in the pattern of Christ."[2] Over time and within the context of worship, preaching forms a fellowship of faith and gives cruciform shape to the character of persons in community. As it maintains its rootedness in liturgy, the lectionary, and the church year, preaching is the Scripture-driven, worship-centered act (art) that makes meaning for a community's life together as it strives to bear witness to the truth of the gospel in the world. The making of meaning is not the mere relaying of theological information or the dissemination of biblical facts and ideas or even the call to personal fulfillment; it is, instead, the Spirit-filled process of discerning the Word of God in ways that render the Logos alive and present to the community gathered to receive it—"the Word which can no longer exist in isolation from the humanity it has assumed."[3] Before it is anything else (if it should be anything else at all), preaching is proclamation: the annunciation of who God is and of what

God has done, is doing, and will do. The sermon, situated as it is in the drama that is the church's liturgy, reiterates that dramatic narrative—the complex, multilayered story of creation, redemption, and future hope—giving formal articulation to what is expressed in Scripture, song, and sacrament.

The preacher interprets the Word for the community, placing the day's appointed texts within the larger narrative scope of the biblical witness; allowing Scripture to interpret Scripture; acknowledging the multistranded nature of any given text's meaning for the life of the community; recognizing the partiality and self-interest that undergird all our interpretations of the biblical texts; and letting the Word of God interrogate the community as much as the community, through the preacher's own hermeneutical practices, scrutinizes the text. In interpreting Scripture for the community, the preacher speaks a word that is local and specific, particular to the context and circumstances out of which it arises and to which it must speak, attentive to the ways in which the ordinary aspects of our daily lives are caught up in and transformed by the extraordinary design of God's redemptive purposes. But the preacher also interprets the world, surveying it through the lens of Scripture and using the "language world" of the Bible "so that reality is redescribed for us by Scripture"[4]—so that biblical language and categories shape and inform our understanding of the world rather than the other way around. Scriptural preaching allows the hearers to discover themselves as participants in the ongoing narrative, rather than as distant spectators of it or as those who would seek merely to "apply" the Bible's "principles and precepts" to contemporary experience.[5]

Even as they wield words in new ways and shape ancient images for contemporary listeners, scriptural preachers trust biblical language to do its transformative work. As Adam Nicolson has suggested: "Language which is not taut with a sense of its own significance, which is apologetic in its desire to be acceptable to a modern consciousness, language in other words which submits to its audience, rather than instructing, informing, moving, challenging, and even entertaining them, is no longer a language which can carry the freight the Bible requires." If language is shaped, Nicolson goes on to say, by "an anxiety not to bore or intimidate," then "it has, in short, lost all authority."[6]

Preaching and Imagination: Transforming Vision

Scriptural preaching, like the liturgy in which it is situated, evokes a world: the sermon uses words "to make and to move and to accomplish."[7] In this sense preaching is an act of *imagination*, which is to say not that it is about the imaginary but that it participates in the communal (rather than individual) practice of "construing reality according to a particular vision, in full awareness of other options."[8] Imagination understood this way is a hermeneutical practice that functions not arbitrarily or capriciously but *strategically*, as a way of reading texts and construing worlds. That is, the power of imagination lies not in the subjective experiences of individuals but in the community's transformative vision of what God calls the church to be. *Faithful imagination* names the capacity of a people who in their worship together enact, perform, and give life to a story that subsumes all other stories.

Preaching and worship are always products of imagination, but this does not mean that they are therefore fanciful, whimsical, or illusory. Imagination, rather, is a community's capacity for envisioning an alternative way of being, doing, seeing, and living in the world. The preacher's task is to help cultivate such a capacity so that worshipers who imagine differently "can (and will) *act* differently, personally and publicly."[9] In this the homiletical and the catechetical are brought together as one enterprise. Imaginative preaching, which means preaching not that is merely clever or inventive but that evokes and envisions a counterworld, helps to form in each hearer the *reimagined self*—not the self of mindless overconsumption or of unthinking patriotism; not the narcissistic self or the media-saturated self; but "a self rooted in the inscrutable miracle of God's love,"[10] a self that knows by being known, that recognizes that it is most fully constituted in and through prayer and praise.

Catechesis, historically, was concerned with the work of imagination and the shaping of the self-in-community; the catechumenate of the early church was not only a means of formation in doctrinal purity but a practice intent on the reimagined self.[11] The object was not merely a more informed intellect but a transformed life lived out as a counterwitness to the world's construal of what was good or moral or true. Thus to recover in our own time a sense of the catechetical force of worship and preaching is to recognize that the power of proclamation lies not in its didactic or moralizing function but in its participation in the Christian community's ongoing work of imagination, of "seeing with new eyes" the church, the world, and our place in both. The liturgy imagines and enacts for us—and the preached Word formally articulates—a vision of God's reign in which we exist both as recipients and as members of the body of Christ. We come to know that our lives are gifts for the purposes of praise and communion. Preaching tells the story of the gospel so that in the liturgy after the liturgy[12] we might embody the story concretely and materially. To be shaped by the Word is to enact the practices it enjoins: forgiveness in a world of retribution, justice in a world of inequity, prayer in a world of mindless chatter. These are not acts of pious people trying to be good but signs of God's inbreaking reign in the world. Making evident these signs is the work of imagination in worship and of the proclamation of the Word.

The capacity of imagination, moreover, is linked inextricably to *knowing*: "I pray that the God of our Lord Jesus Christ, the Father of glory, may give you a spirit of wisdom and revelation *as you come to know him*, so that, *with the eyes of your heart enlightened, you may know* what is the hope to which he has called you, what are the riches of his glorious inheritance among the saints" (Eph. 1:17–18). Such knowing is not Cartesian certitude but *abiding*, resting and trusting in the truth of the triune character of God, a truth that "organizes a comprehensive view of all things, and especially of human nature, history, and destiny."[13]

Yet we do not start with the Trinity, or even with doctrine at all; rather, we begin with worship and the proclamation of the Word in worship, which gives us the language and teaches us the patterns of relationship (baptism, Eucharist, prayer, hospitality, mission) that embody a vision of human flourishing founded on the pattern of relations that exist among Father, Son, and Holy Spirit. The triune pattern is love: God's nature is ceaseless donation, the endless giving of love, the outflow of generosity that seeks to share its perfect joy with all of creation. To preach faithfully is to proclaim this vision; it is to imagine the world as this way and not any other way.

Imagination, therefore, is a valid way of knowing.[14] As was noted in an earlier chapter, this kind of knowledge is understood as participation, not mere contemplation; as *ontos*, not mere *epistēmē*. Such knowledge, in other words, is not self-evident in a fallen world, nor is it the result of depositing theological data into a receptive mind; rather, it requires bodily participation in the forms of life that shape persons in the virtues and habits that make such knowing meaningful and actual. It is *corporate knowledge*—"the knowledge which comes from participation in a way of life, and in which we are sharers with others, past and present."[15] Such knowledge presumes the unity of doctrine (what is taught, what is preached) and practice. That is, Christian doctrines find their coherence and intelligibility as they are lived out and witnessed to—not as self-contained theological formulas objectively analyzed from the outside. We cannot, contra Moran, step outside of or rise above doctrines or beliefs in order to understand them. For example, we do not know that we are sinners saved by a merciful God because we have a vague awareness that *sin* names our moral failings as human beings, but because the call to live in communion with God and one another reveals to us our estrangement from God.

To know in this way is to imagine new possibilities for existence; it is the conversion of the deepest self. The proclamation of the Word, as it dwells within the liturgy as this imaginative drama, intends our conversion to a new way of seeing and knowing, which is manifest in what we do in worship and how we live together in Christian community and in the world beyond. The transformation that is the goal of Christian catechesis is the process (pilgrimage, journey) by which the proclamation of the Word invites us "into a counterstory about God, world, neighbor, and self. This slow, steady process has as counterpoint the subversive process of *unlearning* and disengaging from a story we find no longer to be credible or adequate."[16] For example, if we enter into worship with patriotism too readily wedded to our faith, the Word rightly preached (and there is not only one way to preach rightly!) invites us to unlearn the beliefs and behaviors that venerate flag above cross. If we enter into worship governed by consumerism and its destructive patterns and practices, the Word rightly preached teaches us that the gospel is not a commodity nor the church a marketplace of consumable goods and services, but both are gifts to be received, blessed, and shared.

The knowledge that we gain from the proclamation of the Word—the catechesis that takes place through preaching—cannot be abstracted from the kinds of practices that define and constitute such knowledge. This knowledge is not a systematically organized body of general truths but is instead *practical* knowledge: it is "fruit which can grow only in the soil of a person's [and a community's] experience and character."[17] Proclamation in worship helps to cultivate the soil that makes possible the bearing of fruit in the lives of Christians.

While imagination is exercised as the capacity to "see" differently, it is also manifested, as suggested above, in our use of language. As philosopher Sabina Lovibond puts its: "The faculty of moral 'imagination,' by which speakers represent to themselves how things might be different and better, [is] a distinct species of linguistic competence."[18] This emphasis on the connection between imagination and language serves to challenge two facile and erroneous assumptions alluded to earlier: one, that imagination is concerned primarily with "make believe," and two, that it is the property of individuals. For as Lovibond also points out, imagination "is a faculty which cannot be exercised in isolation, but only within an organic grouping of persons who are participants in a common mode of activity."[19] The juxtaposition of imagination and language is compelling and suggests that imagination, as a hermeneutical category or moral faculty, can never be divorced from the way a community has "learned to talk"—how it learns to name and describe itself and its future vision for itself. Lovibond notes how a community's linguistic competence is a matter of practical skill: "'Knowing how to talk'—either absolutely, or with reference to some specified subject-matter—is something that admits of degree. . . . We can work on our discursive skills and build them up."[20] Something like this is at work, I suggest, when we learn the language of worship (praise, lament, thanksgiving, judgment, forgiveness, intercession, and so on) and when the preacher uses the language of Scripture and Christian tradition to teach us how to "talk better," how to speak (with words and lives) the truth of our existence as Christ's body in the world. Such teaching and learning are the heart of catechesis.

Yet the connection between imagination and language reminds us that "speech is not merely descriptive, but it is in some sense evocative of reality and constitutive of reality."[21] The reality evoked through liturgical speech is an imagined one, but all worlds are, in fact, constructs of imagination: "what we have taken for granted in economics, politics, and everywhere else is an imaginative construal."[22] Such constructs are real, of course, in the sense that they are tangibly identifiable, they exert influence, they function for good or ill, and so on, but they are not natural and inevitable—rather, they are contestable, subject to challenge, debate, and critique.

These claims echo the argument made by Talal Asad, explored in chapter two, that the very category of religion is a construct that emerged out of particular interests and agendas and was shaped by particular construals of knowledge, privilege, and power. *All* claims of reality, we must say, finally, "are fully under negotiation."[23] Thus preaching and worship are not about preparing us for or teaching us about life in the "real world" or for giving us refuge for a little while from the "real world"; for Christians, the liturgy (not as text only but as its embodied performance) *is* the real world. We are freed from the burden of thinking that worship (and Christianity in general) have to do with being relevant to the "real world." Worship and Christianity in general are about inhabiting this new world and witnessing to it in the midst of other worlds, other realities. The language of the liturgy and of the preached Word signify differently, creating a new set of possibilities for human existence. Yet if our proclamation in worship draws more on the imaginings of our surrounding culture or on other languages and systems of meaning than on the scriptural and liturgical traditions entrusted to us, then worship risks failing to embody the counterstory that is the gospel's good news (Rom. 12:2).

Preaching and Catechesis: Challenging the Myths

What has been briefly described thus far—the power of preaching to form and shape persons and communities as imaginative witnesses to the church's counterstory—suggests perhaps a more recognizable connection between proclamation and catechesis than actually exists in much contemporary Christian practice. As I noted in the prologue, the very impetus for this project is the undeniable *disconnect* between worship and formation—the sense among many Christians that worship is something we do in the sanctuary and formation (education) is something that occurs elsewhere: in Sunday school classrooms, Bible study groups, and the like. This false distinction deeply informs our ideas about preaching and its purpose, and so part of the task of extraliturgical catechesis is to expose the erroneous assumptions at work in such a dichotomy, to address the difficulties they present to the actual practice of forming disciples, and to imagine faithful and creative ways to unify the proclamation of the Word in worship and the formation of the worshipers gathered to hear and receive it.

Much of the difficulty surrounding the separation of worship and Christian catechesis (and thus of preaching and formation) can be traced, as Janet Fishburn's work helps us see, to Victorian ideals of home, family, and personal piety. Though we now live in an age characterized by unprecedented sexual openness, astonishing innovations in technology and science, and much commented-upon social and familial dysfunction, American culture and churches in America continue to be shaped by the nineteenth-century Victorian vision of "the Christian family" as the cornerstone of civilization and the church as the foundation of American democracy. As indicated in the previous chapter, the nationalistic, patriotic tendencies that enter with us into the worship space are linked directly to the peculiarly Protestant view that church and nation are morally identified. From within such a position, it is assumed that it is the role of the family to provide the moral stability to allow the Christian nation to thrive, while it is the function of the church to support and nurture family life.

While we may as a culture and as the church appear to openly eschew many of the "values" associated with Victorian piety (the view of women, for example, as paragons of moral virtue and as "keepers of the springs"[24]), we do, in fact, continue to promote a privatized, domesticated Christianity that tends "to uncritically identify loyalty to family with loyalty to church."[25]

Fishburn rightly notes that the dualisms operative in Victorian thinking (masculine-feminine, mind-body, private-public, church-family) continue to influence the organization of congregational life, especially around issues of education and moral formation. For example, Victorian attitudes about male and female roles—the father as strict authoritarian, the mother as pious moral teacher—are unwittingly perpetuated in the division of labor that exists between the Sunday school and church:

> These attitudes [about prescribed male and female roles] still affect the way pastors feel about tasks they associate with Christian education. Many pastors, male and female alike, have an aversion to any association with the Sunday School. Like the father in the Victorian family, the pastor was edged out of a role in educational ministry in the congregation. The outcome is a dualistic attitude about preaching and teaching. Ordination is associated with preaching and a primarily masculine authority in the pulpit, while the domestic or feminine task of teaching is associated with laity who teach—Sunday School teachers and non-ordained Christian educators.[26]

Such dualisms are rooted, of course, in Enlightenment thought; the Victorians, like their philosophical predecessors, "had confidence in their own intellectual and moral righteousness, born of a philosophical assumption that truth is self-evident."[27] As Enlightenment ideas about progress, reason, morality, and so on found a comfortable fit within Victorian sensibilities regarding home and family, the alliance of the Protestant impulse (freedom and individualism) and the American religion of empire (God and country) shaped a vision of the American dream that depended on the family to form moral citizens schooled in Christian virtues and democratic ideals.[28] As Fishburn argues:

> According to the script of the American Dream, the family was essential to the hope for a "Christian America." Since parents were expected to nurture citizens according to a Christian standard of moral behavior, church leaders assumed that children would learn Christian attitudes from their parents at home. Parents were also expected to teach their children about the Bible and Christianity. The Sunday School was started to provide Christian nurture and knowledge of the Bible for poor children who lacked the advantages of middle-class family life. In this sense the home

and the Sunday School were both expected to be "a little church" in which children and young people could learn the moral values of Christian citizens.[29]

Two important trends related to our purposes are worth exploring here: one, that the "Christian home" usurped the church (and its worship) as the locus for shaping the lives of Christians and for nurturing discipleship; and two, that the teaching task associated with women in the home moved gradually into the church in the role of the Sunday school teacher and later in the role of professional Christian educator.

In regard to the first: While it may be true that we are less sentimental about the "American family" and the "Christian home" than were previous generations (though this is perhaps a debatable point), it is still quite clear that among both evangelical and nonevangelical Christians, the myth of the family as "a little church" continues to hold sway. The phrase *family values*, now a part of our cultural lexicon, presupposes the belief that the home is the site at which Christians are made and citizens are formed. Only in a climate in which "adults continue to refer to the family life of individual church members as 'the Christian home' would pastors, educators, and theologians have continued to believe for so long that parents are more important than the church is to the faith of children."[30] For Victorian Protestants the education of Christians was believed to occur principally in the home, primarily in the form of moral instruction meted out by devoted mothers. (This was, of course, the ideal—whether or not it always matched actual practice).

Such an understanding of formation had the unintended consequence of dislodging Scripture and its interpretation from its rightful setting—corporate worship—and relocating it to the family devotions of the home. Of course, Enlightenment religion had already put the Bible in the hands of individual believers; the Victorians simply represented the logical extension of the privatistic, pietistic approach to biblical interpretation born in the Age of Reason. The assumption that a mother could teach the Bible to children at home reinforces the common belief (widely held then and now) that any Christian can understand and teach the Bible. It also raises the question of why a pastor/preacher is needed at all.[31] Indeed, the separation of Christian formation from the proclamation of the Word in worship has had the effect, even into our own time, of diminishing "the importance of the teaching office of ordained ministry."[32] It has given the lie to the church's historic belief that, as David Steinmetz has put it, "the offices of preaching, teaching, and discipline are inseparable from the single office of the ministry of the Word of God."[33]

Although contemporary life in the twenty-first-century United States bears little resemblance to the Victorian ideal of family piety and moral purity, our imaginations continue to be captivated by this vision of Christian formation as primarily an affair of hearth and home. That is, so the reasoning goes, if we can just get our family life "in order"—if we can instill in our children Christian virtues and shape their behavior and character according to biblical principles—then we can have hope that we will be a moral people, a faithful church, and a nation under God's continuing protection and favor. On this view, the church is understood not as the counterpolitics to such a (thoroughly unbiblical) construal of home and nation but as a spiritual agency in service to the moral edification of the family and the ideals of democracy. While much of this way of thinking goes unarticulated in many ecclesial settings, it remains, as Fishburn points out, the presupposition of educational ministries in most congregations. As she notes: "A modern mother would not think of herself as the priest of the family. Change in family living patterns makes it difficult for a family to gather daily for a common meal, let alone set aside time for family devotions. Nevertheless, there is still more concern about the dwindling importance of the family meal than evidence of desire among Protestants to gather more often at the Table of the Lord."[34]

The fact that we now recognize (as the Victorians did not) that the "Christian nation" is not an empirical reality—that the United States has always been inhabited by persons and communities who reflect a variety of religious convictions—does not discourage this idealization of family, nation, and God. It is simply recast in more generalized, amorphous terms. Politicians and presidents now speak of "religious values" as opposed to specifically Christian ones, with the understanding that the descriptor *religious* names a universally recognizable disposition or orientation operative in all religions, toward the human quest for transcendence, the obligation to live morally, and the duty to strive for peace and justice. These religious values are invoked primarily because they are thought to work in concert with the aims and objectives of the political order—freedom, democracy, justice, and so on; and the appeal is made that these values be taught in the home.

In regard to the second trend: When the mother-as-teacher-of-Christian-virtue moved from the home into the Sunday school and education was "institutionalized" in Anglo-Protestantism, the wall between worship and catechesis, proclamation and formation, preaching and teaching was further solidified. Along gender lines, the Christian educator (usually a woman) took on the task of teaching while the ordained minister (almost always a man) assumed the responsibility of preaching. Christian education took place during Sunday school in the education wing or building; worship and preaching occurred in the sanctuary and were seen as separate from (though in some ways more important than) the "educational" activities.

The Religious Education Association, founded in the early decades of the twentieth century, represented formal acknowledgment that the teaching role of women had become professionalized in the church. The task of educating, nurturing, shaping, and forming Christians was now beholden more to the ideas of modern educational philosophy and the growing literature of pedagogical theory (written mostly by men) than to the practices of Christian discipleship, learned in worship and in Christian community and embodied in the church and beyond. The critiques of Gabriel Moran, Thomas Groome, and Mary Boys, undertaken in the first part of this book, demonstrate how readily this "professionalization" became a scholastic endeavor with little connection to actual Christian theology and practice, and how as it developed in academic circles through the decades, it paid insufficient attention to the problematic cultural and philosophical assumptions at the heart of its enterprise.

Because the Christian education undertaken in the Protestant Sunday school was (and is) tutorial and didactic in nature, it has been difficult—as I have been suggesting all along—to broaden notions of formation and catechesis to include what we *do* in worship. Because generations of churchgoers have been "schooled" (literally) in Scripture and doctrine primarily in the Sunday school classroom (and also in the "opening assembly" popular in many churches),[35] *and* because they have been trained to view preaching itself as tutorial and didactic, it is deeply challenging to proffer an alternative imagining of what the proclamation of the Word might accomplish catechetically in the worshiping assembly.[36]

Historically, much evangelical Protestant preaching was centered on forceful, moral persuasion meant to lead to the "saving of souls." While it is outside the scope of my purposes here to analyze that phenomenon, it is important to note that such preaching often assumed that one's conversion to the Christian faith occurred at a datable moment in history and was a dramatic, immediate, and often emotional experience. Once you were "saved," the Sunday school or Bible study group was the locus for your ongoing Christian education. Preaching was intended to stir you to belief; Sunday school inculcated biblical knowledge. The former was exhortative, the latter educative.

As the church continued to come under wide-ranging theological influences—liberalism, the social gospel, and neo-orthodoxy, for example—preaching took different forms and shapes. For example, the impulse in the mid- to late nineteenth century toward social reform movements (abolition, suffrage, temperance) was driven largely by preaching meant to stir the action of the larger public (not just the Christian church) and to marshal the necessary resources to ensure wholesale political and social change.

The point of the foregoing discussion regarding the relationship between preaching, formation, and "the Christian home" has not been to advocate a dismantling or abolishing of that most Protestant of ecclesial institutions, the Sunday school, but to do two other things. First, to help us recognize that the rhetoric of "the Christian home" and "family values"—along with the practices associated with such rhetoric—have helped to create and foster the disconnect between preaching and formation (and more broadly between worship and catechesis) that Sunday school continues unwittingly to perpetuate. Second, to aid us in imagining and implementing practices that address the resultant problems, so that the formative power of preaching can be emphasized in meaningful ways *and* so that Sunday schools and Sunday school–like structures can work in accord with, not in isolation from or in competition with, the church's worship.[37]

Crucial to these objectives is the task of naming and describing the problem correctly—seeing what is going on, what has gone on for a very long time—so that we might know how to begin the process of meaningful change. Something as simple as making a congregation aware of the history and theology of the American Sunday school movement can prepare persons not only to expect but to desire a reformation that seeks deliberately to connect efforts at making disciples to the larger life of the worshiping community and to a more disciplined, cruciform ecclesiology. Lectionary-based Sunday school curricula, increasingly common in a variety of traditions and denominations, help not only to unify the course content across the age spectrum but also to situate and saturate the Sunday school learning experience in the worship and liturgy in which all will participate following the Sunday school hour. There is the potential, as Westerhoff envisions, to transform the Sunday school "into an intergenerational preparation for the Sunday Eucharist based upon an experience of and reflection on the lectionary texts."[38]

Moreover, reconceiving the Sunday school education (and/or the confirmation process) of the young along the lines of a master-apprentice relationship can help to communicate that Christian discipleship is a journey of formation and transformation that requires not (just) book learning in a classroom setting but the patterning of one's life after flesh-and-blood exemplars, ordinary women and men of one's own worshiping community whose faithfulness attests to the extraordinary power of God. Such endeavors teach young people that Christianity is not a series of propositions to be believed in (as current configurations of Sunday school might lead them to believe) but a set of habits and skills to be acquired and sharpened.

Finally, a Sunday school paradigm that intentionally works in concert with the liturgical life of the community, that is informed by and infused with the doxological, can highlight the formative power of preaching and of the liturgy as a whole by continually calling our attention to how it is that the Word proclaimed in worship shapes our living in the world beyond our worship. It is worth giving careful consideration to how Sunday school might be meaningfully reinvigorated as the forum in which preparation for and reflection on preaching and worship can lead us out of the sanctuary and out of the classroom into the wider world to offer radical witness of the extravagant goodness of God.

Preaching as Counterformation: Reshaping Character and Community

In our own time, the homiletical temptation is often toward the therapeutic, with disastrous implications for the formation and nurture of Christians. Instead of proclaiming a vision of Christian community informed by the triune relations of love and mutuality, instead of rigorously exploring the scriptural texts in all their depth and complexity, instead of challenging worshipers to a deeper engagement with the disciplines of the church, instead of calling into question our love affair with comfort and affluence, the preacher frequently (though usually unwittingly) takes on the persona of a self-help guru, dispensing pseudo-theological advice in a format that is congenial, entertaining, and, most important, brief:

> In a New England Episcopal church, where a Thanksgiving cornucopia of pumpkins, squash, Indian corn, and apples bedeck an altar, the pastor opens the Sunday service with a sermon on overcoming self-destructive thinking. It lasts fourteen minutes. At a crowded Methodist church down the street, the sermon comes at the end of the hour, a commentary on maintaining gratitude in a materialistic culture. It spans sixteen minutes. Both services illustrate a trend that has quietly crept into American church life over the past twenty years: the shorter sermon.[39]

The brevity of sermons today, compared to those of a generation ago, is not in and of itself a sign that preaching as therapy has become the norm. Neither is my criticism of the modern sermon rooted in a nostalgic longing for a past when preaching was faultless—there has never been such a time. But the shorter sermon of today does fit into an overall pattern in which the proclamation of the Word in worship is often reduced to a patchwork of amusing anecdotes, bereft of the depth and subtleties of biblical and theological language, and intended primarily to comfort and uplift. On this view, preaching is conceived of and practiced as an offering of consumable "wisdom" to be stored, remembered, and put to use in tough times. Our formation in the wider culture as discriminating consumers is reproduced in the relationship between preacher and worshipers, when what is needed are the modes of a counterformation that assumes we have as much to unlearn as to learn. Because contemporary worshipers are trained by television and other media to have ever-shortening attention spans, the Sunday morning sermon often caters to this condition rather than attempting to tackle the deep-seated problems associated with it. Because declining membership in churches is often addressed by appeals to marketing techniques meant to bolster church attendance, preachers are easily seduced into "pitching" their "product" to an increasingly savvy "audience."

One of the things that the liturgy teaches well is that in worship our lives are ordered by a different sense of time. We tell time differently through the church's liturgical year; we inhabit time in countervailing ways to the culture's ordering of the temporal, cultivating attention to the sabbatical rhythms of work and rest, creation and recreation. The liturgy also presumes to tell time from the perspective of its end: in the Eucharist, especially, past and present are defined and taken up by the eschatological—the consummation of all things.

As a foretaste of eternal time—the continuous heavenly worship—the Sunday morning service gives us, among other things, the time to tell the story. Preaching is the gift of articulating the gospel's meaning for a community over time. We do not have to say it all at once if we recognize that the catechetical task before us is to help cultivate a community of worshipers capable of hearing the story and of embodying it in their daily work and witness; capable of sustained attention and active engagement, not just for fifteen minutes on Sunday morning but for the lifelong pilgrimage that is the Christian journey. Preaching always forms its hearers (for good and ill), but liturgically centered preaching also presumes a community formed through time in the holy habits of worship and prayer, justice and charity, study and hospitality, so that the proclamation of the Word can do its transformative, redemptive work and the Word can go forth as love and action into the world.

Preaching that seeks to form character and community recognizes that the sermon must not take the struggle out of theology. When the proclaimed Word imagines for and with the community the gospel's counterstory of God's sovereignty in the world—not the sovereignty of nations or of our solipsistic selves—then preaching can never be reduced to pious promises that we will be fulfilled or happy or even that our lives will have meaning. Rather, preaching offers only "the promise of God's ongoing rule in the world."[40] It is false and arrogant to believe that the preacher is responsible for the effects—the results, the outcome—of the proclamation of the Word. She or he is responsible only for its faithful performance.

Imaginative preaching recognizes that the Christian vision, the imagined counterstory of God's eternal reign, might not be welcome news. This is an alien truth in the times in which we live, for therapeutic preaching presumes that the sermon should be agreeable and easily digestible—that while it may have enough of an edge or bite to cause mild discomfort, it is, after all, meant to cure the ailment, not aggravate it. But it is the intent of the gospel, of course, that the Word kill us, that we might die to our old ways and be raised to new life and new understanding. Always the *telos* of preaching is transformation. Preaching strives toward this goal by the power of the Holy Spirit and in collaboration with the community gathered in anticipation of the Word, eager to share in its proclamation.[41]

Response to the Word: Baptism and Identity

The proclamation of the good news leads to baptism, the sacrament of the church in which "the beginning of God's saving work in us is both signified and accomplished."[42] Baptism discloses the paradox at the heart of the gospel we preach: the cross leads not to isolation, annihilation, despair, or defeat but to abundant new life. Jesus' risen presence inspired and authorized his disciples to make more disciples, to go into all the world and baptize in the name of the Father, and the Son, and the Holy Spirit (Matt. 28:19). Immersed into his death, Christians are now those who, like Jesus, are "alive to God" (Rom. 6:11), who share in the divine life of the Trinity, and whose identity is not now separable from Jesus'. As Rowan Williams puts it: "What the believer says is, 'I live because of Jesus, in Jesus. The person I am cannot be understood apart from Jesus. I am baptized: I received my name, my identity, in the process of immersion in the Easter event.'"[43]

And while baptism is received by the individual believer, the new life in Christ to which she or he is raised is a shared life, a life of mutuality that can be fully realized only in community, in the network of relations that bears witness to the presence of Christ as a living encounter with the powers and principalities of this world. For as Bonhoeffer insisted, baptism implies a break: "I am deprived of my immediate relationship to the given realities of the world, since Christ the mediator and Lord has stepped in between me and the world. Those who are baptized no longer belong to the world, no longer serve the world, and are no longer subject to it. They belong to Christ alone, and relate to the world only through Christ."[44]

Despite the sentimentality that habitually permeates the "mild christening ceremonies" of our time, the baptismal rite is, first and last, a ritual about dying. "In baptism we receive both community with Christ and our death as a gift of grace. . . . It is the death in the power and community of the cross of Christ. Those who become Christ's own must come under his cross."[45] These can be unfamiliar and unwelcome images in baptismal celebrations in our own time. As one preacher has described it: "In the domestic beauty of our lovely ritual of baptism, with proud parents and grandparents and godparents beaming joyfully at the innocent charm of a white-gowned child, it can be hard to recognize the radical nature of the act of baptism. But if your nostrils were spiritually energized, they would be filled with the smell of death."[46] In baptism we die to sin and to self, and in that death we share in the passion of Christ: baptism joins us with Jesus "in a visible community of suffering."[47] It sets us on a lifelong journey in which suffering is a sign of faithfulness and a mark of true discipleship. The suffering that baptism brings about is not that of one's personal misfortune, though experiencing pain and affliction can be redemptive. Rather, it is the price for noncomformity in a world scandalized by the cross of Christ. To be baptized is to join the communion of saints through time who have been rejected for the sake of the gospel.

Baptism, then, is a subversive act. It is, like the Eucharist, an act of disaffiliation. It confers an identity at odds with the ways we are named and claimed by family, nation, and ideology. It begins a process of conversion whereby old allegiances are shattered, previous loyalties negated. In this way, baptism can also be understood to be a profoundly political act, for if, as I have said, the church itself constitutes a *polis,* an alternate ordering of human relations governed by the trinitarian pattern of love-in-communion, then baptism forms a people whose politics are shaped not by suspicion and self-interest but by trust and mutuality, thanksgiving and generosity. To be a baptized Christian is not so much to have *been baptized* at a particular time as it is to lead a baptismal life—"a life of daily renunciation, of daily drowning, of daily dying and rising."[48]

Baptismal Crisis: Family Idolatry and the Dangers of Parody

Once again we can see a stark disparity between historic understanding and contemporary practice, between the origins and purposes of Christian baptism—what it produces, what it promises, what it costs—and the shallowness of much current baptismal practice. Misunderstanding about the meaning of baptism abounds, a direct consequence of the failure of catechesis (and of poor performances of the rite itself). Baptism is often entered into lightly by candidates and/or their families and performed promiscuously by clergy. In churches where baptizing infants is more common than baptizing older children and adults, the risk of betraying the rite's radical implications for discipleship is especially serious. In a culture (and church) that sentimentalizes children, the baptism of an infant can too easily be turned into a family-centered spectacle (replete with flash photography or roving videographer), a domesticated, status-conscious rite of passage having little to do with repentance, conversion, mutual accountability, and the sober desire to attain "the measure of the full stature of Christ" (Eph. 4:13).

Victorian ideas about the primacy of the family for faith formation in children continue to exert powerful, if sometimes subtle, sway over current views on the nature and purpose of baptism. Most affluent American Christians, especially, "have known only a Christianity in which God has been identified with prosperity and family stability."[49] Jesus' acerbic warnings about family idolatry are incomprehensible to the sentimental Christianity that tempts the middle class, and thus his harsh words are either ignored or subjected to a tortuous, desperate logic that strives (in vain) to align them with the popular rhetoric of "family values." The life-altering import of the apostle Paul's vision of baptism as adoption into a new family and immersion into Christ's death is at times all but lost (Rom. 6:4; 8:15–16). Children (and adults) are, as the liturgical language suggests, *presented* for baptism, but seldom are they actually *entrusted* to the care and tutelage of the Christian community in a meaningful way, as the liturgy also declares they should be.[50] Because the subversive political nature of baptism is rarely communicated in the ritual act itself or in preaching and teaching about the rite, baptismal practice is often in danger of becoming parody.

This danger, however, has as much to do with a flawed ecclesiology—a distorted view of the church and its mission—as it does with confusion about the practice of baptism itself. If the operative assumption, implicit or explicit, is that the church gives form and expression to the politics of modernity (privatized moralism, the priority of the individual, the identification of Christianity and nationalism) rather than to the politics of the cross (suffering love, resistance to all other powers and allegiances), then baptism can unwittingly serve to initiate persons into "a loose confederation of individuals who take no responsibility for the conversion and nurture of others, who do not act as if they really believe that the promises of baptism are true, and who lack confidence in their ability, by God's grace, to 'make disciples.'"[51] The sacrament of baptism must be located within an ecclesiology rooted in the mystery of the triunity of God and in an understanding of the baptized as partakers of that divine life—with all of the real-world, nitty-gritty implications of such a claim (social, political, moral, economic; implications of race, gender, and class). Baptism brings persons into a relationship with God, with each other, and with the world that is no longer determined or constrained by family connections or historical circumstances: Baptism supersedes biology, ecclesiology overcomes ontology, in the story we tell of ourselves as Christians.

And yet this truth must not be accounted as merely "spiritual" or metaphorical but also as material and corporeal, having to do with human relations on the most basic level and with the very *telos* of human existence in the created order: "The Christian through baptism stands over against the world, he [*sic*] exists as a relationship with the world, as a person, in a manner free from the relationship created by his biological identity. This means that henceforth he can love not because the laws of biology oblige him to do so—something which inevitably colors the love of one's own relations—but *unconstrained* by the natural laws."[52] This is the christological, trinitarian dimension of the sacrament: our being baptized into Christ affirms our new existence as founded on a relationship with God, "identified with what Christ in freedom and love possesses as Son of God with the Father."[53]

The consequence of this is that our new "nature," our ecclesial identity, allows us, summons us to, the freedom to love beyond the bounds of kith and kin. This is the nature of the *ekklesia* itself—the community of the baptized whose love for the world (for the neighbor, the stranger, the enemy) glimpses the eternal self-giving among Father, Son, and Holy Spirit. It is a love without partiality because its source is the trinitarian love-in-communion that transcends every exclusiveness. It is not a love that we muster on our own power, through will or personal resolve; rather, it is a love imputed to us and efficacious through us. We are its vessels, not its wellspring.

Therefore when the church fails to love as it should—when it fails to be what it is—we attribute that failure not to an inability to measure up to a modern, secular standard of justice-as-equity (à la Groome et al.) but to a disavowal of baptismal identity and vocation, personally and communally. The failure to give witness to the love of God in Christ that is our calling in baptism is a failure to enact a politics in which, for instance, racism, violence against women, class divisions, and economic injustice cannot take root. Such a politics is not the product of better-organized efforts at education but is the actualization of who we already are by God's grace: a pilgrim people who have been washed in a common bath, welcomed to a common table, and invited to share in a common life so that others might be drawn into the very fellowship of God. Again, the church's negligence in battling injustice, confronting oppression in its myriad forms, and so on is not to be construed as a failure to help secure the rights of individuals in a free society but as a betrayal of our ecclesial identity and vocation and as infidelity to our common humanity as sisters and brothers in the body of Christ.

The common life made possible by baptism and Eucharist is always, of course, a witness *against* the powers of darkness as much as it is a testimony *to* the love and life of God. The baptism of infants, for example, when followed by serious, ongoing efforts at their nurture and formation, is a powerful witness against the victimization of innocent children everywhere. Our ability to enact a meaningful baptismal politics, sustained through time by eucharistic fellowship, is born of a desire to take seriously the baptismal vows we make ourselves or on behalf of others. The Lutheran rites for the catechumenate address the heart of the matter in this pointed question: "Your work and your rest are now in God. Will you endeavor to pattern your life on the Lord Jesus Christ, in gratitude to God and in service to one another, at morning and evening, at work and at play, from this day until the day of your death?"[54]

Baptismal Catechesis: Christian Initiation in the Early Church

Baptism is usually characterized, with some scriptural warrant, as a once-and-for-all event. If by such a description we mean that baptism is an unrepeatable sacrament—effectual not because of the faith of the individual being baptized but because of the historic faith of the church and the work of the Holy Spirit—then the description is fitting. But too often the once-and-for-all characterization serves to sever the sacrament from what the early church understood to be an entire complex of rites of Christian initiation—rituals and actions that in the very doing shaped identity and imparted knowledge.

While baptismal practices in the earliest Christian communities (and the theologies behind them) were hardly uniform, there did emerge, after the conversion of Constantine, something of a "fourth-century synthesis": relative consistency in practice and doctrine across East and West.[55] For our purposes, it is worth not-

PROCLAMATION AND RESPONSE

ing how the baptismal liturgy of late antiquity sought to embody the Christian life in miniature, and how it was that in the rituals and actions performed during the baptismal rite—along with the requisite prebaptismal and postbaptismal catechesis—Christian character and the Christian community were formed. Baptism, as response to the proclamation of the Word, is seen here to be (per)formative: in the doing of certain things, the baptized come to know certain things.

Yet in recalling the rites of initiation of the early church and encouraging their retrieval for current practice, it is important to note that I am not advocating anything that has not been previously urged and attempted; various Christian communions already have begun the process of recovering for our own time the wisdom of early church baptismal theology and practice.[56] My efforts here are congruent with theirs, but are also, I hope, a profitable attempt to do several other things: to give more visibility to the already established efforts that have yet to become mainstream in any Protestant tradition; to make clear that the invitation to the ongoing process of daily conversion is extended always to the *entire* community, not just to newly baptized infants or adults; to bring the discipline of Christian education into the conversation about worship and catechesis, particularly to speak to misunderstandings about and misappropriations of education and formation in the church; to nullify the false divisions that stubbornly persist between education, theology, catechesis, and liturgy; and to offer deeper and more rigorous theological reflection on the work of catechesis in the life of the church.

As we survey the sixfold pattern of baptism in the early church, below, we might imagine possibilities for reform and renewal in our own day.[57]

After having their lives (habits, occupations, social relationships) carefully scrutinized, candidates for baptism entered into a three-year catechumenal process during which they received systematic instruction in the doctrines and tenets of the faith and participated regularly in the first part of Sunday worship. After the sermon and before the Eucharist they were dismissed from the assembly for further catechesis. When the three-year period ended, and following that year's Lenten fast, the catechumens underwent the sacrament of baptism during the Easter vigil.

The experience was meant to be dramatic, even theatrical, in order to communicate the stark transformation of identity and vocation that baptism effected.

First is the renunciation, in which the candidates strip off their clothing as a symbol of peeling off the old nature with its old ways. Cyril of Jerusalem writes that the candidates are to face west, renounce Satan and all his works, and then turn around toward the light of the baptistry to be anointed with the oil of exorcism. Set free from the tyranny of evil, the candidates then approach the baptismal waters. Second comes the ritual drowning, going under the baptismal waters—three times—as a sign of Christ's dying and rising. The waters of baptism are thought of as both tomb and mother. Theodore of Mopsuestia considered the font the womb of the sacramental birth. Third, the candidates are clothed in a white baptismal robe—they "put on Christ." Fourth, the newly baptized receive the sign of the cross. The word for signing is the same term used to refer to a wax sealing, indicating possession or ownership: the Christian is sealed with the sign of Christ, bearing in his or her body the marks of Christ. The fifth act is the baptismal anointing. The oil signifies our participation in Christ: we are *Christ-ened*. Having become worthy of the holy chrism, says Cyril of Jerusalem, you are now called Christians. Sixth, the candidates are given a candle, the sign of Christ's resurrection light. With this act the rite of initiation is completed, and the newly baptized are received into the fellowship of the Eucharist, the holy meal of the church in which baptism reaches its climax.

The life of discipleship that the newly baptized will henceforth live out is prefigured in microcosm in these ritual acts of initiation. The physical, bodily movements and gestures of the acts are richly emblematic of the daily, real-world, lived commitments of faithful Christian practice: renunciation of false paths and turning to the light; daily dying to sin and self; putting on the Christ-nature; bearing the name of Christ; anointing of the Spirit; and standing in the light of Christ.[58] Thus while the candidates have undergone rigorous prebaptismal instruction and will receive further teaching after the sacrament, the rite of initiation itself is catechetical; it imparts a knowledge that can be known only in the doing of it. In doing certain things, the baptized come to know certain things—about themselves, the nature of God, and the character of Christian community.

Extraliturgical Catechesis: Teaching about the Baptismal Life

If the sacrament of baptism itself can be formative—if it can shape sensibilities, produce Christian bodies, fashion ecclesial character, and so on—then extraliturgical catechesis works in concert with the rites of initiation to accomplish ongoing Christian nurture in the lives of persons and communities. This can include everything from catechism classes to small-membership accountability groups to an intensive, parishwide study of the history and meaning of baptism.

Even studies or classes not overtly centered on the topic of baptism can be framed baptismally. For example, following the U.S. invasion of Iraq in the spring of 2003 I taught a class with a minister friend in a local church, "Christianity and War." While the four-session study was not directly related to the sacrament of baptism, we deliberately shaped the course and its contents around the notion that our identity as baptized Christians is the most determinative factor in deciding how we are to speak—what we can and cannot say—about war, violence, peace, justice, and the military. Knowing that the members of this class were itching to articulate their (widely disparate) personal views about the current military situation, we gently, and with liberal doses of humor, insisted that the group would spend the first three sessions learning as much as we could about the church's historic teaching on war. We agreed that we would refrain from stating our personal positions on the current conflict, whether we were for or against our nation's foreign policy, until we had some history behind us and the theological language with which to articulate our views as baptized Christians.

Anne and I began and ended each session with carefully chosen prayers and hymns, giving, as much as possible, a liturgical cast to our discussions of war and violence. We probed the Scriptures; we noted the unequivocal pacifist stance of the early church; we examined Augustine's attempt at forging a doctrine of just war and Aquinas's efforts at furthering that same task; we studied the Crusades of the Middle Ages and the Reformation's teachings on war; we scrutinized current denominational resources dealing with issues of war, justice, and serving in the military.

At the end of the four weeks, we were struck by two things. One, almost all the members of the class expressed astonishment, sometimes incredulity, that they had never before been exposed to these aspects of Christian history and doctrine. (We took this as confirmation of our belief that the church generally, not just this particular congregation, has failed to provide substantive, historically engaged catechesis to its members.) Two, when the time came for persons to articulate their views on the current military situation, the members of the class more often than not couched their convictions in the discourse we had been attempting to learn and inhabit. There was very little of "Well, this is my own opinion . . ." and much more of "Like Augustine, I think that force should be used only to protect innocents from harm, never for self-defense" and "Pacifism is not a withdrawal from politics but a redefining of the political."

Within this very eclectic group of very bright people gathered to discuss one of the most divisive of all theological and political issues, there was also a very evident spirit of community, friendship, and generosity. We learned in our four weeks together that our unity as Christians is not dependent on our like-mindedness but on our willingness to live into and out of our baptismal identities as those who follow the One who is truth and who enables us to speak truthfully to one another.

My point in the above example is to say that not all efforts at baptismal catechesis are directly centered on baptism. Sometimes the kinds of catechesis that appear to be the least connected to baptism can teach us the most about what it means to be a people baptized in the name of the Father, Son, and Holy Spirit.

Catechesis about baptism also includes less overtly didactic forms of influence that can exert formative power: locating the baptismal font prominently in the worship space to communicate its centrality for faith and practice; offering congregations opportunities for baptismal renewal, even when no baptisms take place; allowing baptismal themes to regularly inform the Sunday sermon, whether or not baptism is celebrated.

Of most importance, however, are significant preparation and instruction before baptism and sustained, meaningful reflection afterward. When infants are being baptized, this means catechesis for parents and godparents, in which their own faith is nurtured and given opportunities—through worship, study, fellowship, mission—to mature and flourish. Entering the catechetical process assumes that the commitment of the parents and godparents to the community is genuine and visible. Postbaptismal catechesis elucidates the adults' long-term responsibility in nurturing the child in Christian community.

For older children and adults a catechumenal period is in order. John Westerhoff and Will Willimon outline a fourfold process. Stage one is precatechumenal *inquiry,* in which persons determine whether they desire to enter into the Christian life. It is a time for those attracted to the Christian community to reflect seriously on the demands and joys of discipleship and the implications of Christian living. Stage two, *preparation,* is the formal entering into the catechumenate, celebrated as a public liturgical act during the Sunday Eucharist. "During this stage the catechumen is expected to attend worship regularly, to acquire a knowledge of salvation history as revealed in the Holy Scriptures of the Old and New Testaments, to grow in the spiritual life of prayer and devotion, and to practice a life of Christian service and social action in accordance with the Gospel."[59] The third stage is baptismal *candidacy,* the period of weeks before baptism in which the catechumen and his or her sponsor(s) engage intently in the disciplines of fasting, prayer, and study. The fourth and final stage is *postbaptismal reflection,* a time "devoted to formal and informal activities that will assist the newly baptized to understand the meaning of the sacraments and to experience the fullness of corporate life in the Church."[60]

Yet it must be made clear that formation in the life of Christian discipleship is not merely a program or curriculum offered to newly baptized children and adults, something that they can "graduate" out of at a certain point.[61] The invitation to embark on the journey of Christian discipleship—the ongoing process of "daily dying," of conversion, transformation, regeneration—is extended to all, newcomers and longtime Christians alike. All are in need of continuous formation, and catechesis is a lifelong endeavor for all who would be followers of Jesus. Indeed, the

current, increasingly popular practice of dividing Christian communities into insiders and outsiders, veterans and "seekers," has
the grievous consequence of denying the fundamental truth that
all of us, old and young, the seasoned disciple and the beginner
Christian alike, are, as Luther put it at the end of his life, beggars
in continual need of God.[62]

Summary

The proclaimed Word in worship imagines the world that
baptism invites us to eternally inhabit. Like the community St.
Benedict envisions in the *Rule,* the body of Christ gathered lo-
cally in worship and work is the setting out of which we grow
in holiness. Preaching seeks to transform persons into faithful
worshipers of the Triune God, set apart to live true to the holiness
of God; baptism initiates us into the lifelong process of having
our lives shaped in holiness. But preaching and baptism must
also engender the cultivation of holy habits so that we might live
true to one another. For the journey we make toward holiness
is a collective one, and the formidable challenge for pilgrims on
this path is to create the kind of community where familiarity
will not breed contempt, where disagreement will not lead to
distrust and despair, where we recognize that unity and unifor-
mity are not the same thing.

The habit of weekly worship affords us the time and teaches
us the skills to learn to regard the other with the kind of patient
charity with which God esteems each of us. It is less a living
out of who we are and more a living into who we will become,
for ecclesial identity is always also eschatological. In gathering and greeting one another in Christ's name, in proclaiming
God's praises in speech and song, in heeding the call to new life
through baptism, we witness to a new kind of human community
that, even in the midst of its struggles with pettiness, cynicism,
self-righteousness, and superficiality, is able to glimpse a bit of
heaven.

7

THANKSGIVING AND COMMUNION

The Formative Power of Prayer and Eucharist

Lord, teach us to pray.

> Luke 11:1

All our prayer, all our worship, is within the struggle of the suffering Lamb of God, faced with the destructive forces of the old world. We pray with our vision of the coming Kingdom of justice, love, and peace before us.

> Kenneth Leech

Blessed are you, Lord God of all creation.
Through your goodness we have this bread to offer.

> The Roman Mass

Introduction

Christian prayer is, of course, many things.

We speak of personal prayer and corporate prayer; prayers of adoration and thanksgiving and prayers of supplication and intercession; contemplative prayer, meditative prayer, praying the Scriptures, praying the rosary, praying with icons; formal, written prayers and extemporaneous, spontaneous prayer; pastoral prayers, prayers of confession, prayers of blessing, silent prayer, the Lord's Prayer. Without reducing all manner of Christian praying to one easily identifiable and manageable thing, we can at least say that at its heart Christian prayer is a disposition of the self toward God, an openness and intentionality that seeks to receive, paradoxically, what cannot be fully contained.

Prayer for the Christian is not so much the result of faith as its source and sustenance. That is, we do not learn to pray after we have gotten our "spiritual life" in order or after we have perfected our faith. Prayer is a skill we cultivate and practice in the midst of our fumbling *toward* faith, in our halting, hesitant steps toward mature discipleship. And while prayer is performed by individuals, all Christian prayer—even that of the closet or the cloister—is always an act of church; it is in every case corporate and ecclesial. Our prayer, as Kenneth Leech suggests, can never be purely individualistic, because "it is rooted in *koinonia*, sharing, in the life of God."[1]

Because prayer is social it is also political; it is subversive of the status quo, disruptive of the stable order that we everywhere take for granted. As I have noted in previous chapters, the church is a political arrangement that stands over against all other polities. This is its eternal calling, however well or poorly it may actually embody this truth. Christian worship imagines this *polis* as the instantiation of the very life of God—the material, embodied witness of trinitarian love and communion. Therefore it is also true, as many Christians through the ages have insisted, that the prayer of the church at worship is profoundly countercultural. To pray in Jesus' name is to disavow the powers and principalities that mock his lordship; it is to recognize the scandalous nature of all our bidding. To utter "Thy will be done" is no small thing.

But living as we do in a compromised church in an accommodated age, we have lost much of the sense of power and risk and holiness that the pursuit of a prayerful life requires. As poet and essayist Annie Dillard has wryly observed:

On the whole, I do not find Christians, outside of the catacombs, sufficiently sensible of conditions. Does anyone have the foggiest idea what sort of power we so blithely invoke? Or, as I suspect, does no one believe a word of it? The churches are children playing on the floor with their chemistry sets, mixing up a batch of TNT to kill a Sunday morning. It is madness to wear ladies' straw hats and velvet hats to church; we should all be wearing crash helmets. Ushers should issue life preservers and signal flares; they should lash us to our pews. For the sleeping god may wake someday and take offense, or the waking god may draw us out where we can never return.[2]

The first part of this chapter will explore the formative nature of prayer in Christian worship—what it means to invoke this power Dillard speaks of. We will seek to discern how prayer and the act of praying form, instruct, and nurture those who worship; how prayer challenges and chastises; how it moves us beyond the walls of the worshiping space into the work of prayer in the world. Two catechetical concerns will underscore my efforts here. First is the need to understand how prayer itself shapes identity: how it acts, in Roberta Bondi's memorable phrase, as formation in love of God and neighbor.[3] How do we learn to pray? What does prayer teach us? What do worshipers learn by how they pray and by what they pray for? Second, I will note the necessity of extraliturgical catechesis to teach *about* prayer in the life of the church and the worshiping community. What must be done to counteract superficial, privatistic notions of prayer and the self-help, wish-list approach to prayer? How is it possible to discourage the view of prayer as a leisure-time activity, a diversion from the world, a commodity—something we strive to possess or achieve? What forms of catechesis are necessary to encourage a deeper engagement with the practices of prayer, both personal and corporate?

The second half of the chapter takes up the formative power of eucharistic prayer and of the eucharistic celebration itself. Few practices within the Christian church have generated more wide-ranging interpretations—or more outright conflict—than that of Holy Communion, the Lord's Supper, or the Eucharist. Controversy over the proper way to understand this sacrament has persisted through the centuries; theologians of almost every era have constructed elaborate and complex systems in efforts to explain the mechanics and meaning of this seemingly simple act of eating bread and drinking wine. Systematic treatment of the Eucharist has centered on a wide variety of themes, including memorial, thanksgiving, sacrifice, real presence, eschatology, communion, and mystery. Historical and ethnographic studies have produced complex portrayals of eucharistic practices in particular times and places and have revealed the multiplicity of meanings ascribed to this ritual act across Christian history.[4] The present discussion of the Eucharist is not meant to diminish this rich variety (nor is it intended to address the assortment of problems that may attend it). Rather, the objective here is to underscore the centrality of eucharistic worship for understanding how Christian identity is constituted and how the sacrament itself is implicated in any theological account of catechesis.

Eucharist, it will be argued, is the central act of ecclesial life which constitutes Christians as an eschatological community of mutuality and solidarity—a community embodying nothing less than the divine life of the Triune God. To make such a claim is to say that the church has no "essence" apart from communion; the life of the Eucharist is the church's life in communion with God. Thus the Eucharist is "understood primarily not as a *thing* and an objectified means of grace but as an *act* and a *synaxis* [assembly] of the local Church."[5] The Eucharist, as John Zizioulas suggests, *constitutes* the being of the church—it enables it to *be*.[6] This way of being made possible by the gift of the Eucharist is reflective of God's own being as relational: "Without the concept of communion it would not be possible to speak of the being of God. . . . The substance of God, 'God,' has no ontological content, no true being apart from communion."[7]

The church then is not ontologically prior to the act we call Eucharist, but neither is the relationship between the two one of causality. The Eucharist does not cause the church to exist—the Eucharist, rather, is the perfect expression of the triune mystery that is the church's identity. William Cavanaugh puts it this way: "The church does not simply perform the Eucharist; the Eucharist performs the church."[8] In the end, and for the purposes of catechesis, we cannot talk about any of these things—church, God, sacrament, humanity—without talking about all of them. Ecclesiology, theology, and anthropology are all implicated in a view of the Eucharist as "the life of *communion* with God, such as exists within the Trinity and is actualized within the members of the eucharistic community."[9]

All of this can sound lofty and overly complex. It can seem like abstract theological reflection for its own sake. It can appear to have little to do with the education of Christians and the nurture of Christian community. And it can seem especially bewildering to Protestant sensibilities shaped by the notion that the Eucharist is something the church *does* (and usually not very often), rather than something that makes the church what it is. But this vision of the Eucharist as the life of God is at the heart of the catechetical enterprise for all Christian communities. This is true because the Eucharist is the site at which the community (*laos*) of the baptized and the work (*ergon*) of the Holy Spirit are joined to effect the transformation of persons into an image of the divine fellowship of the Triune God. The Eucharist produces a people who live out of the giftedness of their creatureliness, who make actual the love and generosity, fellowship and freedom that characterize the life of God (1 Corinthians 11). Baptism initiates us into and the Eucharist sustains us in the life we were created for: participation in the ceaseless flow of *caritas* between Father, Son, and Holy Spirit.

Yet because the church lives for now in anticipation of the fullness of this truth, it remains acutely aware of its failure to wholly embody this divine reality. In the Eucharist we are always a people *becoming*, in a sense, what we already are—what we have been called to be and made to be but have yet to fully actualize. Rather than being far removed from the day-to-day affairs of real-world, human existence, this view of the Eucharist as life in communion with God situates the church firmly within the social, political, moral, and economic exigencies of the real world. Indeed, eucharistic worship shapes the church as a counter-*polis* to the dominant cultural powers. A eucharistically centered ecclesiology is a powerful critique of and bold witness against the bureaucratic, managerial, consumer-capitalist models of church that are so prominent today and that purport to be more "socially relevant" than so-called liturgical churches.

The concern in the latter part of this chapter will be twofold. First, we will examine the formative power of the Eucharist itself—how it constitutes identity, shapes character, nourishes

community, produces bodies, instantiates its own politics, and
so on. Second, we will explore the necessity for more rigorous
and responsible catechesis about the sacrament itself. What
does it mean to teach that the Eucharist is constitutive of the
church's very existence within Christian communities habituated to infrequent celebrations of Holy Communion, who regard
the sacrament as an "activity" that the church (occasionally)
engages in? How can we begin to communicate and then enact
the radical social, political, and economic implications of eucharistic worship? What forms of catechesis are necessary to
contest the privatization of eucharistic piety and the view that
Communion is an isolated, individualistic, and somber affair?
How can churches implement forms of catechesis that work
in harmony with lived liturgical practice and help to nurture
a desire for more frequent celebrations? And finally, how can
faithful catechesis work to move communities toward this more
holistic, synergetic vision of eucharistic worship and Christian
formation?

But first we begin with prayer.

The Opening Prayer: "Collecting" Ourselves before God

After we have gathered together as the body of Christ for
worship, after we have greeted one another in Jesus' name,
acknowledging that the Lord is present with us and that it is
he who empowers our worship, after we have sung a hymn
that expresses joy, gratitude, praise, and thanksgiving, we pray
together an opening prayer.[10]

> Almighty God,
> to you all hearts are open, all desires known,
> and from you no secrets are hidden.
> Cleanse the thoughts of our hearts
> by the inspiration of your Holy Spirit,
> that we may perfectly love you,
> and worthily magnify your holy name,
> through Christ our Lord. Amen.[11]

This prayer, the collect for purity, does what all opening prayers are meant to do: it invokes the name and the presence of God, before whom the people of God stand without pretense, and it distinguishes (implicitly) between the sovereign God whom we worship, the one from whom "no secrets are hidden," and the false gods (of power, money, self-will . . .) that lure us into secrecy and deception, that vie daily for our affection, attention, and loyalty. When we pray this prayer we express a desire and willingness to be transformed so that our true end might be realized: to love and worship God. This prayer at the beginning of worship signals our availability to the working of the Holy Spirit that such a transformation might occur. And we do this corporately, communally, and openly. Our prayer is not a turning inward; it is not an invitation to a deeper interiority but an outward gesture of openness toward God and each other.

We may come to worship wrapped up in ourselves; the culture we live in trains us, as we well know, in the myriad practices of self-preoccupation. But the prayer of the church, as Gail Ramshaw says, is a "prying open" of the closed system of the self. "I come to the liturgy bound up in myself. But the prayer of the liturgy inserts me into a narrative older and deeper than myself, giving me language for myself that I would not have discovered looking at myself in the mirror."[12]

Collects or opening prayers that are specific to the celebrations and observances of the liturgical calendar (unlike the collect for purity) have the added effect of situating our prayer within the broader scriptural themes of the day—themes that, again, often set us at odds with dominant cultural assumptions and practices. Consider, for example, the collect for the second Sunday of Advent from *The Book of Common Prayer:*

> Merciful God, who sent your messengers the prophets to preach repentance and prepare the way for our salvation: Give us grace to heed their warnings and forsake our sins, that we may greet with joy the coming of Jesus Christ our Redeemer; who lives and reigns with you and the Holy Spirit, one God, now and for ever. Amen.

The wide-ranging themes of Advent and the scriptural narratives and images that give rise to them are encapsulated in this brief opening prayer: repentance, salvation, sin, judgment, joy, anticipation of Christ's final coming. These may be common, familiar biblical themes, but when they are voiced in prayer by worshipers who find themselves on the second Sunday of Advent besieged by the consumer culture's frenzied Christmas countdown, they become subversive speech. The prayer prays us, so to speak, that we might learn what it means to be an Advent people in a Christmas-carnival world; that we might learn to have our lives shaped by scriptural patterns and practices that locate the pathway into the mystery of the incarnation in patient and hopeful vigilance rather than in the restless, rootless activity of cultural overconsumption. Thus as we begin worship with this prayer, we acknowledge—and we enact—our resistance to the wider world's rush to frivolity that would have us deny Advent's call to prepare for the Christ Mass with waiting and penitence.

The prayer we pray at the outset of worship, whatever the day or season, prepares us for what is to follow in the remainder of the liturgy. It shapes the worship to come, just as it shapes our thoughts and sensibilities in the ongoing work of transforming us into the likeness of the Son, in whose name we pray.

Prayers of Confession: Telling the Truth about Ourselves

We live in a confessional age: an era in which "telling all"—especially in front of an anonymous television audience of millions—is deemed an act of heroism and a kind of therapy for the guilt-ridden and humiliated. Countless politicians, corporate executives, actors, and athletes have in recent years confessed openly to past misdeeds, often winning newfound respect for their purported honesty and bravery. Some of these public displays of regret may be rooted in sincere penitence; others are most likely crafted and calculated attempts at career damage control. Either way, authentic confession can never take place in the anonymity that television and other mass media create and foster. Confession requires a context and a community, and the confession of our sins, personally or corporately, is more than simply lamenting them.

In the church, confession and pardon are linked inextricably to the proclamation of the gospel and to baptism. To confess our sins is not merely to recite a litany of our faults, nor even to feel something—guilt, shame, remorse—about our wrongdoing. It is instead to locate our sins and our sinfulness within the gospel's story of estrangement and loss, forgiveness and restoration—to recognize ourselves as creatures separated from our Creator and to seek renewal of relationship and communion. Repentance is, as Luther suggests in his *Large Catechism*, a "walking in baptism," a return to the root of our identity as new creatures in Christ. Thus sin is a *theological* category—not a generic label for whatever wayward, ill-conceived behavior a person might engage in—and our confession of sin as Christians is an act of the whole body of Christ. "The praying I," as Ramshaw puts it, "stands before the Triune God. Not only am I before the living God, but I am not standing alone."[13]

Augustine's recounting of his sins in *The Confessions*, for instance, is not one lone individual's cataloging of his youthful indiscretions for the interest of the prurient reader; nor is it a display of obsessive introspection by an overly self-conscious intellectual. *The Confessions* is Augustine's prayerful attempt to situate the story of his sinfulness within the larger narrative of the grace of the gospel and in the context of his baptismal faith, the reality that brings meaning and coherence to all of Augustine's life—past, present, and future. For Augustine's is a story told from the perspective of its end and utterly within the bounds of Christian community, despite the narrative's seemingly individualistic cast. The disparate, fragmentary sins of his past are gathered together into the fabric of a shared baptismal life that is lived out as an ongoing process of conversion.

So too with us. Prayers of confession allow us, as Don Saliers suggests, "to speak the truth about ourselves in order to find the truth in Christ. True confession of sin before God is . . . directed toward amendment of life."[14] We confess our sins not that we might feel better about ourselves but that our lives might be changed, that we might learn to bear faithfully the mark of Christ received at baptism. When we confess our sins before God and one another and seek pardon for our offenses, we participate in the mystery of Christ's reconciling work. Christ's forgiveness is made real to us. "The grace of the baptismal event is restored to us, and we are again received into the fellowship of Christ's body."[15]

Personal and corporate confession, while practiced differently, are really of a piece, for all our prayers of confession are meant to restore us to communion with the whole body of Christ. When personal confession is reduced to a sheepish acknowledgment of our private vices, the radical edge of its communal implications is diminished; similarly, when public confession is turned into a muffled, embarrassed admission of corporate guilt, we evade the self-scrutiny necessary to confront all our sin.[16]

Catechesis *about* prayer can help to hold these two truths in a necessary tension. The first truth: the conversion of the self that confession seeks to effect is "a practical matter, a social matter, with material conditions [that] . . . cannot occur through the mere exercise of will power, or through wistfully wishing that it were so."[17] And the second truth: confession presupposes self-examination—not self-condemnation or self-abasement, but "the honest, fearless confrontation of the self, and its abandonment to God in trust."[18] Catechesis about prayer nourishes a community in the truth that genuine *metanoia*—literally, a turning around of the mind or heart—is sought in fellowship, not in isolation from it, and that self-examination can be carried out, paradoxically, only within accountable Christian community, among persons who resolve not to live as strangers to one another.

The catechetical challenge is a daunting one because of the many ways we allow false ideas about prayer, repentance, self-knowledge, and so on to inform the practices of confession and conversion and our understandings of them. Thus efforts at teaching about prayer have the responsibility of drawing attention to the disparity between liturgical practice and lived commitments—that is, between what and how we pray in the worshiping assembly and how our lives often betray flawed understandings of prayer and its purpose. For example, when we pray with Jesus the Lord's Prayer we seek the forgiveness of our sins. But such forgiveness is not a two-way proposition "between Jesus and me." Rather, we are forgiven "as we forgive those who trespass against us." Our own forgiveness is linked to (though not held hostage by) our willingness to forgive others. The implication here is that we cannot know what it is to experience the forgiveness of God apart from the forms of life that bind us one to another in faithful covenant community.

Such community, however, is not an easily attained romantic idyll. The community in which forgiveness is possible is one in which persons struggle to learn over time—over a lifetime, perhaps—the linguistic skills, virtuous habits, and gestures of reconciliation and peaceableness necessary to risk the truth for the sake of love. Worship is the primary locus for learning such skills, habits, and gestures (e.g., sharing the peace of Christ, breaking bread at a common table, confessing sin openly and corporately). When our lived commitments do not correspond to our liturgical practices, when we do not "practice what we preach" (the description of the problem really isn't any more complicated than that), intentional, sustained catechesis can help a community achieve more coherence between liturgy and life, with the goal always of learning to live in the love and joy of God.

The first task of good catechesis, then, is naming and describing the problem correctly—knowing what it is that needs to be taught *and* what needs to be unlearned. Whether with denominational curricula on prayer and Scripture, or a course on how to use the daily office for personal prayer, or instruction on learning to pray the psalms, catechesis is situated within a worshiping community and does its work in concert with the prayerful practices of the liturgical assembly. It encourages active engagement in and critical reflection on the church gathered in prayer and praise and seeks to cultivate disciples whose whole lives are prayers offered to God with joy and thanksgiving.

Prayers of the People: Remembering the World before God

Prayer and worship together form, as Saliers has put it, a "school of gratitude."[19] But the gratitude, joy, praise, and thanksgiving that prayer schools us in must also make room for the less than joyful, the less than grateful—the doubt, despair, struggle, grief, rage, and lament that at one time or another accompany all truthful prayer. We know this intuitively when we confess our sins, when we anguish over the harm we have wrought, the wounds we have caused, and when we sense God's distance or even absence in the midst of strife, pain, or fear. But we know it also when we pray for others, when we do the prayerful work of intercession—what Rowan Williams defines at its simplest as "thinking of something or someone in the presence of God."[20] How is it possible to hold together, we may be compelled to ask, God and the brutal murder of a child; God and the cancer-ravaged body of a spouse; God and terrorism, natural disaster, genocide, AIDS? "'This present darkness' is often so dark," says Williams, "that it seems empty formalism to put the name of God beside some appalling atrocity. How pointless, how unconnected it is."[21] But it is precisely in the struggle to hold together what seems incongruous and irreconcilable that we come to know that "there is no place where the love of God can't go."[22]

This is the task that the prayer of intercession calls us to and the truth it schools us in: as Christ's body we are called to share in the continuing work of carrying his cross—which has already overcome suffering and defeated the powers of darkness—into "the remotest and bleakest places."[23] In worship the liturgy calls us to pray for "all those who suffer in body, mind, or spirit."[24] We do this even when we cannot see what hope there might be, because *not* to pray thus is to draw back from the full implications of faith in Jesus crucified.[25]

In the liturgy, our prayers of intercession—the prayers of the people as they are sometimes called—summon us to a deeper engagement with the world that we "hold together" with the reconciling work of the cross of Christ. We do not intercede for others as vaguely interested bystanders; intercession is not a utilitarian act of passively putting in a request and waiting idly by for a simple yes or no.[26] Intercession implicates us, draws us in, entangles us in the healing and restoration for which we pray. Intercession is, according to Leech, "more than a mere recital of names: it is a literal standing between, an act of reconciliation, a sacrificial, priestly work in which Christ allows us to share."[27] It is a call to ministry and action, a call to love with the radical, impossible love of Christ.

Roberta Bondi notes how the Lord's Prayer, often recited to conclude liturgical prayers of intercession, is Jesus' gift to the church that asks "no less than a total transformation into the love of God and neighbor of our entire persons, interior and exterior, public and private, social and personal, hearts, minds, strength, and souls."[28] This transformation of character becomes possible when intercessory prayer directs us to those for whom we pray—when our prayer becomes work and witness in the lives of the lost and broken. We pray with closed eyes that our eyes might be fully open to the suffering world, that we might "know in *ourselves* how God's mercy breaks barriers, remakes and renews."[29]

Even our bodies are implicated in the formation and transformation that prayer effects. Kneeling in worship is an act of the production of Christian bodies. Kneeling, bowing, genuflecting, closing the eyes, and clasping the hands do not so much express or communicate certain subjective inner states as much as they produce particular kinds of people. Kneeling and other liturgical bodily postures are not mere *displays* of ritualized behavior. Rather, the act of kneeling itself "generates a body identified with subordination."[30] This is not the subordination of forced enslavement or quiescent obedience—despite the lamentable abuses and misunderstandings in the church's past—but is the willing surrender, inscribed on one's very body, to the will of God. It is a (literal) molding of the body that discloses the knowledge, tacitly and over time, of who we are in relation to the God whom we worship and pray to. Thus prayer, as does all of worship, produces persons who have an instinctive knowledge *embedded in their bodies* of what it means to be Christian.

Persons raised in the Catholic Church, for example, learn the practice of genuflecting when approaching the altar—a kind of bodily, performative knowledge that in many ways operates subconsciously and that runs counter to the ways bodies and identities are constructed and normed in the wider culture. For even in the brief ritual gesture of genuflection (situated as it is within the larger set of speech-acts that are the liturgy) there is the configuration of the body as attentive to and desirous of the holy. In the culture of consumption and mass entertainment, by comparison, the body is constructed as a receptacle and communicator of consumeristic values, an object for the visual display of wealth, power, and beauty (nice car, nice body). Christian bodies, in contrast, are to enact resistance to such configurations of the corporeal and bodily. For instance, when fasting is practiced in association with prayer it "may serve to produce bodies that can withstand the seductions of a culture of consumption and desire."[31]

The production of our bodies in worship has important implications for the catechesis of youth, perhaps that of girls and young women especially. The culture of fashion, like the culture that is the church, engages in the discursive production of bodies. Fashion constructs female bodies as objects of male desire, regards female bodies as discrete body parts, and encourages the "enhancement" of female bodies through surgery, chemical injections, and/or extreme physical training. The church, however, through worship, prayer, fasting, and other disciplines, teaches that bodies are holy, that they bear in them the *imago Dei*, even that sexuality can be in some sense sacramental (the biblical view of human beings, we must remember, is not that we *have* bodies but that we *are* bodies). This is true even though the church through most of its history has been easily swayed by a puritanical squeamishness about women's bodies and by the Enlightenment's outright contempt for them. Christian theology and practice through the centuries has been, without doubt, insufficiently materialist and corporeal. Retreating into what Kathleen Norris calls a "comfortable gnosticism,"[32] the church has been undeniably scornful of the human body generally and of women's bodies in particular. This is one of the church's enduring ironies, given that Christianity is inescapably incarnational and given that Christians believe that "the Word became flesh" through the flesh-and-blood, very real body of a young woman.

But Western misogyny takes its most pernicious form in popular culture's exertion of a subtle yet fierce disciplinary power that seeks to control women through their bodies and to manipulate very young girls with false images of bodily beauty and health. Christian catechesis for the young must make obvious the profound difference. To fast and pray as a Christian, for example, for the purposes of self-discipline and solidarity with the hungry, is a strikingly different bodily act from starving oneself in order to meet the unattainable goal of super-thinness set by the culture of fashion. Moreover, any church teaching that communicates a prudish embarrassment about the human body must be resisted with a catechesis that celebrates the giftedness of our creatureliness, even as it teaches that our bodies are utterly implicated in the gospel's call to holiness and discipleship.

To be more aware of our bodies in prayer can remind us that the physical postures we assume in the act of praying are themselves a part of the holiness that conversion calls us to—a holiness of mind and body, spirit and matter.

Finally, in teaching about intercessory prayer we would do well to remember and instruct others that intercession cannot be separated from all that we are and do as Christians. "It is a great mistake," Williams points out, "to regard intercession as 'bread and butter' prayer, while adoration is left to a few professionals, holy and remote souls. In the long run, prayer is one act, not several—the act of opening ourselves as best we can to the glorious life of God, letting God live in us."[33] Catechesis about prayer must continually strive against the notion that intercession keeps us at a safe distance from those for whom we pray—that we bring the request to God, who then does all the work. All Christian prayer, finally, is rendered authentic in action. Like the Benedictines in the *Rule*, we must come to see that prayer is "the living idiom of the community."[34] Prayer transforms us because it has everything to do with everything we do—being, thinking, seeing, feeling, and acting in the world around us.

The Eucharist as Imaginative Act

As we have noted repeatedly, the church at worship imagines a world that is fundamentally at odds with "the world." But this enacted world—this world that is prayed, sung, and spoken into being—is the real world after all. Worship, as Jacques Maritain once said of poetry, is "the 'recomposition' of a world more real than the reality offered to the senses."[35]

In the discussion of preaching in the last chapter, I drew on Garrett Green's treatment of imagination, which he describes as a community's capacity to practice the world according to a particular vision, in full awareness of other options, other visions, other ways of seeing.[36] We will return to this strategic element of imagination and the Eucharist soon, but there is another critical point from Green's project that is helpful here: the connection between imagination and paradigms. Following the scientific work of Thomas Kuhn, but also building on the linguistic philosophy of Ludwig Wittgenstein, Green defines a paradigm as "the constitutive pattern according to which something is organized as a whole-in-parts."[37] Paradigms are holistic rather than piecemeal, and their distinguishing feature, according to Green, is their exemplary function. "Something serves as a paradigm—that is, as an exemplar or ideal type—because it shows forth a pattern, a coherent nexus of relations, in a simple and straightforward manner."[38]

The relationship between imagination and paradigms allows us to see one thing *as* another. To see one thing *as* another—to say that the world is this way and not that way—is to recognize that all claims to truth, reality, and so on can only be argued out; there is no privileged, essential "realness" or "rightness" for or against which alternative visions can position themselves. In theological terms we can say that "the Christian gospel is a counter-'as' to the long-accepted 'as' that is widely and uncritically accepted as objectively real."[39] The Apostles' Creed is an example of a paradigm within the Christian faith—a holistic pattern that "sketches the grammar of Christian belief in capsule narrative form."[40] "Christians have imagined the world," Green observes, "according to the paradigm exemplified by the creed."[41] To claim to live as persons created by and dependent on a sovereign God who is "maker of heaven and earth" is to refuse to be defined as self-made, self-governing, independent individuals.

If the Apostles' Creed is an example of a paradigm, then I suggest that the eucharistic meal—the centerpiece of the church's worship—is another example, perhaps the preeminent one, of how Christian imagination functions paradigmatically. The Eucharist is the paradigm through which Christians interpret the church and the world; it "shows forth a pattern" after which the church is called to order its common life—a pattern marked by habits (generosity, hospitality, thanksgiving) that govern the lives of its members. The Eucharist actualizes the nexus of relations that enables the imagining of the church as the suffering body of Christ, broken for the world; as an eschatological community of hope and reconciliation; and as a counterpolitics to the cultural forces of consumerism, nationalism, narcissism, violence, oppression, and injustice. In this way the Eucharist is an imagined, paradigmatic practice construed as one "way of seeing" among others.

Indeed, the belief that it is one possibility among others is what gives the Eucharist its subversive and scandalous character. For in a world that values individuality, autonomy, interiority, and independence, Christians, when they participate in this communal meal, witness to the truth that their identity is constituted through mutuality, solidarity, openness, and dependence on God and on each other. Against a culture shaped by the vacuous, alienating politics of consumer capitalism, the Eucharist forms a community of persons called to live in the abundance and generosity of a grace-giving God. The Eucharist *transforms* all human imaginings as it *conforms* the community to the image of God.

Eucharistic imagination, moreover, is *strategically* deployed; it is a strategy of resistance to the dominant powers and practices of any given social setting. To come to the Lord's table is to be shaped by a story of forgiveness, reconciliation, and communion; it is to refuse to participate in the forces of destruction (however subtle they may be) that deny that all of creation is God's good gift. Within the context of other ways of knowing and acting, Christians bear witness to the truth that the body of Christ gathered together in eucharistic fellowship is not the way of the world; it is a sign of the inbreaking reign of God. The Eucharist is, as Leech puts it, a subversive act, an act of disaffiliation. "It is the sacrament of equality in an unequal world."[42] Or, as William Cavanaugh suggests, in celebration of the Eucharist "the secular imagination is radically called into question."[43]

This is true because the Eucharist, and the vision of church and world that it enacts, is an *eschatological* reality. The Eucharist does not merely commemorate past events; it makes available a foretaste of the future kingdom of God in the midst of human history. The Eucharist is an interruption of the *saeculum,* but it is also the encompassing of it, for there is nothing outside the renewing work of Christ that the Eucharist performs. Chronological time is not done away with, of course, but it is measured from the perspective of its end, since the culmination of history is already accomplished in the cross and in the breaking of the bread, and awaits only its final consummation. "What we call the beginning is often the end / And to make an end is to make a beginning. / The end is where we start from."[44]

Chronological time, from a eucharistic, eschatological perspective, is beside the point. This is not to say that when the church celebrates the Eucharist it is somehow beyond or outside the scope of time, occupying a spiritual, ethereal plane of existence. To the contrary, the body of Christ is a body enmeshed in all the travails of the temporal: the Eucharist is justice in the midst of injustice, peace in the midst of violence, reconciliation in the midst of strife and division. Chronological time is beside the point in the sense that it is not the time in which the church lives; its measurements (clocks and calendars) do not order the church's life. The church lives instead by another time: *kairos*—time redeemed by the saving work of Christ and measured by the rhythm of fasts and feasts that orders the church's common worship. The eschatological retelling of time has wide-ranging implications for catechesis in the life of the Christian community—matters we will get to shortly.

Strategic Imagination: Ritual and Resistance

What occurs when a community of Christians celebrates the Eucharist, indeed when it worships, is often described broadly as "ritualistic." Often, particularly within Protestant circles, the term carries pejorative overtones, connotations of mindless, rote behavior, robotic action, hollow ceremony. However, the concept of ritual—especially within anthropological and cultural studies—is generally understood "in the descriptive sense of regular patterns of behavior invested with symbolic significance and efficacy."[45] Recent critical theory in the anthropology of ritual has focused less on mechanistic or functional analyses of behavior and more on explication of the *meaning* of particular human activities. Understanding not only ritual but all cultural activity as essentially *semiotic*, ritual theory has been concerned with the sorting out of signs and their meanings. In this vein, eucharistic doctrine from Augustine onward has been built on the theory of the *signum*, which, as Aquinas maintained, "conveys something else to the mind, besides the species which it impresses on the sense."[46] For the study of sacramental worship, one of the important questions has been how liturgical rituals encode the world for those who engage in them.

Catherine Bell, whose work has been alluded to in other parts of this book, offers a helpful way to sort through these matters because her account of ritual is less encumbered by common assumptions about "thinking" and "acting" and more disclosing of the *strategies* by which ritualized activities do what they do. Traditional ritual theory often bifurcates thinking and acting within religious symbol systems: thoughts, beliefs, and ideas are deemed to be of primary significance, while ritual is understood as the secondary expression of these "mental" processes. (Clifford Geertz's anthropology of religion was critiqued in chapter 2 for displaying this very tendency.) Traditional ritual theory is also often caught up in an intractable debate over whether ritual is distinct and set apart from ordinary human action or is itself an aspect of all human activity. To avoid the impasse created by understanding ritual as either a separate structural category within cultural systems or constitutive of all human activity and behavior, Bell proposes an approach that refers to

> the particular circumstances and cultural strategies that gener-ate and differentiate activities from each other. This approach, which assumes a focus on social action in general, [looks] to how and why a person acts so as to give some activities a privileged status vis-à-vis others. Rather than impose categories of what is or is not ritual, it may be more useful to look at how human activities establish and manipulate their own differentiation and purposes—in the very doing of the act within the context of other ways of acting.[47]

"Ritualization," then, is a "way of acting that specifically es-tablishes a privileged contrast, differentiating itself as more important or powerful."[48]

This understanding of ritual action is helpful in considering the strategic, formative dimension of the Eucharist—how the sacrament shapes Christians in particular and powerful ways. The act of sharing the eucharistic meal does indeed establish and manipulate the meal's own differentiation and purposes, for it is "within the context of other ways of acting" (refusing solidarity with the poor, for example, or pledging one's ultimate loyalty to the nation-state, or aligning the Christian gospel with the aims and agendas of democratic social orders) that Christians, when they celebrate the Eucharist, bear witness to a "privileged contrast"—the sovereignty of God's inbreaking reign in the world. This may be cumbersome, unwieldy language for describing the sacraments, but it does help to articulate the formative power of the Eucharist as a strategic practice in the midst of other formative practices.

To cite a historical example: The eucharistic theology of John Wesley—which was centered on not only frequent but "constant communion"—was an attempt to differentiate between the increasingly lax standards applied to Anglican eucharistic practices and Wesley's own view that partaking of Holy Communion several times a week was indispensable for nurturing the life of faithful discipleship. According to James White, the sacraments in Wesley's day had been reduced to "social propriety (in the case of baptism) or ethical motivation (in the case of eucharist), with little thought that either sacrament might be divine intrusion into this well-ordered universe."[49] At a time when the Anglican Church was experiencing a general decline in eucharistic worship (in most parish churches there were only three celebrations a year), Wesley counters with this admonition: "Whoever therefore does not receive . . . either does not understand his duty or does not care for the dying command of his Saviour, the forgiveness of his sins, the strengthening of his soul, and the refreshing of it with the hope of glory."[50]

For Wesley to situate the Eucharist (and all Christian practices) within the context of accountable communities of discipleship indicated his belief that the sacraments are intelligible only within the bounds of ecclesial practice and are subversive of—not cooptable by—the status quo. "Methodist worship," as White observes, "was a countercultural movement in the midst of the English Enlightenment."[51] For Wesley to maintain the synthesis between sacramentalism and evangelicalism, between Holy Communion and holy living, was a strategy of resistance to the dominant practices of his day—an attempt, in Bell's words, at the "production of differentiation." His insistence on celebrating Communion frequently was also a strategic interruption of the individualist impulse of Anglican sacramental theology and was especially subversive of the personal autonomy at the heart of much of early American revivalist Methodism. While later Methodism would align itself more with the privatization and interiority of Enlightenment religion than with Wesley's own communal vision of piety and practice, Wesley's model of accountable discipleship, embodied most definitively in the class meeting, assumed the corporate nature of faithful sacramental practice. Moreover, John and Charles Wesley's emphasis on the *eschatological* nature of the Eucharist (evident especially in many of their hymns) offered a privileged contrast to the commonplace view that limited the meaning of Holy Communion to mere memorial.[52] As Bell reminds us, "The significance of ritual behavior lies not in being an entirely separate way of acting, but in how such activities constitute themselves as different and in contrast to other activities."[53]

Bell also describes how strategic practices are able to "reconfigure a vision of the order of power in the world."[54] She labels this ability "redemptive hegemony" and locates its significance in a community's attempt to construct its reality in ways that upset normalized power relations. Once again we can bring the notion of imagination into play—the church's capacity to reconfigure reality and the ordering of power in light of scriptural faith and the claims of the gospel. By attending to Bell's idea, it is possible to understand the Eucharist as an imaginative, strategic negation of the power structures everywhere taken for granted: powers that prize profitability above human flourishing, that seek to render invisible the poor and dispossessed, that place all hope in the unchecked advances of science and technology, that glamorize obscene displays of wealth and stigmatize simplicity and frugality, that desecrate the natural world in the name of progress and free enterprise.[55] As the embodied proclamation of the gospel, the Eucharist turns secular power on its head: "Blessed are the poor in spirit," the invitation to the banquet reads, "and those who mourn, the meek and those who hunger for righteousness; the merciful, the pure in heart, the peacemakers, and those who are persecuted" (Matt. 5).

This is *not* a matter of the church's marshaling its resources to create or support power structures that, as Thomas Groome would have it, are "capable of promoting the values of the Kingdom."[56] Neither is the gospel proclaimed in the Eucharist a private word spoken to the public sphere for the purpose of mitigating or mediating existing relations of power that are assumed to be necessary and inevitable, as Mary Boys suggests.

Rather, in the celebration of the Eucharist the church embodies a visible politics as an imaginative, utterly real alternative to the false and destructive powers and principalities. The Eucharist *is* the politics of the church, a Christian economy (*oikonomia*) in a world of economic folly and injustice. And in the celebration of the Eucharist Christians are reminded that they are claimed by a power and politics not of their own choosing.

The Great Thanksgiving: Prayer and Communion

This reordering of the relations of power in the world is dramatically evident in the historic texts we know as the eucharistic prayers. The pattern of these prayers is remembrance and thanksgiving, and their forerunners are the ancient meal blessings of Judaism. In these table prayers it was not the bread or wine that was blessed but God, for it was recognized that Yahweh was the source and power behind all human and cosmic affairs. This same sovereign God, moreover, was intimately involved in the day-to-day lives of his people. And so in the ordinary table blessing (*berakoth*) "God was blessed or thanked for what he had done, in rescuing the people from slavery in Egypt, in giving them the promised land and the law to direct their lives, in bringing forth food from the earth and creating the fruit of the vine."[57]

These were prayers of remembrance (*anamnesis*) of God's mighty acts of salvation. All meals were considered hallowed occasions, but the most sacred meal in Judaism, the Passover, was to be a special day of remembrance and a feast to the Lord (Exod. 12:14). Yet the events of Israel's deliverance from Egypt in this meal were not merely recalled; they were (and are) relived as an immediate reality. Remembrance was not simply nostalgia for the past but a proleptic, performative work that celebrated the great mystery of God's salvation in a ritual meal joining together past, present, and future. What's more, the prayer of *anamnesis* presumed the *continuing* work of God (the one who freed Israel from slavery would surely also liberate them from their present sufferings), and it sought God's aid in the present time of trial: "Jewish prayers of remembrance frequently led into a second half that involved invocation (in Greek, *epiclesis*), calling upon God to continue his saving work."[58]

Early Christianity eased naturally into these Jewish patterns of prayer and blessing, and Passover was the (theo)logical backdrop for understanding both the cross and the Communion meal: "For our paschal lamb, Christ, has been sacrificed. Therefore, let us celebrate the festival" (1 Cor. 5:7–8). And while it is beyond the scope of my purposes here to analyze precisely how the Jewish *berakoth* became the template for the eucharistic prayer and the Passover the framework for understanding the eucharistic action, there are several things of importance about the prayer itself—with implications for catechesis and formation—that we can take note of.

There are no complete eucharistic prayer texts in the New Testament—only hints of them in various places—and the late-first-century document known as the *Didache* contains Christian meal prayers that may or may not have been part of a eucharistic liturgy.[59] The earliest written text of a full eucharistic prayer is found in Hippolytus's *Apostolic Tradition* from the early third century. As Saliers notes, since its publication in the late nineteenth century this document "has become a paradigmatic model for nearly every major Christian body undertaking reform of its rites during the past twenty years."[60] In it the *anamnesis* and *epiclesis* from the Jewish table blessing are retained, yet they are now given christological, trinitarian content. The prayer begins with the presider and the gathered community in an exchange of dialogue:

> The Lord be with you.
> *And with your spirit.*
> Up with your hearts.
> *We have (them) with the Lord.*
> Let us give thanks to the Lord.
> *It is fitting and right.*[61]

After recounting the events of Jesus' birth, life, death, and resurrection, the formal *anamnesis* occurs: "Remembering, therefore, his death and resurrection, we offer to you the bread and the cup, giving you thanks because you have held us worthy to stand before you and minister to you."[62] And then immediately the *epiclesis:*

> And we ask that you would send your Holy Spirit upon the offering of your holy Church; that, gathering her into one, you would grant to all who receive the holy things (to receive) for the fullness of the Holy Spirit for the strengthening of faith in truth; that we may praise and glorify you through your child Jesus Christ, through whom be glory and honor to you, to the Father and the Son, with the Holy Spirit, in your holy Church, both now and to the ages of ages.[63]

In regard to the formative, catechetical aspects of the Eucharist, at least three things are noteworthy about this prayer, which we now commonly call the Great Thanksgiving: It is participatory in nature, it conveys a spirit of doxological joy, and it offers an eschatological vision of the church. While liturgical reform efforts in the last generation or so have put the Great Thanksgiving at the heart of the eucharistic celebration, there remains in many Christian communities a troubling disconnect between what and how we pray and what we have been taught, directly and indirectly, about the meal and its meaning. As we look briefly at these three characteristics of the prayer we can observe important catechetical challenges and opportunities.

First, in regard to the participatory character of the prayer: the Great Thanksgiving calls for the whole people of God to take part (*leitourgia* = work of the people). As just noted, it begins as a dialogue between presider and people. From the start it seems to enjoin what the reforms of Vatican II sought to encourage: "full, conscious, and active participation of the faithful."[64] For Christians schooled in passivity during worship, the call to such dynamic engagement presents a formidable challenge.

For traditions rooted in evangelical Protestantism especially, the task often involves overcoming a view of Holy Communion as "a private meal for me," something that I alone receive or take, rather than a common meal we share together as the body of Christ. Whether or not this way of thinking is overtly taught, it is subtly (or perhaps not so subtly) communicated in various ways—most notably through the use of individual cups and individual pieces of bread. Stacked trays of miniature shot glasses alongside a platter of wafers do not constitute a faithful symbol of the oneness that the Eucharist embodies and calls the church to. Their presence on the altar and use in the meal convey a sense of separation and isolation that undermine the truth of communion as a shared, participatory act. Individual communicants huddled over their own plastic cup and bit of bread are less a sign of the convivial fellowship of the kingdom and more a metaphor for the privatized spirituality, religion-as-commodity sensibility that pervades both church and culture. But if this is what we *do*, then this is what we *learn*. If in the Eucharist we consider ourselves autonomous individuals communing privately with Jesus, it is a short and logical step toward the consumeristic, gospel-as-therapy way of thinking that faithful eucharistic practice calls into question and that catechesis should strive to name, describe, and root out.

Part of the problem is logistical: our current movements and actions at the Table have not caught up with how the prayer would have us behave. For many church communities, the Great Thanksgiving has come into currency only fairly recently. In the United Methodist Church, for example, baptism and Communion liturgies based on early church texts and the ecumenical work of liturgical commissions and committees appeared for the first time in the denominational hymnal published in 1989.[65] The implementation of these "new" liturgies and services without sufficient teaching about the history and the theology behind them has created a gap between what we say we are doing in the prayer and how we actually behave as we consume the elements at the Table.

This disconnect is the result of a failure of catechesis—which is not to say that all teaching about the Eucharist must be done in a didactic, information-driven sort of way. Much of the catechetical work that is needed can be accomplished through imaginative preaching; in some situations a more extensive study of eucharistic theology and practice is necessary; often giving more prominence to the gestures, movements, and physical objects themselves can help to create a more communal, participatory ethos that subverts the impulse toward individualism and passivity. But in communities where the disparity between speech and action is apparent and ongoing, much more care and attention must be given to encouraging and establishing the patterns and practices (gestures, movements, postures, etc.) that cohere with the words we say and pray in the rite and to explaining the necessity of such reforms.

Second, the Great Thanksgiving sets a tone of praise and joy:

> Lift up your hearts . . .
> It is right, and a good and joyful thing . . .
> We praise your name and join their unending hymn . . .
> Hosanna in the highest . . . [66]

As Hippolytus's text and the revised liturgies derived from it make clear, the celebration of the Eucharist is just that: a joyous, thankful, praise-filled celebration.

It is interesting to consider that the earliest Christian communities thought of and practiced the Eucharist in this way, given that many contemporary Christians have been trained to regard the sacrament as a somber, funereal occasion and the meal itself as something to be approached in a spirit of unworthy dread. Such an understanding has a long history, of course, emerging from the Communion liturgies of the late medieval church and the Reformation, liturgies that were "heavily penitential, sin-obsessed, [and] limitedly focused."[67] Certainly there is room at the Table for reverence and repentance; to say that the meal is a joyful occasion does not mean that it is a frivolous, giddy one. Genuine praise, thanksgiving, and joy encompass the weightier states of contemplation, reflection, serious-mindedness. But the Great Thanksgiving is doxological through and through and calls for a response of gladness and gratitude. If our bodies (face, eyes, posture, gait) communicate gloominess or tedium, if the music that accompanies the celebration is mournful and dirgelike, if we make our way to the Table in a kind of reluctant, half-hearted shuffle, then we fail to enact the jubilant gratitude at the heart of *eucharistia*, and we are "produced" as a people who deny the very gift that makes us what we are.

More will be said shortly about how catechesis can help address these matters, but I can mention here that the use of pasteurized, unfermented grape juice works against this notion of the Eucharist as a festive celebration. While there may be complicating issues like alcoholism to consider, and while the tired (and useless) debate about the chemical properties of the wine in Jesus' day will no doubt continue, Welch's grape juice simply cannot function—in the same way that wine does—as a potent, living sign of communal pleasure and rejoicing.[68] Wine, chemically speaking, is "alive"; grape juice, because it undergoes a process that halts natural fermentation, is "dead." Wine in a common cup and a common loaf of bread are signs that exert the full power of that which they signify. To consume wine at the Lord's table, moreover, is to swallow a potentially dangerous drink; we are offered the same wine that can make us drunk, that can lead to addiction. But the implicit danger in consuming alcoholic wine can be a powerful reminder of the riskiness of the Eucharist itself: To take into our bodies this bread and wine is to be changed into a people who recognize the perils of being church in the world and who seek to live faithfully even at great cost.

Yet moving a congregation entrenched in practices of using grape juice in individual Communion cups, of approaching the sacrament with solemnity, and so on, is a challenge of catechesis that cannot be met successfully with swift, sweeping, wholesale changes. As I will soon note more fully, raising awareness of the need for reform and implementing changes in practice require persistence tempered by patience, grace, and much good humor.

Third, the Great Thanksgiving offers an eschatological vision of the church. It glimpses, as I have already discussed, the heavenly feast to come and implores the unity of the body of Christ across time and space. As the current Lutheran rite puts it:

> Believing the witness of his resurrection, we await his coming in power to share with us the great and promised feast. . . . Join our prayers with those of your servants of every time and place, and unite them with the ceaseless petitions of our great high priest until he comes as victorious Lord of all.[69]

Because eucharistic liturgies from the Middle Ages and the Reformation stressed the memorial aspect of the meal and tended to lean heavily on language and imagery of death, sacrifice, immolation, sin, guilt, and atonement, the eschatological aspect of the meal was often minimized. The recovery of this future-oriented dimension of the earliest liturgies does not nullify the memorial aspect of the Eucharist but rather situates it within the comprehensive drama of salvation: crucifixion *and* resurrection, suffering *and* joy, death *and* life. The eschatological dimension of the Eucharist is the basis for its doxological character: we anticipate with joy and thanksgiving the banquet that awaits the whole people of God, as we acknowledge that the bread we share gives us the risen Christ.

> That's why this bread is
> so lovely in shape and fragrance,
> so weighty,
> so substantial in taste and texture,
> a gift worth giving,
> a gift worth receiving.
> That's why we carry it
> so proudly to the altar,
> why we lift it so eagerly to God,
> pray over it so intently,
> take it so tenderly in our hands,
> so gratefully into our bodies.
> This bread
> from the Great Harvest Bakery
> today becomes for us
> the Bread of Heaven,
> Holy Food for Holy People.[70]

Eucharistic Catechesis: Teaching about Communion

So far we have noted how the Eucharist is formative of identity and catechetical in a most basic sense: it is the locus of truth for the church, the act that constitutes the church as the eschato-logical body of Christ, and the means by which Christians are nurtured and sustained through time in the covenant community created at baptism. We have observed that while early eucharis-tic liturgies have been recovered and revised for contemporary use, there often exists a notable disparity between speech and action—between the participatory, doxological, eschatological character of the Great Thanksgiving and the solemn, dispirited piety that has held sway for centuries. We have noted something already of the catechetical challenge that this dilemma presents. But we need to look more directly at how a meaningful theology of catechesis must hold together the formative capacity of the ritual itself *along with* intentional, sustained reflection on and teaching about the Eucharist. As with baptism, extraliturgical catechesis about the Eucharist takes as its working context the actively engaged, worshiping community.

Two examples show how attention to the rite's own formative power and to catechesis about the rite can help to foster a deeper understanding of what we do in worship and why we do it. The sharing of the peace, for one, is a bodily act by which we gesture our willingness to be reconciled to a sister or brother before partaking of the Eucharist (Matt. 5:23–24). It is an eschatological sign through which we foreshadow the reconciliation that characterizes the reign of God, the peaceable love-in-communion that embraces, redeems, and transforms a sinful humanity. Sharing the peace of Christ produces a people for whom peace is both gift and command; we must learn to receive it and also to practice it (John 14:27). Within the liturgy, the sharing of the peace follows the prayers of the people and the prayer of confession. Having been formed into a community by holy baptism, having heard the Word proclaimed, and having responded with the words of one of the historic creeds, the people pray for peace in the church and in the lives of all people everywhere. They then offer signs and tokens of that peace to one another. The peace that is shared is not a conjured feeling of goodwill toward one's nearest neighbor in the pew, nor does it connote tidy agreement among the sharers in all matters ecclesial. It is not a human feat or a moral achievement but is "the form of our relations in the church as we seek to be in unity with one another."[71] It is the sign of our baptismal oneness as members of the household of God, and it bears witness to the risks (and joys) of living truthfully together as the body of Christ.

But because this practice easily and often devolves into little more than a momentary exchange of pleasantries before the offertory, serious reflection on it and ongoing catechesis about it are of crucial importance. Explaining the origins of the practice, its scriptural warrant, and its theological significance are all necessary and can be carried out in a variety of ways. But deeper questions can also be probed: Whom do we greet when we share the peace, and whom do we avoid? How does the segregated nature of many Christian churches hinder genuine reconciliation and peaceableness? How can we learn to worship in proximity to sisters and brothers with whom we have differences that need to be reconciled? How do we carry out the work of reconciliation and peaceableness in communities where even those with whom we worship are as strangers to us? What do we risk when we approach the table unreconciled?

Sharing the peace of Christ in the Sunday liturgy is a bodily, material reminder (replete with gestures of touching and embracing, face-to-face encounters, verbal promises made) that "peacemaking is a virtue intrinsic to the nature of the church."[72] And because this practice has been recovered only fairly recently, it is of great educative benefit when brief explanatory rubrics are offered (orally or on the printed page of a bulletin or worship guide) to situate this practice within the larger context of the church's unity in Christ and the eschatological hope of a final and lasting peace. Such explanations can serve to counter the (understandable) tendency to view the exchange of peace as little more than a friendly morning greeting.

As most denominational resources indicate, a brief description/clarification can be placed in the Sunday morning bulletin where the sharing of the peace appears in the order of worship:

> SHARING OF THE PEACE
> The peace of Christ be with you.
> And also with you.

> *(It is not simply our peace but the peace of Christ that we offer; therefore let us offer one another signs of peace and reconciliation.)*

Another possibility is an oral directive, something like this: "It is not our peace but the peace of Christ that we offer; let us greet one another in his name with the signs of a people who seek to live in reconciliation." Whether such cues are given orally or in written form, they teach worshipers that the sharing of the peace is not to be confused with other gestures of friendship or with the welcoming of visitors.[73] If done with an eye and ear toward textual (or verbal) economy, these kinds of catechetical directives—which are useful for other practices as well—can be informative without being disruptive of the liturgical language and gestures they aim to illuminate.

Second, we can look at the fourfold action of the Eucharist itself—taking, blessing, breaking, and giving—beginning with the offertory. After the exchange of peace, material gifts are taken and offered to God. Monetary gifts are brought forward, and bread and wine are offered as fruits of the earth and the labor of human hands. In this oblation the people too are offered, that they like the elements on the Table might be consecrated and transformed. In the eucharistic prayer that comes after the offertory, the church prays that its offering of praise and thanksgiving, betokened in the gifts placed on the altar, might be favorably received. From *The Book of Common Prayer* (form 2 of the "Order for Eucharist"):

> Accept, O Lord, our sacrifice of praise,
> this memorial of our redemption.

In the Great Thanksgiving from *The United Methodist Book of Worship* the people pray that

> in remembrance of these your mighty acts in Jesus Christ,
> we offer ourselves in praise and thanksgiving
> as a holy and living sacrifice,
> in union with Christ's offering for us,
> as we proclaim the mystery of faith.
> Christ has died; Christ is risen; Christ will come again.[74]

And from the order of holy communion in *The Lutheran Book of Worship:*

> Merciful Father,
> we offer with joy and thanksgiving what you have first given
>   us—
> our selves, our time, and our possessions,
> signs of your gracious love.
> Receive them for the sake of him who offered himself for us,
> Jesus Christ our Lord. Amen.[75]

These prayers make evident that in the bringing forth of the gifts of bread and wine is the offering of the people themselves.

Historic practice, however, has generally not given preeminence to this understanding, tacitly assuming instead a sharp distinction between the gifts on the Table and the people gathered to receive them. Catechetical instruction can and should be offered to correct such misunderstanding, but when attention is drawn in the liturgy to the connection between the gifts of bread and wine and the offering of ourselves, the act of offertory can provide its own powerful form of catechesis. Having representatives of the congregation bring the gifts forward from the back of the sanctuary and place them ceremoniously on the altar is a potent visual sign of the offering we make of ourselves; it draws the worshiping body into the dramatic action of the eucharistic sacrifice, linking our offering with Christ's offering of himself for us. When the ritual gestures of offering are done with a kind of extravagant deliberateness, they can help to produce this sense of the corporate offering the community makes of itself.

The second action, the blessing or the eucharistic prayer, has been treated in some detail already, but it bears noting that in the words of *epiclesis,* the invoking of the Holy Spirit, we pray not only that the bread and wine might be blessed and transformed but that we ourselves might also be changed and sanctified as a holy people. As Eucharistic Prayer 2 of the Roman Mass has it:

> Let your Spirit come upon these gifts to make them holy, so that they may become for us the Body and Blood of our Lord Jesus Christ, . . . [and] may we who share in the Body and Blood of Christ be brought together in unity by the Holy Spirit.[76]

Ordinary bread and wine are presented; our lives in all of their ordinariness are offered. And our prayer is that all of these ordinary gifts will be transformed by the extraordinary power of the Holy Spirit.

This leads to the third action—the breaking of the bread—in which we see the fractured loaf as a symbol of Christ's broken body but also as a sign of the Christian body, the church, broken that it might be scattered abroad throughout the world. This is the paradox of the symbol: in brokenness is the possibility for wholeness, and in brokenness we give witness to the world of Christ's power to reconcile all things to himself (Col. 1:20, 22), to unite with a perfect love what has been shattered, divided, and estranged.

In the breaking of bread, moreover, the church makes "a sacrifice of its own body" that it might exist "as gift and sustenance for others."[77] Just as the Eucharist enacts the inexhaustible gift of God's mercy to us, we become the locus of that mercy for others. To share in this feast of plenty is to give real bread to the hungry; it is to respond as Christ's body to suffering bodies everywhere; it is to greet the stranger and the unannounced guest with the same generous hospitality by which we have been welcomed, nourished, and sustained. And yet in the breaking of the bread we are also reminded that the church remains a broken body in need of healing and repair. Our failure to enact forgiveness and reconciliation, our collusion with evil and injustice, our own role as oppressors and traitors are signs of the church's inability to live eucharistically. This failure "should make very plain to us the indispensability within the Church not merely of a mentality of self-criticism and penitence, but of *signs* which continually impress on the Church that it is called to penitence."[78] In such signs, I have noted, we come to know who we are and who we are called to be.

In the fourth action, the shaping of selves-in-communion reaches its *telos* (this side of the eschaton) as we become sharers in the divine life through the sharing of Christ's body and blood. We consume the bread and wine that we might become what it makes us: participants in the very life of God.

Thus in the fourfold action of the Eucharist we can see the pattern of our own formation and transformation: offering, blessing, breaking, and sharing. As Leech puts it: "Our lives are *offered* to God within the redemptive offering of his Son. They are laid open to the *sanctifying,* consecrating power of the Spirit. They are *broken* and *poured out* in union with Christ for the life of the world."[79] And all of this is the work of the Trinity—the creative, redemptive, and sanctifying work of God in Christ through the Spirit.[80]

The catechetical challenge before us is to give renewed attention to the formative power of the Eucharist itself, even as we engage in substantive, meaningful, wise, and discerning forms of catechesis that allow persons to learn and to reflect critically *while* they are being shaped by the worship they offer. These forms of catechesis, as I have noted in earlier chapters, can vary widely—from denominational curricula to original materials designed to speak to the specific needs of a given time and place. In most congregational settings the difficulty in doing catechesis of consequence is not so much a problem of locating adequate educational resources as one of approaching the task of catechesis in a way that captures the imagination of would-be learners, inspiring them to envision catechesis as a lifelong adventure in growing in Christian discipleship—an adventure grounded in baptismal and eucharistic fellowship.

The unique challenge in teaching about the Eucharist stems from the problem in many communities of infrequent celebrations of the sacrament. It is difficult to catechize that Eucharist is foundational for Christian identity and constitutive of the church's very existence among persons who cling resolutely to the belief that Holy Communion loses its "specialness" if it is celebrated too often. The impasse created by the entrenchment of each side in this debate (clergy and catechists who are "for" more frequent Communion and laypersons who are "against" it) can bring to the surface the latent and unarticulated mutual suspicion that often exists between the church's leadership and the laity. Trying to talk people into celebrating the Eucharist more frequently is usually a futile exercise; intellectual arguments meant to educate and enlighten often have the effect of putting persons on the defensive. A more promising approach—entered into with the understanding that it is a long-term endeavor carried out, most likely, in fits and starts—is to demonstrate the significance of the Eucharist for the flourishing of Christian community (in ways I have already discussed) and, more important, to make its absence from worship keenly felt. When we are taught that the larger life of the community is eucharistically shaped—when our preaching and all our conversation about worship, fellowship, missions, prayer, Bible study, hospitality, and so on are intentionally couched in the language of *eucharistia*, the rarity of Communion during worship becomes something no longer tolerable. Eucharistic catechesis at its best trains persons not merely to endure, even happily, more frequent celebrations—that is, to give in intellectually to the argument that more (often) is better—but rather to *desire* in their inmost being the sacrament as the source of all life and the locus of all truth.

Summary

All Christian prayer is in some sense eucharistic—an opening up of the self to God in praise and thanksgiving—and the eucharistic prayer of the community gathered at the Table of the Lord is the center of all Christian prayer. "To be formed in the language and gesture of this prayer is to acknowledge that all other forms of prayer and, indeed, all forms of contemplation and action, are within the great embrace of praise and thanksgiving."[81] All of the liturgy shapes us as a people of prayer and thanksgiving, but not that we might cocoon ourselves in the safety of worship that is familiar and comfortable. Rather, from the shared life that the Eucharist both creates and bears witness to, our prayer and thanksgiving flow outward into the unfamiliar, the uncomfortable, perhaps even the dangerous, that the work of Christ might be accomplished in the world. The Eucharist, as the sign of the kingdom of God in our midst, "is always in some sense celebrated on the altar of the world."[82] And it gives us nourishment for our sending forth into the world from which we came, for the liturgy after the liturgy.

8

———

SENDING FORTH

The Liturgy after the Liturgy

Go into all the world and proclaim the good news to the whole creation.

Mark 16:15

Worship ascribes glory to God alone; but unless the glorification is shown in works of justice, mercy and love faithful to God's commands, Christ's liturgy is not fully enacted.

Don Saliers

Go forth in the name of the Lord. This is God's charge: to give our allegiance to Jesus Christ and to love one another as he commanded.

The Book of Common Worship
(Presbyterian Church USA)

Introduction

We gather that we might go forth.

Worship is the church's gift to God, but worship is also where God's gift to the church is received—a gift that transforms and commissions the receivers for action in the world. "The Eucharist," as Matthew Whelan suggests, "is the redemptive self-gift of Jesus in the form of his body . . . [which] transforms the bodies of participants into gifts for others."[1] We go forth to be gifts for others. "The church is the church," Bonhoeffer reminds us, "only when it exists for others."[2] The Eucharist, the sacrament that constitutes the church's being as life in communion with God, shapes and undergirds the whole of the liturgy as preparation for witness of that divine fellowship in the world: it leads us from the gathering to the proclamation of the Word and our responses to it, through the confession of sins and the prayers of the people, to the heart of worship—eucharistic fellowship—and, finally, back into the world for mission and ministry.

The "Sending Forth" prepares us for dismissal—not the mere conclusion of the Sunday morning service but the continuation of the people's work in the world. Both *mass* and *dismissal* come from the Latin root word *mittere,* meaning "to send," indicating the strong conceptual link between the service we render in worship and the service we offer in, to, and for the world. The blessing we receive as we are sent out (*benedictus*) is a call to connect in the most immediate and practical ways prayer and mission, baptism and justice, Eucharist and hospitality—to see liturgy and life as all of a piece, a seamless, organic whole. Duncan Forrester puts it this way: "There is not, and should not be, a clear mark or frontier between the cult and the life of the community, between the liturgy and the liturgy after the liturgy, between the Lord's table and the common table."[3] Said another way, we leave worship not so that we might retreat into our own inner sanctuaries, but to bear witness to the presence of God in Christ reconciling the world to himself (2 Cor. 5:19).

We sometimes speak of this as the connection between liturgy and ethics, though it must be made clear that it is not a causal one. That is, we do not "do" worship so that we can then go out and "do" ethics or good works. Worship, as has been suggested throughout this book, *is* our ethic: it is the enactment, the ritual performance, of a moral vision out of which the people of God are called to live justly and ethically. Thus liturgy is not a *resource* for ethics; it is, rather, as Vigen Guroian contends, "its ontological condition."[4] Construed this way, Christian ethics is less about intractable moral quandaries debated ad nauseam in the church and the public arena and more about *a way of envisioning* church and world (and the Christian's place in both) that is rooted in the ongoing narrative of Israel, Jesus, and the church—a narrative that is given formal and dramatic expression in the church's liturgy. The task of Christian ethics, then, is "to assemble reminders from the training we receive in worship that enable us to rightly see the world."[5] It is to be formed by the truthful habits of speech and gesture, learned in worship, that shape the character of persons and communities for faithful witness in the world. And while the liturgy is not a tool for the moral formation of Christians, in and through worship the baptized "become what they are already by grace, the holy people of God."[6]

Yet there is a sense among many in our time that much of this talk about liturgy and ethics has a hollow ring. In light of sexual abuse scandals, financial improprieties, the continued racial and ethnic segregation of churches, rampant sexism, and corruption of all kinds, positioning the terms *church* or *worship* and *ethics* in proximity to one another often evokes reactions of cynicism, disdain, incredulity, and anger. From this perspective, the church is lamented (and often dismissed) as a human institution easily given to the kinds of crookedness and shady dealing that have come to define much of the culture of corporate America and the spheres of politics, professional sports, and mass entertainment.

That the church is a human institution—a motley collective across time and space of human beings who are subject to weakness, sin, and unfaithfulness—is, of course, true. The church is, as Lesslie Newbigin observes, "a sinful community . . . [and] during most of its history, [it has been] a weak, divided, and unsuccessful community."[7] But the church is more than the mere sum of its human members; it is, as we have noted, an eschatological reality. As the earlier discussions of baptism and Eucharist hopefully have made clear, the church is the body of Christ as *sign,* as the continuing presence of Christ in the world. "The reign of God is present," Newbigin goes on to say, "in the midst of this sinful, weak, and divided community, not through any power or goodness of its own, but because God has called and chosen this company of people to be the bearers of his gift on behalf of all people."[8]

So the church's moral failings and ethical breaches can be traced, at least in large measure, to its inability or unwillingness to live true to this calling—its inability or unwillingness to enact a cruciform politics, and thus an "ethic," of truthfulness and holiness in the midst of falsehood, deception, and all manner of unholiness—an ethic predicated on *eucharistia* and on the call to be the gift of Christ's body for others. "The unfaithfulness of the church in the present age is based to some extent," William Cavanaugh argues, "on its failure to take itself seriously as the continuation of Christ's body in the world and to conform itself, body and soul, not to the world but to Christ (Rom. 12:2)."[9]

In the first part of this chapter we will return briefly to where we began: to the "problem" of religious education. In the earlier examination of the work of Gabriel Moran, Thomas Groome, and Mary Boys, we learned that the ethical, activist impulse is considered foundational for understanding what religious education or Christian education is about. But such ethics and activism, we noted, are insufficiently rooted in ecclesial practice—in the church's worship of the Triune God. Contrary to the views of Gabriel Moran, Thomas Groome, and Mary Boys, and to much present work in the field of Christian education, the formation of Christian disciples *in worship* is the church's primary ethical task, and in the sending forth from the liturgy disciples are authorized and empowered for work and witness, ethics and activism, in the world.

The second part of this concluding chapter will retrace the contours of a Christian catechesis rooted in the liturgical life of the church. As each chapter has offered suggestions about practical forms of catechesis related to preaching, prayer, and sacraments, here we will take a more general look at the norms that ought to undergird efforts at discipleship/formation grounded in the people's worship of God. The intent is not to present a program or formula or curriculum that would micromanage the education of Christians in particular church settings but to stake out the parameters of an *approach* to liturgical catechesis that can allow for flexibility, creativity, and imagination.

Sent Forth: Liturgy and Ethics, Worship and Witness

The sundering of the intrinsic connection between liturgy and ethics has created conditions in which Christians are unsure about what it is that makes their ethics distinctive. Rather than understanding the church as the locus of an alternative ethic—and worship as the embodiment of that ethic and the "training ground," so to speak, for living it out in the world—many Christians continue to assume an all-too-easy compatibility between Christian convictions and, say, the ethics born of liberalism's championing of privacy and individualism. Guroian contends that this situation has resulted from the church's loss of its eschatological vision, which has had the "effect of blurring the boundaries between church and world . . . [so that] some Christians are even persuaded that Christian ethics is not at all distinctive and that Christian moral formation can take place almost anywhere."[10]

Because the discipline of Christian education historically has been conceived of and implemented as too tidily distinct from the patterns and practices of Christian worship, systematic efforts at the formation of Christians, those of children especially, have been rooted in discourses and methods drawn primarily from the fields of pedagogical theory, philosophy of education, and human development. The turn to secular disciplines is not by itself a misguided move; it matters, for example, that Sunday school teachers of three-year-olds know the kinds of cognitive, motor, and interpersonal skills their charges possess. The wrong-headedness has been in the all-too-willing surrender of the church's teaching office to a theoretical agenda invested utterly and unquestioningly in the orthodoxy of modern liberalism and only minimally, if at all, in trinitarian worship and the sacramental life of the church.

Gabriel Moran, we recall, locates religious education's raison d'être in a transcendence of all distinctiveness and particularity that he believes will allow fruitful contact and conversation among various religious traditions. Specifics of doctrine, narrative, tradition, and worship, while internally important to each religion, can be sidestepped in this larger enterprise so that the real work of religious education can be undertaken: engendering an awareness and appreciation of commonality that will lead to the healing of bitterness and division. As noted in chapter 1, Moran's desire for peace and understanding among the world's religions is noble. But his means, finally, are insufficiently radical for his ends, for his project unwittingly serves to dissolve the very differences he wishes rightly to honor. An account of religious education that assumes we can communicate meaningfully with the other apart from inhabiting and embodying a story that renders otherness comprehensible in the first place is an account of the flimsiest sort. If we are sent forth from worship to bear witness to the love of Christ to our neighbor—friend or stranger, Jew, Muslim, Buddhist, or Hindu—our witness, in order to be true, must be shaped by the worship of the One whom we believe heals all wounds and overcomes all divisions.

The work we are sent forth to do, the witness we offer in Christ's name, is not, moreover, an enterprise of our own undertaking. It is always the work of the Spirit and something in which we participate rather than something the church by its own power initiates and accomplishes. Indeed, we can speak of the liturgy after the liturgy as rooted not only in the work of the Spirit but more comprehensively in the triunity of God: we witness to the sovereignty of the Father, through the love of the crucified Son, by the power of the Holy Spirit, whose presence offers us a living foretaste of the kingdom in order that we may be a sign of the kingdom in the world beyond our worship. In addition, the justice that we believe to be at the heart of the church's work and witness derives its intelligibility and authority from the triune nature of God.

Justice is a hallmark of the accounts of Christian education put forth by both Groome and Boys. For Groome, we remember, "educating for justice" (along with freedom) is a central mandate of the Christian religious education enterprise.[11] For Boys, the discipline of religious education functions at its best when it prompts the church to work in partnership with social institutions to promote justice and enhance responsible, ethical citizenship in the public realm.[12] The difficulty with such seemingly admirable stances, as noted in my earlier critiques, is their troubling identification of the justice of God with the justice of the modern democratic social order. That is, for Groome and Boys (and a host of other educators, philosophers, and theologians), justice, as a term and a cause, is emptied of its biblical and theological content, particularly its cosmic, cruciform import, and is defined instead as the desired social condition that grants everyone equal access to the market economy and the culture of consumption. That is the best such construals of justice can do, despite their being couched in the rhetoric of virtue, dignity, equity, harmony, and the common good.

In contrast, the justice that Christians are sent forth to live out, work for, and witness to is based on the absolute reciprocity, generosity, and equality that constitute the relations among Father, Son, and Holy Spirit. The Trinity is the source of all justice, all striving for liberation, well-being, and wholeness, because "in this Trinity none is afore, or after other; none is greater, or less than another; But the whole three Persons are co-eternal together and co-equal."[13] This is a doctrine of God with the most radical consequences for what it means to do justice in the world; it has evident implications for the organizing of human communities and for the material conditions for human flourishing. And yet, as we have seen, Christians through the centuries and into our own time have been easily seduced by powers and programs that locate justice in discourses far less radical and life-changing. When we are sent forth from worship with the words of the apostolic blessing[14] and then neglect to enact a politics that manifests trinitarian justice—that is, when the church in the world fails to be what it already is by God's grace—we fail to do justice to the justice of God. And we are also in danger of rendering the worship we offer untrue, for work and worship are, as Nicholas Wolterstorff observes, "mutually authenticating."[15]

The liturgy after the liturgy is work, moreover, performed from a position of vulnerability rather than strength or dominance, because the faithful church always exists in alien territory ("power is made perfect in weakness," 2 Cor. 12:9). "The real triumphs of the gospel have not been won," Newbigin contends, "when the church is strong in a worldly sense; they have been won when the church is faithful in the midst of weakness, contempt, and rejection."[16] The attempts by Moran, Groome, Boys, and others to render Christianity more respectable (more relevant, more "public") assume mistakenly that it is the church's first task to be "effective" and "successful" in its engagement with the wider culture. In order to be so, they argue, the church must bracket its particular, parochial idiosyncrasies and "join the public discourse and the political struggle for a better world."[17] Education's task, on this view, is to assist churches in regaining "a sense of their public role as corporate citizens," that they might contribute to the transformation of the social order and the "repair of the world."[18] But such an understanding fundamentally misconstrues the nature of the church's witness in the world. The church's task, contra positions like that of Moran, Groome, and Boys, is to engage the world by being faithful to its own story and its own convictions, even when that story and those convictions are at odds with the reigning public discourse. The church is more likely to be "successful" in its witness, as Newbigin reminds us, when it is marginalized, persecuted, ridiculed, or written off.[19]

Sent Forth: Catechesis after the Liturgy

I began this book by lamenting the current state of affairs in the field of Christian education. But the failures and disappointments of the church's efforts at the formation of children and adults cannot be separated from the deeper deficiencies in Christian worship, many of which have been outlined in the foregoing pages. It is a catch-22 dilemma: Christian education—what I have preferred to call catechesis—will be better when the church's worship improves, but catechesis has an indispensable role to play in ensuring that worship improves. Those concerned with teaching the tradition, with "communicating the living mystery of God" (John Paul II), can remind pastors, preachers, and liturgists of their obligation to preside over worship that faithfully enacts a countervision, a countertruth, and a counterpolitics to the business-as-usual approach to Christian worship in the current North Atlantic context. This will mean, among other things, that the training of Christian educators will need to be more rigorously theological (and liturgical and biblical and historical).

But the *form* that Christian catechesis takes cannot always be delineated a priori or summarily outlined for the purpose of a neat, tidy deployment in any given ecclesial setting. This is true because the practice of catechesis requires much more than the application of technique. Catechesis is carried out in and through practices that are "densely embodied, linguistic, and historical."[20] A catechesis that takes as its working context the worshiping community attempting to live faithfully in the world is always adaptable to the contingency and haphazardness of concrete situations. It is an enterprise that is decidedly, and perhaps to some lamentably, ad hoc. Which is to say not that it lacks rigor, design, or substance, but that the ongoing formation of Christian disciples can never be reduced to the programmatic mastery of doctrine or data. The truth of God—what catechesis seeks to impart—is not a thing to be grasped but a way of life to be embodied. This way of life—living true to the cruciform pattern of Jesus' own life—is a doxological practice, learned over time in the worshiping body gathered regularly for prayer and praise.

Efforts at catechesis must resist the "lure of technique" (Joseph Dunne) by which we assume that knowledge is possible apart from the conversion of character and community. Because catechesis takes as its starting point the trinitarian character of the Christian life and the centrality of worship, the methods, strategies, and principles we employ must be those already embedded in the texts and traditions we seek to transmit. We must strive to recover a vocabulary and an accompanying set of practices currently absent from the writings of prominent Christian educators: the language of *holiness* and *witness, discipleship* and *doxology, gift* and *grace.*

With these reminders in place, the following directives, while not exhaustive, can help to sketch the parameters of faithful Christian catechesis.

- Worship catechizes, and worship is the matrix and milieu from which all other catechesis takes place.
- While extraliturgical catechesis is best thought of as an ecology of practices whose aim is the formation and ongoing nurture of Christian disciples, any and all such practices derive their intelligibility and their legitimacy from the church's worship. And while catechesis assumes a variety of forms, from the intentionally didactic to the more

experiential and praxis-oriented, the formative power of worship must be maintained as primary.

- Catechesis, historically, has been about the reshaping of identity and the transformation of the self into the likeness of Christ. The catechumenate of the early church was an endeavor in such transformation, an attempt at an intentional, ongoing, communally centered, liturgically driven transformation of persons so that they might become icons of the risen Christ. Contemporary catechists, clergy, and other leaders can draw on (always with discernment, not uncritically) the resources of the early catechumenal process, allowing the selection and implementation of current educational materials to be shaped and informed by the practical wisdom of the early church.

- The transforming work that catechesis is about is accomplished not by the catechist, nor by the clergy, nor by the catechumen herself, but by the Father, who through the power of the Holy Spirit wills our conformity to the Son. Therefore catechesis is a process of creating the conditions that help to make the baptized *available* to the working of the Holy Spirit. This means habituating persons over time to the practices and disciplines of Christian community, primarily the church's worship of the Triune God.

- Catechesis is concerned with teaching that strives to be transformative, so that what is taught is "not simply that which [the teacher] has come to know but how she has come to know it and the difference this knowing makes."[21]

- Catechesis helps to cultivate the church's distinct witness in the world, pressing us to ask and answer specific, pointed questions like: Which is more prominently displayed in our worship space, the American flag or the baptismal font? What holiday is likely to receive more attention, Mother's Day or Epiphany? Who is a greater hero to American Christians, George Washington or Oscar Romero?

- Catechesis that is wedded to the doxological is carried out in the context of *vocation*. That is, the attempt to nurture lifelong discipleship is an active response to God's call to be a people of praise and thanksgiving who bear witness in the world to Christ's joy and peace. Catechesis works to bring the baptized into the fullness of life in Christ and to nourish the whole people of God for faithful witness and work in the world.

- When there is a clear understanding between those who lead worship and those who are teachers and catechists that their respective efforts are mutually informing, worship can be conducted so that it is more intentional about its power to shape, form, and transform, and extraliturgical efforts at catechesis can work more deliberately to enliven and illumine what is learned in worship.

- And finally, since Christians are those who worship the Triune God, what we know and how we know are bound up together in doxology. The longing to know the truth of God and of ourselves is not merely intellectual but is the deepest desire of our souls, a desire fulfilled only in community, in communion—in the fellowship of Christian sisters and brothers and in the eternal mystery of the God whose life is our life.

Summary

As worship shapes us as a people of praise and thanksgiving, it also equips us for the mission of sharing with the world a "deep vision of the extravagant splendor of God."[22] Our task is to witness to this God and not any other god; to show forth in our common life and in our individual encounters with others the lavish goodness of the divine fellowship of Persons whose nature is ceaseless *caritas* and whose desire is to share that perfect love and joy with all of creation. Catechesis, in its various forms, helps prepare us to fulfill our mission in the world, for the work of the people—*leitourgia*—is never done.

NOTES

Prologue

1. Don E. Saliers, "Liturgy and Ethics: Some New Beginnings," in *Liturgy and the Moral Self: Humanity at Full Stretch before God*, ed. E. Byron Anderson and Bruce T. Morrill (Collegeville, Minn.: Liturgical Press, 1998), 17.

2. Consider this comment from an article on second language learning: "If learners invest in a second language, they do so with the understanding that they will acquire a wider range of symbolic and material resources, which will in turn increase the value of their cultural capital. Learners will expect or hope to have a good return on their investment—a return that will give them access to hitherto unattainable resources." B. N. Pierce, "Social Identity, Investment, and Language Learning," *TESOL Quarterly* 29, no. 1 (1995): 17. Quoted in David Smith and John Shortt, "Editorial: Images of Christian Reflection," www.stapleford-centre.org.

3. John Westerhoff, "A Call to Catechesis," *The Living Light* 14, no. 3 (Fall 1977): 354.

4. John Paul II, Apostolic Exhortation *Catechesi Tradendae* (On Catechesis for Our Time), 1979, para. 1.

5. Marva Dawn, *A Royal "Waste" of Time: The Splendor of Worshiping God and Being Church for the World* (Grand Rapids: Eerdmans, 1999).

6. St. Benedict, *The Rule of St. Benedict*, ed. Timothy Fry (New York: Vintage, 1998).

7. Catherine Pickstock, *After Writing: On the Liturgical Consumma-tion of Philosophy* (Oxford: Basil Blackwell, 1998), 171.

8. Gail Godwin, *Father Melancholy's Daughter* (New York: Avon, 1991), 274.

9. Nicholas Lash, *Easter in Ordinary: Reflections on Human Experi-ence and the Knowledge of God* (Notre Dame, Ind.: University of Notre Dame Press, 1988), 261 (emphasis in original).

10. Norma Cook Everist, *The Church as Learning Community: A Comprehensive Guide to Christian Education* (Nashville: Abingdon, 2002), 10.

Chapter 1

1. Gabriel Moran, *Religious Education as a Second Language* (Bir-mingham, Ala.: Religious Education Press, 1989), 23.

2. Maria Harris and Gabriel Moran, *Reshaping Religious Education: Conversations on Contemporary Practice* (Louisville: Westminster John Knox, 1998), 30–31.

3. Ibid., 8.

4. Moran, *Religious Education as a Second Language*, 26, 27.

5. James W. Fowler, *Stages of Faith: The Psychology of Human Development and the Quest for Meaning* (New York: Harper & Row, 1981), 14.

6. George Lindbeck, *The Nature of Doctrine: Religion and Theology in a Postliberal Age* (Philadelphia: Westminster Press, 1984), 22.

7. Moran, *Religious Education as a Second Language*, 46.

8. Gabriel Moran, *Uniqueness: Problem or Paradox in Jewish and Christian Traditions* (Maryknoll, N.Y.: Orbis, 1992), 58–59.

9. John Paul II, Apostolic Exhortation *Catechesi Tradendae* (On Cat-echesis for Our Time), 1979, para. 3.

10. Michel Foucault, *Power/Knowledge: Selected Interviews and Other Writings, 1972–1977*, ed. Colin Gordon, trans. Colin Gordon et al. (New York: Pantheon, 1980), 119.

11. Hubert Dreyfus and Paul Rabinow, *Michel Foucault: Beyond Structuralism and Hermeneutics* (Chicago: University of Chicago Press, 1982), 106.

12. Clifford Geertz, *The Interpretation of Cultures* (New York: Basic Books), 90.

13. Ibid., 95.

14. Talal Asad, *Genealogies of Religion: Discipline and Reasons of Power in Christianity and Islam* (Baltimore: Johns Hopkins University Press, 1993), 53.

15. Ibid., 33.

16. Ibid., 35.

17. Ibid.

18. Norman Sykes, "The Religion of Protestants," in *The Cambridge History of the Bible*, vol. 3, S. L. Greenslade, ed. (Cambridge: Cambridge University Press, 1976), quoted in Asad, *Genealogies of Religion*, 41.

19. Immanuel Kant, *Political Writings*, ed. Hans Reiss, trans. (Cambridge: Cambridge University Press, 1991), 114. Quoted in Asad, *Genealogies of Religion*, 42.

20. Asad, *Genealogies of Religion*, 42.

21. Ibid., 28.

22. Harris and Moran, *Reshaping Religious Education*, 30.

23. John Paul II, *Catechesi Tradendae*, para. 5.

24. Stanley Fish, *There's No Such Thing as Free Speech, and It's a Good Thing, Too* (New York: Oxford University Press, 1994), 295 (emphasis in original). As Fish goes on to say, "Most people who come to the point of talking about critical self-consciousness or reflective equilibrium or being aware of the status of one's own discourse are also persons who believe strongly in the historical and socially constructed nature of reality; but somehow, at a certain moment in the argument, they are able to marry this belief in social constructedness with a belief in the possibility of stepping back from what has been socially constructed or stepping back from one's own self. I don't know how they manage this. I think, in fact, that they manage it by not recognizing the contradiction" (295).

25. John Milbank, "The End of Dialogue," in *Christian Uniqueness Reconsidered: The Myth of a Pluralistic Theology of Religions*, ed. Gavin D'Costa (Maryknoll, N.Y.: Orbis, 1990), 139 (emphasis in original).

26. Moran, *Religious Education as a Second Language*, 218.

27. Harris and Moran, *Reshaping Religious Education*, 38.

28. Lesslie Newbigin, *The Open Secret: An Introduction to the Theology of Mission*, rev. ed. (Grand Rapids: Eerdmans, 1995), 162–63 (emphases in original).

29. Fish, *There's No Such Thing*, 297.

30. Ibid. (emphases in original).

31. Moran, *Uniqueness*, 59.

32. Ibid., 42, 56.

33. John Milbank, *The Word Made Strange: Theology, Language, Culture* (Oxford: Basil Blackwell, 1997), 250 (emphasis in original).

34. Moran, *Uniqueness*, 77.

35. Ibid., 82.

36. Ibid., 79.

37. Ibid., 92.

38. Ibid., 132.

39. Ibid., 131.

40. Rowan Williams, *Resurrection: Interpreting the Easter Gospel* (Harrisburg, Pa.: Morehouse, 1982), 72.

41. Ibid., 71.

42. Phillip D. Kenneson, *Beyond Sectarianism: Re-imagining Church and World* (Harrisburg, Pa.: Trinity Press International, 1999), 52.

43. Peter Ochs, "The God of Jews and Christians," in *Christianity in Jewish Terms,* by Peter Ochs et al. (Boulder, Colo.: Westview 2000), 59.

44. Ibid., 60.

45. Stanley Hauerwas, "Remembering as a Moral Task: The Challenge of the Holocaust," in *The Hauerwas Reader,* ed. John Berkman and Michael Cartwright (Durham, N.C.: Duke University Press, 2001), 341. Hauerwas's essay was originally published in *Cross Currents* in spring 1981.

46. Moran, *Religious Education as a Second Language,* 26.

Chapter 2

1. Emmanuel Katongole, *Beyond Universal Reason: The Relation between Religion and Ethics in the Work of Stanley Hauerwas* (Notre Dame, Ind.: University of Notre Dame Press, 2000), 202.

2. Thomas H. Groome, *Christian Religious Education: Sharing Our Story and Vision* (San Francisco: Harper & Row, 1980), 149.

3. Groome, *Educating for Life: A Spiritual Vision for Every Teacher and Parent* (New York: Crossroad, 1998), 96–98.

4. Ibid., 148.

5. Ibid.

6. Ibid., 178.

7. Ibid., 13 (emphases in original).

8. Groome, *Christian Religious Education,* 22.

9. Ibid., 25.

10. Ibid., 23.

11. Richard McBrien, "Toward an American Catechesis," *The Living Light* 13, no. 2 (Summer 1976): 167–81. Quoted in Groome, *Christian Religious Education,* 23.

12. Groome, *Christian Religious Education,* 27.

13. Ibid., 49 (emphases in original).

14. Ibid., 37.

15. Ibid., 43.

16. Ibid., 47.

17. Ibid., 48.

18. Ibid., 43.

19. Daniel M. Bell Jr., *Liberation Theology after the End of History: The Refusal to Cease Suffering* (New York: Routledge, 2001), 44–45.

20. Thomas H. Groome, *Sharing Faith: A Comprehensive Approach to Religious Education and Pastoral Ministry—The Way of Shared Praxis* (San Francisco: Harper & Row, 1991), 150.

21. John Howard Yoder, *The Priestly Kingdom: Social Ethics as Gospel* (Notre Dame, Ind.: University of Notre Dame Press, 1984), 40. Quoted in Kenneson's *Beyond Sectarianism*, 51.

22. Groome, *Christian Religious Education*, 82.

23. Groome, *Educating for Life*, 101 (emphases in original).

24. Groome, *Christian Religious Education*, 96.

25. Ibid.

26. Ibid., 97. Groome's threefold definition of freedom is similar to (though not the same as) that of liberation theologian Gustavo Gutiérrez, who distinguished three levels or dimensions of liberation in Christ: "First there is liberation from social situations of oppression and marginalization. . . . [Second] is a personal transformation by which we live with profound inner freedom in the face of every kind of servitude. . . . [Finally] there is liberation from sin, which attacks the deepest root of all servitude; for sin is the breaking of friendship with God and with other human beings" (*A Theology of Liberation*, rev. ed., trans. Caridad Inda and John Eagleson [Maryknoll, N.Y.: Orbis, 1988], xxxviii).

27. Groome, *Christian Religious Education*, 98.

28. Groome, *Sharing Faith*, 22.

29. Ibid.

30. Groome, *Christian Religious Education*, 87.

31. Dietrich Bonhoeffer, *Dietrich Bonhoffer Works*, vol. 4, *Discipleship*, Geffrey B. Kelly and John D. Godsey, eds. Barbara Green and Reinhard Krauss, trans. (Minneapolis: Fortress, 2001), 285 (emphases in original).

32. Michel Foucault, "Truth and Power," in his *Power/Knowledge: Selected Interviews and Other Writings, 1972–1977*, ed. Colin Gordon, trans. Colin Gordon et al. (New York: Pantheon, 1980), 119.

33. John Howard Yoder, *The Original Revolution* (Scottsdale, Pa.: Herald, 1971), 165–66. Quoted by Stanley Hauerwas, *The Hauerwas Reader*, ed. John Berkman and Michael Cartwright (Durham, N.C.: Duke University Press, 2001), 388.

34. Groome, *Sharing Faith*, 24 (emphases in original).

35. Ibid., 22.

36. As mentioned, Groome acknowledges his indebtedness to liberation theology in formulating his arguments about Christian education. Nicholas Wolterstorff, in criticizing the tendency in liberation thought to view freedom as an end in itself, makes this fitting observation: "The

paradigmatic biblical event for the liberation theologian is the Exodus. Yet the hexateuch does not use *freedom* to describe the end-state of this great liberation. Characteristically when it wants a single word to describe that rich and complex reality which Israel found in the promised land, that word is *rest*. Is there a clue in that? . . . Genesis does not say that [hu]mankind's uniqueness lies in our call to freedom; it lies in our being responsible, in our being created for responsible action: to be human is to be *called*. Is there a clue in that?" Nicholas Wolterstorff, *Until Justice and Peace Embrace* (Grand Rapids: Eerdmans, 1983), 53 (emphases in original).

37. Dietrich Bonhoeffer, *The Cost of Discipleship* (New York: Touchstone, 1995), 89.

38. Groome, *Educating for Life*, 369.

39. Ibid., 370 (emphasis added).

40. Ibid.

41. Ibid.

42. Ibid., 371.

43. Ibid.

44. Ibid.

45. Ibid., 371–72.

46. Ibid., 373.

47. Ibid., 374.

48. Ibid.

49. Bell, *Liberation Theology*, 103.

50. Ibid., 105.

51. Ibid., 124.

52. Ibid.

53. Ibid., 125.

54. Ibid., 127.

55. Bonhoeffer, *Discipleship*, 197.

56. Rowan Williams, "Administering Justice," in *A Ray of Darkness: Sermons and Reflections* (Boston: Cowley, 1995), 210.

57. Ibid., 211 (emphasis in original).

58. Ibid., 212.

59. Groome, *Sharing Faith*, 21.

60. Williams, "Administering Justice," 212.

61. Groome, *Educating for Life*, 379.

Chapter 3

1. W. A. Huesman and Johannes Hofinger, eds., *Die Frohbotschaft, the Good News Yesterday and Today* (New York: Sadlier, 1962), 3. Quoted in

Mary C. Boys, *Biblical Interpretation in Religious Education* (Birmingham, Ala.: Religious Education Press, 1980), 78.

2. Boys, *Biblical Interpretation,* 250.

3. Ibid., 251.

4. Ibid., 282.

5. Ibid., 289.

6. Ibid., 284.

7. Ibid., 327.

8. Ibid., 161.

9. Ibid., 300.

10. Nicholas Lash, *Easter in Ordinary: Reflections on Human Experience and the Knowledge of God* (Notre Dame, Ind.: University of Notre Dame Press, 1988), 44.

11. Ibid.

12. Boys, *Biblical Interpretation,* 300.

13. Lash, *Easter in Ordinary,* 46 (emphasis in original).

14. Boys, *Biblical Interpretation,* 315–16.

15. Stephen E. Fowl and L. Gregory Jones, *Reading in Communion: Scripture and Ethics in Christian Life* (Grand Rapids: Eerdmans, 1991), 29–55.

16. Ibid., 20.

17. Mary C. Boys, Sara S. Lee, and Dorothy C. Bass, "Protestant, Catholic, Jew: The Transformative Possibilities of Educating across Religious Boundaries," *Religious Education* 90, no. 2 (Spring 1995): 255–56.

18. Mary C. Boys, *Has God Only One Blessing? Judaism as a Source of Christian Self-Understanding* (New York: Paulist, 2000), 8.

19. Ibid., 9.

20. Ibid., 42.

21. Ibid., 177 (emphasis in original).

22. Richard B. Hays, *The Moral Vision of the New Testament: A Contemporary Introduction to New Testament Ethics* (San Francisco: HarperSanFrancisco, 1996), 430–31 (emphasis in original). Similarly, George Lindbeck has argued that "Christians need to be reminded that biblical denunciations of God's people in both Testaments were voiced, unlike most contemporary ones, by prophets unshakably committed to the community. . . . The prophets constituted a loyal opposition, not an adversarial one." George Lindbeck, "What of the Future? A Christian Response," in *Christianity in Jewish Terms,* by Peter Ochs et al. (Boulder, Colo.: Westview 2000), 364.

23. Boys, *Has God Only One Blessing?* 184.

24. Ibid., 185.

25. Ibid., 183.

26. Hays, *Moral Vision*, 421–22.
27. Ibid., 424 (emphasis in original).
28. Ibid., 427.
29. Ibid., 432.
30. Ibid., 430.
31. Ibid., 414–15 (emphasis added).
32. Boys, *Has God Only One Blessing?* 267.
33. Ibid.
34. Ibid., 216.
35. Ibid., 211.
36. Mary C. Boys, *Jewish-Christian Dialogue: One Woman's Experience* (New York: Paulist, 1997), 76.
37. Lindbeck, "What of the Future?" 360.
38. Ibid., 364–65.
39. Ibid., 365.
40. Hays, *Moral Vision*, 439.
41. Boys, *Jewish-Christian Dialogue*, 85.
42. Lindbeck, "What of the Future?" 365.
43. Boys, Lee, and Base, "Protestant, Catholic, Jew," 256.
44. Mary C. Boys, "The Tradition as Teacher: Repairing the World," *Religious Education* 85, no. 3 (Summer 1990): 349–50.
45. Thomas H. Groome, *Christian Religious Education: Sharing Our Story and Vision* (San Francisco: Harper & Row, 1980), 47.
46. Boys, "Tradition as Teacher," 351.
47. Ibid.
48. Ibid., 352 (emphasis in original).
49. Ibid., 354 (emphases in original).
50. Martin Marty, *The Public Church* (New York: Crossroad, 1981), 103. Quoted in Mary C. Boys, *Educating in Faith: Maps and Visions* (New York: Harper & Row, 1989), 176.
51. Marty, *Public Church*, 136–37; quoted in Boys, *Educating in Faith*, 176.
52. Boys, *Educating in Faith*, 176.
53. Ibid., 181.
54. Ibid., 180.
55. Talal Asad, *Genealogies of Religion: Discipline and Reasons of Power in Christianity and Islam* (Baltimore: Johns Hopkins University Press, 1993), 2.
56. Asad offers an insightful observation of how this kind of "orthodoxy" (my term, not his) has a taken-for-granted quality that makes it incapable of seeing its own biases: "Saudi theologians who invoke the authority of medieval Islamic texts are taken to be local; Western writers who invoke the authority of modern secular literature claim they

are universal. Yet both are located in universes that have rules of inclusion and exclusion. Immigrants who arrive from South Asia to settle in Britain are described as uprooted; English officials who lived in British India were not. An obvious difference between them is power: the former become subjects of the Crown, the latter its representatives. What are the discursive definitions of authorized space? Everyone can relate themselves (or is allocated) to a multiplicity of spaces—phenomenal and conceptual—whose extensions are variously defined, and whose limits are variously imposed, trangressed, and reset. Modern capitalist enterprises and modernizing nation-states are the two most important powers that organize spaces today, defining, among other things, what is local and what is not" (*Genealogies of Religion*, 8–9).

57. Emmanuel Katongole, *Beyond Universal Reason: The Relation between Religion and Ethics in the Work of Stanley Hauerwas* (Notre Dame, Ind.: University of Notre Dame Press, 2000), 232 (emphases in original).

58. Ibid.

59. Ibid., 231.

60. John Coleman, "Beginning the Civic Conversation" (paper presented to the National Faculty Seminar, Christian Theological Seminary, Indianapolis, February 6, 1987); quoted in Boys, *Educating in Faith*, 180. See also John Coleman, "The Two Pedagogies: Discipleship and Citizenship," in *Education for Citizenship and Discipleship*, ed. Mary C. Boys (New York: Pilgrim, 1989), 35–75.

61. Not unlike the practice on television news shows in which a member of the clergy is invited to serve as a panelist alongside, say, a lawyer, an historian, and a "political analyst," so that all might amicably discuss the "moral" topic of the day—usually something like war or terrorism or marital infidelity among elected officials. (It is telling that a member of the clergy is never invited to a panel discussion on tax reform or the stock market or the crimes of corrupt corporations.) The clergyperson on the panel (almost always a man, interestingly) is respected for the "religious dimension" he brings to the conversation, but his contribution is welcome only so long as it is proffered as one person's harmless, pious opinion—as one interesting theory to ponder among many. In other words, in the world of "political" debate and "civil" discourse, clergy are invited to an argument they are not allowed to win.

62. Boys, *Educating in Faith*, 179.

63. Ibid., 180.

64. John Milbank, *The Word Made Strange: Theology, Language, Culture* (Oxford: Basil Blackwell, 1997), 250 (emphasis in original).

65. Ibid., 244 (emphasis in original).

Chapter 4

1. René Descartes, *A Discourse on Method* (New York: E. P. Dutton, 1951), 28.

2. Susan Bordo, *The Flight to Objectivity: Essays on Cartesianism and Culture* (Albany: State University of New York Press, 1987), 5.

3. Ibid., 95.

4. Parker J. Palmer, *To Know As We Are Known: Education as Spiritual Journey* (San Francisco: HarperCollins, 1993), 30.

5. Joseph Dunne, "Deconstructing a Dilemma: The Need for an Adequate Conception of (Practical) Reason," in *Philosophy of Education Yearbook 1998,* www.ed.uiuc.edu/EPS/PES-yearbook/.

6. Palmer, *To Know,* 40.

7. Augustine, *The Confessions,* trans. Maria Boulding (New York: Vintage, 1997), 3.

8. Ibid.

9. Patricia Hampl, "Preface to the Vintage Spiritual Classics Edition," Augustine's *The Confessions,* xxiii.

10. Ibid., xxii.

11. Joseph Dunne, *Back to the Rough Ground: Practical Judgment and the Lure of Technique* (Notre Dame, Ind.: University of Notre Dame Press, 1993), 358.

12. Wendell Berry, "Sanitation and the Small Farm," in *The Gift of Good Land: Further Essays Cultural and Agricultural* (New York: North Point, 1981), 99.

13. Dunne, "Deconstructing a Dilemma."

14. Stanley Fish, *Doing What Comes Naturally: Change, Rhetoric, and the Practice of Theory in Literary and Legal Studies* (Durham, N.C.: Duke University Press, 1989), 353.

15. Stanley Fish, *There's No Such Thing as Free Speech, and It's a Good Thing, Too* (New York: Oxford University Press, 1994), 295.

16. Fish, *Doing What Comes Naturally,* 353.

17. See, for example, Robert L. Browning and Roy A. Reed's *The Sacraments in Religious Education and Liturgy* (Birmingham, Ala.: Religious Education Press, 1985).

18. Gwen Kennedy Neville and John H. Westerhoff, *Learning through Liturgy* (New York: Seabury, 1978), 91 (emphases in original).

19. Catherine Pickstock, *After Writing: On the Liturgical Consummation of Philosophy* (Oxford: Basil Blackwell, 1998), 181.

20. Ibid., 207 (emphasis in original). See also E. Byron Anderson's "Liturgical Catechesis: Congregational Practice as Formation," *Religious Education* 92 (1997): 349–62.

21. M. Therese Lysaught, "Eucharist as Basic Training: The Body as Nexus of Liturgy and Ethics" (paper presented at College Theology

Society annual meeting, St. Norbert's College, De Pere, Wisc., June 5, 1999).

22. Catherine Bell, *Ritual Theory, Ritual Practice* (New York: Oxford University Press, 1992), 220.

23. Jonathan Z. Smith, *To Take Place: Toward a Theory in Ritual* (Chicago: University of Chicago Press, 1987).

24. John Zizioulas, *Being as Communion* (London: Darton, Longman and Todd, 1985), 21 (emphases in original).

25. Ibid., 81 (emphases added).

26. Ibid., 115 (emphases added).

27. It is worth noting again that the liturgy is not a "tool" used to catechize Christians. Worship is "first and foremost the service of God and needs no other justification. The transformation of worshipers is not its central aim. In fact, we are not apt to be changed by worship if we come to it primarily to be changed, for then we will be back to concentrating on ourselves. The transformation of the church is a by-product of the liturgy. It occurs only when the church is determined foremost to simply worship God." Robert Webber and Rodney Clapp, *People of the Truth* (Harrisburg, Pa.: Morehouse, 1988), 69–70.

28. Walter Brueggemann, *Finally Comes the Poet: Daring Speech for Proclamation* (Minneapolis: Fortress, 1989), 3.

29. Richard Lischer, *A Theology of Preaching: The Dynamics of the Gospel* (Nashville: Abingdon, 1981), 43.

30. Richard Lischer, "Preaching as the Church's Language," in *Listening to the Word: Studies in Honor of Fred B. Craddock*, ed. Gail. R. O'Day and Thomas G. Long (Nashville: Abingdon, 1993), 126.

31. Bell, *Ritual Theory*, 221.

32. Dietrich Bonhoeffer, *The Cost of Discipleship* (New York: Touchstone, 1995), 227.

33. Bruce D. Marshall, *Trinity and Truth* (Cambridge: Cambridge University Press, 2000), 3.

34. Ibid.

35. Ibid., 266.

36. Pickstock, *After Writing*, 208.

37. Teresa of Ávila, *The Way of Perfection*, trans. E. Allison Peers (New York: Image, 1991), 171.

38. Nicholas Lash, *Easter in Ordinary: Reflections on Human Experience and the Knowledge of God* (Notre Dame, Ind.: University of Notre Dame Press, 1988), 275.

39. Paul Ricoeur makes this distinction between verification and manifestation. See his *Essays on Biblical Interpretation* (London: SPCK, 1981). See especially "The Hermeneutics of Testimony," 119–54. See also Rowan Williams's comments on Ricoeur in "Trinity and Revela-

tion," *Modern Theology* 2, no. 3 (1986): 197–212, and in Rowan Williams, *Resurrection: Interpreting the Easter Gospel* (Harrisburg, Pa.: Morehouse, 1982), 63.

40. Williams, *Resurrection*, 63 (emphasis added).

41. Zizioulas, *Being as Communion*, 106.

42. Bonhoeffer, *Cost of Discipleship*, 58–59.

43. Ibid., 86.

44. Ibid., 262.

45. Augustine, *Confessions*, 201.

46. Daniel M. Bell Jr., *Liberation Theology after the End of History: The Refusal to Cease Suffering* (New York: Routledge, 2001), 90.

47. John Milbank, "Postmodern Critical Augustinianism: A Short *Summa* in Forty Responses to Unasked Questions," *Modern Theology* 7 (1991): 234.

48. Ibid.

Chapter 5

1. *Lutheran Book of Worship* (Minneapolis: Augsburg, 1978), 57.

2. *The United Methodist Book of Worship* (Nashville: United Methodist Publishing House, 1992), 33.

3. E. Byron Anderson, "'O for a Heart to Praise My God': Hymning the Self before God," in *Liturgy and the Moral Self*, ed. E. Byron Anderson and Bruce T. Morrill (Collegeville, Minn.: Liturgical, 1998), 113.

4. Collect for the Second Sunday of Easter, in *The Book of Common Prayer* (New York: Oxford University Press, 1990), 225.

5. As noted in the prologue, because I define *catechesis* broadly I also use the term *catechist* broadly. Here it certainly could mean (and in many contexts would mean) a professional educator working in a congregational or parish setting. But I do not want to limit the definition of a catechist to the professional staff person hired to oversee "Christian education." Practically this is true because not all churches have a Christian educator on the staff, and theologically this is true because the task of catechesis is carried out by others besides professional educators. Preachers catechize, for example, as do choir directors and musicians: they form and shape not only the worship but the worshiping congregation that participates in the liturgy. Thus in my broad deployment of the term *catechist* my primary concern is to avoid the narrow view that only educators do the educating.

6. Christopher Lasch, *The Culture of Narcissism: American Life in an Age of Diminishing Expectations* (New York: W. W. Norton, 1979), 10.

7. Neal Gabler, *Life, the Movie: How Entertainment Conquered Reality* (New York: Knopf, 1998).

8. Lasch, *Culture of Narcissism,* 7.

9. Rowan Williams, *Lost Icons: Reflections on Cultural Bereavement* (Edinburgh: T & T Clark, 2000), 65. Williams uses this phrase in connection to the events surrounding the death of Princess Diana in 1997: "The images of her, the images, precisely, that had consolidated her 'iconic' status in the modern sense, often had about them an echo of sacrality—even to the sacredness of the royal touch."

10. Susan Willis, Jane Kuenz, Shelton Waltrep, and Karen Klugman, *Inside the Mouse: Work and Play at Disney World* (Durham, N.C.: Duke University Press, 1997).

11. While it is a given that the story of consumer capitalism has a longer and more complex history than can be explored in these pages, it is worth noting, however briefly, some of the historical precedents that gave rise to the consumerist impulses that have so profoundly shaped both culture and church. The term *conspicuous consumption,* for example, was coined by Thorstein Veblen in his book *Theory of the Leisure Class,* published in 1899. Veblen argued that the increasing accumulation of goods by the Victorian middle class was motivated not so much by their desire to enrich themselves personally as by a longing to achieve the standards of the cultural elite. Moreover, and more relevant to my purposes here, social historian Susan Curtis has pointed out that the social gospelers of the late nineteenth and early twentieth centuries, in their reaction to the emerging industrialist/capitalist ethos of American society, ended up underwriting most of the cultural conventions they claimed to be attacking. That is, while the social gospelers were contemptuous of the competitiveness, alienation, and poverty created by a capitalist economy, they themselves joined the market competition by packaging and promoting their version of the gospel as a commodity available for public consumption. "They believed in the social gospel in much the same way that merchants believed in their products—with zeal for its power to make the user a better person, with conviction that the same results could not be obtained from an off-brand, and with proof of results from the people who had already tried it." *A Consuming Faith: The Social Gospel and Modern American Culture* (Baltimore: Johns Hopkins University Press, 1991), 11.

12. Gabler, *Life, the Movie,* 55.

13. Walter Brueggemann, "The Liturgy of Abundance, the Myth of Scarcity," *Christian Century,* March 24–31, 1999, 342–47. Brueggemann's use of this phrase comes out of his interpretation of Old Testament narratives, particular those in Genesis and Exodus, and his reading of the Psalter. As he says, "The Bible starts out with a liturgy of abundance. Genesis 1 is a song of praise for God's generosity. It tells how well the world is ordered. It keeps saying, 'It is good, it is good, it is good, it is very

good.' It declares that God blesses—that is, endows with vitality—the plants and the animals and the fish and the birds and humankind. And it pictures the creator as saying, 'Be fruitful and multiply.' In an orgy of fruitfulness, everything in its kind is to multiply the overflowing goodness that pours from God's creator spirit. And as you know, the creation ends in Sabbath. God is so overrun with fruitfulness that God says, 'I've got to take a break from all this. I've got to get out of the office'" (342).

14. Ibid., 342.

15. Philip H. Pfatteicher, *The School of the Church: Worship and Christian Formation* (Valley Forge, Pa.: Trinity Press International, 1995), 96.

16. Ibid., 101.

17. Catherine Pickstock, *After Writing: On the Liturgical Consummation of Philosophy* (Oxford: Basil Blackwell, 1998), 176–77 (emphases in original).

18. Barbara Brown Taylor, *The Preaching Life* (Boston: Cowley, 1993), 64.

19. Michael Warren, *At This Time, in This Place: The Spirit Embodied in the Local Assembly* (Harrisburg, Pa.: Trinity Press International, 1999), 53.

20. Michael Warren, *Faith, Culture, and the Worshiping Community: Shaping the Practice of the Local Church,* rev. ed. (Washington, D.C.: Pastoral, 1993), 61.

21. Alexander Schmemann, *For the Life of the World: Sacraments and Orthodoxy* (Crestwood, N.Y.: St. Vladimir's Seminary Press, 1973), 118.

22. Dietrich Bonhoeffer, *The Cost of Discipleship* (New York: Touchstone, 1995), 55.

23. Charles Ess, "Borgmann and the Borg: Consumerism vs. Holding on to Reality," *Techne: Journal of the Society for Philosophy and Technology* 6, no. 1 (Fall 2002): 36.

24. Bonhoeffer, *Cost of Discipleship,* 226.

25. Ibid., 225.

26. I think here of the television commercial for a cellular phone family plan in which households are encouraged to forge closer ties and stay in more intimate contact by purchasing a cell phone for each family member, including children and teenagers ("for just $59.99 a month"!). The now-ubiquitous cell phone serves as a metaphor for the contradictions that plague our disembodied age: we are comforted by this device because it allows us to stay in continuous contact with friends, family, coworkers, clients, and yet its very existence creates and encourages forms of life that hinder the kinds of communal interactions that would make the cell phone less necessary to begin with.

27. John Howard Yoder, *The Priestly Kingdom: Social Ethics as Gospel* (Notre Dame, Ind.: University of Notre Dame, 1984), 142.

28. Lizabeth Cohen, *A Consumers' Republic: The Politics of Mass Consumption in Postwar America* (New York: Knopf, 2003), 397.

29. Ibid., 13.

30. John Milbank, "Sovereignty, Empire, Capital, and Terror," *South Atlantic Quarterly* 101, no. 2 (Spring 2002): 305–23.

31. Ibid., 306–7.

32. The phenomenon of surveying congregations and seeking their input on what would make worship "better" or a "more meaningful experience" is a product of a marketing mentality that "teaches people to inquire incessantly about how any given activity or program meets their always changing list of felt needs." Phillip D. Kenneson and James L. Street, *Selling Out the Church: The Dangers of Church Marketing* (Nashville: Abingdon, 1997), 75. The tendency to equate the formative aspect of worship with how we *feel* about it (what we like, what we don't, what moves us, what bores us) is to fail to take what Philip Pfatteicher calls the long view of the liturgy. It is not the first task of worship, he says, "to speak what is immediately applicable to individual lives and present concerns. This may surely come, but the starting point is less greedy and self-centered. Worship, we learn, is a gift that is grandly and gladly given by creatures to their Creator without thought of its benefit to the worshippers who render it" (*School of the Church*, 75). The purpose of worship is not, as Pfatteicher reminds us, "to *express* our thoughts and feelings but to *impress* them, to shape and form them by shaping and forming our attitudes so that they conform to those of Christ. The congregation gathers to submit to the discipline of the rite, to learn from it, to grow into it and by it" (*School of the Church*, 102, emphases added). But what we also learn is that in the gratituous offering of praise and thanksgiving, and in fidelity to the historic forms of worship bequeathed to us by earlier generations of Christians (appropriated thoughtfully, not uncritically), we find ourselves transformed.

33. Pickstock, *After Writing*, 206.

34. Augustine, *Sermo* 272, quoted in William Harmless, *Augustine and the Catechumenate* (Collegeville, Minn.: Liturgical Press, 1995), 319.

35. *Book of Common Prayer*, 857.

Chapter 6

1. Joseph Dunne's description of tradition is helpful (and wonderfully well said), though he articulates it from within a set of concerns different from those being examined here: "As a knowing, feeling, and acting person in the present, one always carries the weight of the

past—one's own and one's community's: a weight which leans heavily on one's projecting into the future. This is the past as tradition, which means the past as present—all the more present because of its being for the most part implicit and prereflective, active from behind one, as it were, rather than something one can place before one as object. Or, to change the plane of the image, tradition may be thought of as what is *underneath* us, continually exercising a kind of gravitational pull. Not that it necessarily makes for a deadweight; for the ground to which it connects us by a thousand invisible filaments, in our thoughts and in our being, can be a sustaining one, making possibilities substantial and actual." *Back to the Rough Ground: Practical Judgment and the Lure of Technique* (Notre Dame, Ind.: University of Notre Dame Press, 1993), 359–60 (emphasis in original).

2. Marva J. Dawn, *Reaching Out without Dumbing Down: A Theology of Worship for the Turn-of-the-Century Culture* (Grand Rapids: Eerdmans, 1995), 211.

3. Dietrich Bonhoeffer, *The Cost of Discipleship* (New York: Touchstone, 1995), 228.

4. Gail O'Day, "Toward a Biblical Theology of Preaching," in *Listening to the Word: Studies in Honor of Fred B. Craddock*, ed. Gail O'Day and Thomas Long (Nashville: Abingdon, 1993), 18.

5. As John Milbank puts it: "We do not relate to the story of Christ by schematically applying its categories to the empirical content of whatever we encounter. Instead, we interpret this narrative in a response which inserts us in a narrative relation to the 'original' story. First and foremost, the Church stands in a narrative relationship to Jesus and the gospels, within a story that subsumes both. This must be the case, because no *historical* story is ever 'over and done with.'" *Theology and Social Theory: Beyond Secular Reason* (Oxford: Basil Blackwell, 1990), 64.

6. Adam Nicolson, *God's Secretaries: The Making of the King James Bible* (New York: HarperCollins, 2003), 153–54.

7. Philip H. Pfatteicher, *The School of the Church: Worship and Christian Formation* (Valley Forge, Pa.: Trinity Press International, 1995), 121.

8. Garrett Green, *Imagining God: Theology and the Religious Imagination* (San Francisco: Harper & Row, 1989), 140.

9. Walter Brueggemann, *Texts under Negotiation: The Bible and Postmodern Imagination* (Minneapolis: Fortress, 1993), 56 (emphasis added).

10. Ibid., 49.

11. Michael Warren, *Faith, Culture, and the Worshiping Community: Shaping the Practice of the Local Church* (Washington, D.C.: Pastoral, 1993), 29.

12. This phrase is from the Orthodox tradition, and I will say more about it in chapter 8, "Sending Forth."

13. Bruce D. Marshall, *Trinity and Truth* (Cambridge: Cambridge University Press, 2000), 3.

14. Brueggemann, *Texts under Negotiation,* 13.

15. Kenneth Leech, *True Prayer: An Invitation to Christian Spirituality,* 2nd ed. (Harrisburg, Pa.: Morehouse, 1995), 27.

16. Brueggemann, *Texts under Negotiation,* 25 (emphasis added).

17. Dunne, *Back to the Rough Ground,* 358.

18. Sabina Lovibond, *Realism and Imagination in Ethics* (Oxford: Basil Blackwell, 1983), 200.

19. Ibid.

20. Ibid., 198.

21. Brueggemann, *Texts under Negotiation,* 12.

22. Ibid., 17.

23. Ibid.

24. This phrase comes from the title of a sermon by Peter Marshall, a Scottish Presbyterian who became the pastor of the New York Avenue Presbyterian Church in Washington, D.C., in the 1940s. Marshall wrote: "Do not think me fanciful . . . too imaginative . . . or too extravagant in my language when I say that I think of women, and particularly of our mothers, as Keepers of the Springs. . . . There never has been a time when there was a greater need for Keepers of the Springs, or when there were more polluted springs to be cleansed. If the home fails, the country is doomed. The breakdown of home life and influence will mark the breakdown of the nation. If the Keepers of the Springs desert their posts or are unfaithful to their responsibilities, the future outlook of this country is black indeed." Peter Marshall, *Mr. Jones, Meet the Master* (New York: Revell, 1951), 155. Quoted in Janet Fishburn, *Confronting the Idolatry of Family: A New Vision for the Household of God* (Nashville: Abingdon, 1991), 20.

25. Fishburn, *Confronting the Idolatry,* 35.

26. Ibid., 45.

27. Ibid., 13.

28. Ibid.

29. Ibid., 39.

30. Ibid., 40.

31. Ibid., 42. Fishburn observes that "the power attributed to Christian nurture at home implied that the Bible is the book, not of the

church, but of the Christian home. That is one of the reasons that the Bible has been a best seller in America" (ibid., 45).

32. Ibid., 45.

33. David C. Steinmetz, *Memory and Mission: Theological Reflections on the Christian Past* (Nashville: Abingdon, 1988), 70.

34. Fishburn, *Confronting the Idolatry*, 45–46. In the next chapter we will examine more closely the formative aspects of table fellowship.

35. Fishburn observes that those "who participate in the 'opening exercises' of the Sunday School learn an ethos. Their identity as Christians is influenced by that ethos. . . . The Sunday School had, and still has, a worship tradition with its own music. There may be a Sunday School songbook different from the hymnal used in worship. . . . There is a difference in the spirituality, the beliefs, and the language used in the worship of the Sunday School and that of the church" (ibid., 47).

36. As Fishburn notes: "The fact that opening exercises [of Sunday School] are usually didactic and instructional in nature can influence attitudes about worship in the sanctuary. That may be one of the reasons that so many adults like the children's sermon in worship. They may be more comfortable with moralistic teaching about what a child *should* do than they are with proclamation about what God is doing" (ibid., 48, emphasis in original).

37. It has been fashionable in some academic circles for several decades now to promote the wholesale elimination of Sunday school as an institution of the church. John Westerhoff, for example, wrote in 1980 that he did not "see a place of significance for the Sunday School in the future" ("The Sunday School of Tomorrow," *Christian Century*, June 4–11, 1980, 642). As I hope my own critique has shown, I am sympathetic to any and all analyses that demonstrate the blandness and ineffectiveness of most current models of Sunday school education. Moreover, the institution's indebtedness to the public school paradigm, with its emphasis on curriculum, classroom instruction, age- and gender-based segregation, and human development theories, is deeply problematic. But I am less inclined toward an across-the-board dismissal of Sunday school, partly because I see its deep entrenchment in much of rural and small-town Protestantism (the kinds of churches that are usually ignored or written off by observers like Westerhoff) and partly because I believe it is possible to redirect, even subvert, the patterns and practices of Sunday school in ways that can help to create a more worship-centered catechesis, even as enough of the old forms is retained to draw in the skeptics.

38. Westerhoff, "Sunday School of Tomorrow," 641.

39. Robert Marquand, "Sound-Bite Sermon for a Busy Believer," *Christian Science Monitor* 87, no. 251 (November 22, 1995): 1.

40. Richard Lischer, "Preaching as the Church's Language," in *Listening to the Word: Studies in Honor of Fred B. Craddock*, ed. Gail O'Day and Thomas Long (Nashville: Abingdon, 1993), 128.

41. Joseph Dunne's words, again, are fitting: "One cannot determine in advance the efficacy of one's words. . . . Efficacy turns out to be a form of influence; it lies not so much in one's own operation as in the cooperation of others" (*Back to the Rough Ground*, 359).

42. John H. Westerhoff III and William H. Willimon, *Learning through the Life Cycle*, rev. ed. (Akron: OSL Publications, 1994), 10.

43. Rowan Williams, *Resurrection: Interpreting the Easter Gospel*, 2nd ed. (Harrisburg, Pa.: Morehouse, 1994), 62.

44. Bonhoeffer, *Cost of Discipleship*, 207–8.

45. Ibid., 208.

46. Lowell E. Grisham, "The Baptism of Jesus by John," sermon preached at St. Paul's Episcopal Church, Fayetteville, Ark., January 7, 2001, available at www.stpaulsfay.org.

47. Bonhoeffer, *Cost of Discipleship*, 246.

48. Leech, *True Prayer*, 28.

49. Fishburn, *Confronting the Idolatry*, 55.

50. The Baptismal Covenant II service of the United Methodist Church has the presiding minister address the congregation thus: "Members of the household of God, I commend these persons to your love and care. *Do all in your power* to increase their faith, confirm their hope, and perfect them in love." *The United Methodist Hymnal: Book of United Methodist Worship* (Nashville: United Methodist Publishing House, 1989), 43 (emphases mine).

51. Westerhoff and Willimon, *Learning through the Life Cycle*, 13.

52. John Zizioulas, *Being as Communion* (London: Darton, Longman and Todd, 1985), 57 (emphasis in original). Zizioulas's claim that in baptism we are freed from our "biological identity" leaves much unsaid about bodiliness, creaturehood, desire, and sexuality. While Zizioulas is insufficiently attentive to the implications of gender for his ecclesiology and baptismal theology, his work is amenable to feminist theology's crucial insight that the historical identification of men with the mind or spirit and women with the body or nature (biology) is theologically unwarranted and unacceptable. To argue that baptism overcomes biology is not to deny the incarnational implications of ecclesial identity; to the contrary, Christian personhood, life in the *body* of Christ, flourishes only *within* the material and corporeal. For a fuller exploration of the relationship between the Trinity and gender, see Sarah Coakley's *Powers and Submissions: Spirituality, Philosophy, and Gender* (Oxford: Basil Blackwell, 2002).

53. Zizioulas, *Being as Communion*, 56.

54. *Welcome to Christ: Lutheran Rites for the Catechumenate* (Minneapolis: Augsburg, 1997), 59–60.

55. Paul Bradshaw, *Early Christian Worship: A Basic Introduction to Ideas and Practice* (London: SPCK, 1996), 8–30. See also Lars Hartman's *In the Name of the Lord Jesus: Baptism in the Early Church* (Edinburgh: T & T Clark, 1997).

56. The Rites of Christian Initiation for Adults instituted in the 1980s in the Roman Catholic Church have helped generate similar efforts—with varying degrees of success—in some Protestant traditions (Lutheran, Episcopalian, and United Methodist, particularly).

57. Much of the following description of early Church practice comes from Leech's *True Prayer*, 28–32.

58. Ibid., 29–30.

59. Westerhoff and Willimon, *Learning through the Life Cycle*, 20.

60. Ibid.

61. The practice of severing the rite of confirmation from baptism has had the undesirable effect of communicating to adolescent confirmands that once they have been confirmed, they have completed their education in church membership and discipleship.

62. While the early church, of course, separated catechumens from the larger congregation until their baptism at the Easter vigil, such a "division" was for the purpose of providing the uninitiated with the kind of rigorous catechesis that would form them in their new life of Christian discipleship. The current congregational divisions, by contrast, brought about primarily because of the so-called "worship wars," operate on the problematic assumption that the uninitiated ("seekers") should be given *less* substantive teaching, not more. The rationale is that "too much theology" (or liturgy, doctrine, etc.) will turn off and turn away potential church members.

Chapter 7

1. Kenneth Leech, *True Prayer: An Invitation to Christian Spirituality*, 2nd ed. (Harrisburg, Pa.: Morehouse, 1995), 89.

2. Annie Dillard, "An Expedition to the Pole," in *The Annie Dillard Reader* (New York: HarperCollins, 1994), 38.

3. Roberta Bondi, "Praying the Lord's Prayer: Truthfulness, Intercessory Prayer, and Formation in Love," in *Liturgy and the Moral Self: Humanity at Full Stretch before God*, ed. E. Byron Anderson and Bruce T. Morrill (Collegeville, Minn.: Liturgical Press, 1998), 153–67.

4. See for example Miri Rubin's *Corpus Christi: The Eucharist in Late Medieval Culture* (Cambridge: Cambridge University Press, 1991); Carolyn Walker Bynum's *Holy Feast and Holy Fast* (Berkeley: University

of California Press, 1987); and Leigh Schmidt's *Holy Fairs: Scottish Communions and American Revivals in the Early Modern Period* (Princeton, N.J.: Princeton University Press, 1989).

5. John Zizioulas, *Being as Communion* (London: Darton, Longman and Todd, 1985), 145 (emphasis in original).

6. Ibid., 21.

7. Ibid., 17.

8. William T. Cavanaugh, *Torture and Eucharist* (Oxford: Basil Blackwell, 1998), 235.

9. Zizioulas, *Being as Communion*, 81 (emphasis in original).

10. Of course, there is variety in the Sunday morning order of worship—a processional hymn, for example, may be sung before the spoken greeting; the opening prayer (sometimes a collect or prayer of the day) may at times precede the hymn—but prayer usually concludes the preparatory acts from entrance to the hymn of praise/adoration. Our concern here is not to micro-analyze the sequencing of the essential elements of the *ordo* but to pay attention to how the elements themselves form the affections and dispositions, even the bodies, of those who engage in them.

11. There is also a traditional (Elizabethan) form of this collect, and one or both versions can be found in the worship manuals and prayer books of various denominational resources, including *The United Methodist Book of Worship, The Book of Common Prayer,* the *Lutheran Book of Worship,* and *The Book of Common Worship* (Presbyterian Church).

12. Gail Ramshaw, "Pried Open by Prayer," in *Liturgy and the Moral Self: Humanity at Full Stretch before God,* ed. E. Byron Anderson and Bruce T. Morrill (Collegeville, Minn.: Liturgical, 1998), 170.

13. Ibid., 172–73.

14. Don E. Saliers, *Worship as Theology: Foretaste of Glory Divine* (Nashville: Abingdon, 1994), 124–25.

15. Leech, *True Prayer,* 132.

16. Ibid., 133.

17. Nicholas Lash, *Easter in Ordinary: Reflections on Human Experience and the Knowledge of God* (Notre Dame, Ind.: University of Notre Dame Press, 1990), 205.

18. Leech, *True Prayer,* 135.

19. Saliers, *Worship as Theology,* 106.

20. Rowan Williams, *A Ray of Darkness: Sermons and Reflections* (Boston: Cowley, 1995), 117.

21. Ibid.

22. Ibid., 118.

23. Ibid.

24. "A Litany for the Church and for the World," in *The United Methodist Book of Worship* (Nashville: United Methodist Publishing House, 1992), 495.

25. Williams, *Ray of Darkness*, 118–19.

26. Ibid., 118.

27. Leech, *True Prayer*, 164.

28. Bondi, "Praying the Lord's Prayer," 156–57.

29. Williams, *Ray of Darkness*, 119 (emphasis in original).

30. Catherine Bell, *Ritual Theory, Ritual Practice* (New York: Oxford University Press, 1992), 99–100.

31. M. Therese Lysaught, "Eucharist as Basic Training: The Body as Nexus of Liturgy and Ethics" (paper presented at College Theology Society annual meeting, St. Norbert's College, De Pere, Wisc., June 5, 1999).

32. Kathleen Norris, *The Quotidian Mysteries: Laundry, Liturgy, and "Women's Work"* (New York: Paulist, 1998).

33. Williams, *Ray of Darkness*, 120.

34. Mary Ewing Stamps, "Lives of Living Prayer: Christomorphism and the Priority of Prayer in the *Rule of St. Benedict*," in *Liturgy and the Moral Self: Humanity at Full Stretch before God*, ed. E. Byron Anderson and Bruce T. Morrill (Collegeville, Minn.: Liturgical, 1998), 150.

35. Jacques Maritain, quoted in Rowan Williams, "Poetic and Religious Imagination," *Theology*, May 1977, 179.

36. Garrett Green, *Imagining God: Theology and the Religious Imagination* (San Francisco: Harper & Row, 1989),140.

37. Ibid., 52.

38. Ibid., 53.

39. Walter Brueggemann, *Texts under Negotiation: The Bible and Postmodern Imagination* (Minneapolis: Fortress, 1993), 15.

40. Green, *Imagining God*, 67.

41. Ibid., 67.

42. Leech, *True Prayer*, 110.

43. Cavanaugh, *Torture and Eucharist*, 225.

44. T. S. Eliot, "Little Gidding," in *Collected Poems, 1909–1962* (New York: Harcourt, 1963), 200.

45. Geoffrey Wainwright, *Doxology: The Praise of God in Worship, Doctrine, and Life* (New York: Oxford University Press, 1980), 8.

46. Thomas Aquinas, *Summa Theologiae* (New York: Benziger Brothers, 1947), 2347 (3.q60.a4).

47. Bell, *Ritual Theory*, 74.

48. Ibid., 90.

49. James F. White, "Methodist Worship," in *Perspectives on American Methodism*, ed. Russell E. Richey, Kenneth E. Rowe, and Jean Miller Schmidt (Nashville: Kingswood, 1993), 462.

50. John Wesley, "The Duty of Constant Communion," in *The Works of John Wesley*, ed. Albert Outler (Nashville: Abingdon, 1986), 429.

51. White, "Methodist Worship," 462.

52. *The Eucharistic Hymns of John and Charles Wesley*, ed. J. Ernest Rattenbury (Nashville: Abingdon, 1947).

53. Bell, *Ritual Theory*, 90.

54. Ibid., 81.

55. As Leech says, we share the Eucharist in an unsharing world, in a world of waste, in a polluted atmosphere, "a world which treats the seas and rivers as drains and sewers, as receptacles for poisons, radioactive waste, crude oil, sewage, and accumulated rubbish. It is in this wasteful and waste-producing environment that we gather to celebrate the sacrament of shared resources and outpoured life" (*True Prayer*, 110).

56. Thomas H. Groome, *Christian Religious Education: Sharing Our Story and Vision* (San Francisco: Harper & Row, 1980), 47.

57. Paul Bradshaw, *Early Christian Worship: A Basic Introduction to Ideas and Practice* (London: SPCK, 1996), 45.

58. Ibid.

59. Ibid., 46. Bradshaw also makes note of a fragmentary document known as the Strasbourg Papyrus. Originally from Egypt, "it seems to be an early (perhaps even third-century) version of what later became the standard eucharistic prayer of the Coptic church" (ibid., 47).

60. Saliers, *Worship as Theology*, 93.

61. Bradshaw, *Early Christian Worship*, 48.

62. Ibid., 49.

63. Ibid.

64. *Constitution on the Sacred Liturgy*, Vatican II Council Document, para. 27. From the "General Principles" portion of the document comes this "catechetical" directive: "Pastors of souls must therefore realize that, when the liturgy is celebrated, something more is required than the mere observation of the laws governing valid and licit celebration; it is their duty also to ensure that the faithful take part fully aware of what they are doing, actively engaged in the rite, and enriched by its effects" (para. 11).

65. *The United Methodist Hymnal: Book of United Methodist Worship* (Nashville: United Methodist Publishing House, 1989). The first-time inclusion of the Psalter in this edition of the hymnal is also of enormous significance for the worship of United Methodist congregations. Yet very little catechesis has been done to train congregations in the use of liturgical psalters.

66. "Service of Word and Table," *United Methodist Hymnal*, 9.

67. John H. Westerhoff III and William H. Willimon, *Learning through the Life Cycle*, rev. ed. (Akron: OSL Publications, 1994), 35.

68. Frederick Buechner does not mince words when he says, with comic seriousness, "Unfermented grape juice is a bland and pleasant drink, especially on a warm afternoon mixed half-and-half with ginger ale. It is a ghastly symbol of the life blood of Jesus Christ, especially when served in individual antiseptic, thimble-sized glasses. Wine is booze, which means it is dangerous and drunk-making. It makes the timid brave and the reserved amorous. It loosens the tongue and breaks the ice, especially when served in a loving cup. It kills germs. As symbols go, it is a rather splendid one." *Wishful Thinking: A Seeker's ABC*, rev. ed. (New York: HarperCollins, 1993), 120.

69. *Lutheran Book of Worship* (Minneapolis: Augsburg, 1978), 70–71.

70. Janet B. Campbell, "The Story, the Book, the Bread, the Font, the Candle—Pass It On," at www.saintmarks.org/sermons. Taken from a sermon for the third Sunday of Easter, 2002, by the Rev. Janet B. Campbell, director of liturgy and the arts, Saint Mark's Episcopal Cathedral, Seattle, Washington. Reprinted by permission of the author.

71. Stanley Hauerwas, "Peacemaking: The Virtue of the Church," in *The Hauerwas Reader*, ed. John Berkman and Michael Cartwright (Durham, N.C.: Duke University Press, 2001), 324.

72. Ibid. As Hauerwas goes on to say: "Peacemaking among Christians . . . is not simply one activity among others but rather is the very form of the church insofar as the church is the form of the one who 'is our peace.' . . . The unity [that peacemaking seeks] is not built on shallow optimism that we can get along if we respect one another's differences. Rather, it is a unity that profoundly acknowledges our differences because we have learned that those differences are not accidental to our being a truthful people—even when they require us to confront one another as those who have wronged us" (ibid.).

73. *United Methodist Book of Worship*, 26.

74. Ibid., 38.

75. *The Lutheran Book of Worship*, 67.

76. Quoted in Leech, *True Prayer*, 105.

77. Cavanaugh, *Torture and Eucharist*, 232.

78. Rowan Williams, *Resurrection: Interpreting the Easter Gospel*, 2nd ed. (Harrisburg, Pa.: Morehouse, 1994), 58.

79. Leech, *True Prayer*, 109 (emphases added).

80. Ibid.

81. Saliers, *Worship as Theology*, 97.

82. John Paul II, Papal Encyclical *Ecclesia and Eucharistia*, 2003, para. 8.

Chapter 8

1. Matthew Whelan, "The Responsible Body: A Eucharistic Community," *Cross Currents* 51, no. 3 (Fall 2001), www.crosscurrents.org/whelan.htm.

2. Dietrich Bonhoeffer, *Letters and Papers from Prison*, ed. Eberhard Bethge (New York: Simon & Schuster, 1997), 382. Quoted in ibid.

3. Duncan Forrester, "Moral Formation and Liturgy: A Response to Vigen Guroian," *Ecumenical Review* 49, no. 3 (July 1997): 380.

4. Vigen Guroian, "Moral Formation and Christian Worship," *Ecumenical Review* 49, no. 3 (July 1997): 372.

5. Stanley Hauerwas, *In Good Company: The Church as Polis* (Notre Dame, Ind.: University of Notre Dame Press, 1995), 156.

6. Guroian, "Moral Formation," 374.

7. Lesslie Newbigin, *The Open Secret: An Introduction to the Theology of Mission*, rev. ed. (Grand Rapids: Eerdmans, 1995), 53.

8. Ibid., 54.

9. William T. Cavanaugh, *Torture and Eucharist* (Oxford: Basil Blackwell, 1998), 233.

10. Guroian, "Moral Formation," 373. "For example," he goes on to say, "Protestant fundamentalists in America often claim that the 'traditional' middle-class family and its moral values unambiguously reflect or embody the Bible's teachings. Mainline liberal Protestants sometimes too quickly assume a correlation between liberalism's standards of liberty and equality and the essence of biblical faith. Practicable goals of social amelioration and reform are treated as if they constitute the raison d'être and the *telos* of the church's ethics. Meanwhile, some Roman Catholic liberationists assert that Marxist theory and analysis are compatible with the redemptive message of scripture. In this instance, Christian eschatology is flattened as it gets read into economic and political processes, while erroneous claims are made that the people of God come into existence through revolutionary practice" (ibid.).

11. Thomas H. Groome, *Christian Religious Education: Sharing Our Story and Vision* (San Francisco: Harper & Row, 1980), 82.

12. Mary C. Boys, *Educating in Faith: Maps and Visions* (New York: Harper & Row, 1989), 176.

13. The Athanasian Creed, in *The Book of Common Prayer* (New York: Oxford University Press, 1990), 856.

14. "The grace of the Lord Jesus Christ, and the love of God, and the communion of the Holy Spirit be with all of you" (2 Cor. 13:13).

15. Nicholas Wolterstorff, *Until Justice and Peace Embrace* (Grand Rapids: Eerdmans, 1983), 157.

16. Newbigin, *Open Secret*, 62.

17. Thomas H. Groome, *Sharing Faith: A Comprehensive Approach to Religious Education and Pastoral Ministry—The Way of Shared Praxis* (San Francisco: Harper & Row, 1991), 150.

18. Boys, *Educating in Faith*, 180.

19. As Newbigin says: "It has been in situations where faithfulness to the gospel placed the church in a position of total weakness and rejection that the advocate has himself risen up and, often through the words and deeds of very 'insignificant' people, spoken the word that confronted and shamed the wisdom and power of the world" (*Open Secret*, 62).

20. Joseph Dunne, "Deconstructing a Dilemma," www.edu.uiuc.edu/ EPS/PES-yearbook.

21. Jean Bethke Elshtain, "Teaching as Drama," in *Schooling Christians: Holy Experiments in American Education*, ed. Stanley Hauerwas and John H. Westerhoff (Grand Rapids: Eerdmans, 1992), 55.

22. Marva Dawn, *A Royal "Waste" of Time: The Splendor of Worshiping God and Being Church for the World* (Grand Rapids: Eerdmans, 1999), 334.

WORKS CITED

Anderson, E. Byron, and Bruce T. Morrill. *Liturgy and the Moral Self: Humanity at Full Stretch before God*. Collegeville, Minn.: Liturgical Press, 1998.

Aquinas, Thomas. *Summa Theologia*. New York: Benziger Brothers, 1947.

Asad, Talal. *Genealogies of Religion: Discipline and Reasons of Power in Christianity and Islam*. Baltimore: Johns Hopkins University Press, 1993.

Augustine. *The Confessions*. Translated by Maria Boulding. New York: Vintage, 1997.

Bell, Catherine. *Ritual Theory, Ritual Practice*. New York: Oxford University Press, 1992.

Bell, Daniel M., Jr. *Liberation Theology after the End of History: The Refusal to Cease Suffering*. New York: Routledge, 2001.

Benedict. *The Rule of St. Benedict*. Edited by Timothy Fry. New York: Vintage, 1998.

Berry, Wendell. *The Gift of Good Land: Further Essays Cultural and Agricultural*. New York: North Point, 1981.

Bondi, Roberta. "Praying the Lord's Prayer: Truthfulness, Intercessory Prayer, and Formation in Love." In *Liturgy and the Moral Self: Humanity at Full Stretch before God*, edited by E. Byron Anderson and Bruce T. Morrill, 153–67. Collegeville, Minn.: Liturgical Press, 1998.

Bonhoeffer, Dietrich. *The Cost of Discipleship*. New York: Touchstone, 1995.

————. *Dietrich Bonhoeffer Works.* Vol. 4, *Discipleship.* Translated by Martin Kuske and Ilse Tödt. Minneapolis: Fortress, 2001.

————. *Letters and Papers from Prison.* Edited by Eberhard Bethge. New York: Simon & Schuster, 1997.

The Book of Common Prayer. New York: Oxford University Press, 1990.

Bordo, Susan. *The Flight to Objectivity: Essays on Cartesianism and Culture.* Albany: State University of New York Press, 1987.

Boys, Mary C. *Biblical Interpretation in Religious Education.* Birmingham, Ala.: Religious Education Press, 1980.

————. *Has God Only One Blessing? Judaism as a Source of Christian Self- Understanding.* New York: Paulist, 2000.

————. *Jewish-Christian Dialogue: One Woman's Experience.* New York: Paulist, 1997.

————. "The Tradition as Teacher: Repairing the World." *Religious Education* 85, no. 3 (Summer 1990).

————, ed. *Education for Citizenship and Discipleship.* New York: Pilgrim, 1989.

————, Sara S. Little, and Dorothy C. Bass. "Protestant, Catholic, Jew: The Transformative Possibilities of Educating across Religious Boundaries." *Religious Education* 90, no. 2 (Spring 1995).

Bradshaw, Paul. *Early Christian Worship: A Basic Introduction to Ideas and Practice.* London: SPCK, 1996.

Browning, Robert L., and Roy A. Reed. *The Sacraments in Religious Education and Liturgy.* Birmingham, Ala.: Religious Education Press, 1985.

Brueggemann, Walter. *Finally Comes the Poet: Daring Speech for Proclamation.* Minneapolis: Fortress, 1989.

————. "The Liturgy of Abundance, The Myth of Scarcity." *Christian Century,* March 24–31, 1999.

————. *Texts under Negotiation: The Bible and Postmodern Imagination.* Minneapolis: Fortress, 1993.

Buechner, Frederick. *Wishful Thinking: A Seeker's ABC.* Rev. and exp. ed. New York: HarperCollins, 1993.

Bynum, Caroline Walker. *Holy Feast and Holy Fast.* Berkeley: University of California Press, 1987.

Cavanaugh. William T. *Torture and Eucharist.* Oxford: Basil Blackwell, 1998.

Coakley, Sarah. *Powers and Submissions: Spirituality, Philosophy, and Gender.* Oxford: Basil Blackwell, 2002.

Cohen, Lizabeth. *A Consumers' Republic: The Politics of Mass Consumption in Postwar America.* New York: Knopf, 2003.

Curtis, Susan. *A Consuming Faith: The Social Gospel and Modern American Culture.* Baltimore: Johns Hopkins University Press, 1991.

Dawn, Marva. *Reaching Out without Dumbing Down: A Theology of Worship for the Turn-of-the-Century Church.* Grand Rapids: Eerdmans, 1995.

———. *A Royal "Waste" of Time: The Splendor of Worshiping God and Being Church for the World.* Grand Rapids: Eerdmans, 1999.

D'Costa, Gavin, ed. *Christian Uniqueness Reconsidered: The Myth of a Pluralistic Theology of Religions.* Maryknoll, N.Y.: Orbis, 1990.

Descartes, René. *A Discourse on Method.* New York: E. P. Dutton, 1951.

Dillard, Annie. "An Expedition to the Pole." In *The Annie Dillard Reader.* New York: HarperCollins, 1994.

Dunne, Joseph. *Back to the Rough Ground: Practical Judgment and the Lure of Technique.* Notre Dame, Ind.: University of Notre Dame Press, 1993.

———. "Deconstructing a Dilemma: The Need for an Adequate Conception of (Practical) Reason." In *Philosophy of Education Yearbook 1998,* www.ed.uiuc.edu/EPS/PES-Yearbook/1998/dunne.html.

Dreyfus, Hubert, and Paul Rabinow. *Michel Foucault: Beyond Structuralism and Hermeneutics.* Chicago: University of Chicago Press, 1982.

Eliot, T. S. "Little Gidding." In *Collected Poems, 1909–1962.* New York: Harcourt, 1963.

Elshtain, Jean Bethke. "Teaching as Drama." In *Schooling Christians: Holy Experiments in American Education,* edited by Stanley Hauerwas and John H. Westerhoff. Grand Rapids: Eerdmans, 1992.

Ess, Charles. "Borgmann and the Borg: Consumerism vs. Holding onto Reality." *Techne: Journal of the Society for Philosophy and Technology* 6, no. 1 (Fall 2002): 28–45.

Everist, Norma Cook. *The Church as Learning Community: A Comprehensive Guide to Christian Education.* Nashville: Abingdon, 2002.

Fish, Stanley. *Doing What Comes Naturally: Change, Rhetoric, and the Practice of Theory in Literary and Legal Studies.* Durham, N.C.: Duke University Press, 1989.

———. *There's No Such Thing as Free Speech, and It's a Good Thing, Too.* New York: Oxford University Press, 1994.

Fishburn, Janet. *Confronting the Idolatry of Family: A New Vision for the Household of God.* Nashville: Abingdon, 1991.

Foucault, Michel. *Power/Knowledge: Selected Interviews and Other Writings, 1972–1977.* Edited by Colin Gordon. Translated by Colin Gordon et al. New York: Pantheon, 1980.

Forrester, Duncan. "Moral Formation and Liturgy: A Response to Vigen Guroian." *Ecumenical Review* 49, no. 3 (Fall 1997): 379–83.

Fowl, Stephen E., and L. Gregory Jones. *Reading in Communion: Scripture and Ethics in Christian Life.* Grand Rapids: Eerdmans, 1991.

Fowler, James. *Stages of Faith: The Psychology of Human Development and the Quest for Meaning.* New York: HarperCollins, 1981.

Gabler, Neal. *Life, the Movie: How Entertainment Conquered Reality.* New York: Knopf, 1998.

Geertz, Clifford. *The Interpretation of Cultures.* New York: Basic Books, 1973.

Godwin, Gail. *Father Melancholy's Daughter.* New York: Avon, 1991.

Green, Garrett. *Imagining God: Theology and the Religious Imagination.* San Francisco: Harper & Row, 1989.

Groome, Thomas. *Christian Religious Education: Sharing Our Story and Vision.* San Francisco: Harper & Row, 1980.

———. *Educating for Life: A Spiritual Vision for Every Teacher and Parent.* New York: Crossroad, 1998.

———. *Sharing Faith: A Comprehensive Approach to Religious Education and Pastoral Ministry—The Way of Shared Praxis.* San Francisco: Harper & Row, 1991.

Guroian, Vigen. "Moral Formation and Christian Worship." *Ecumenical Review* 49, no. 3 (Fall 1997): 372–78.

Gutiérrez, Gustavo. *A Theology of Liberation.* Rev. ed. Translated by Caridad Inda and John Eagleson. Maryknoll, N.Y.: Orbis, 1988.

Harmless, William. *Augustine and the Catechumenate.* Collegeville, Minn.: Liturgical Press, 1995.

Harris, Maria, and Gabriel Moran. *Reshaping Religious Education: Conversations on Contemporary Practice.* Louisville: Westminister John Knox, 1998.

Hauerwas, Stanley. *The Hauerwas Reader.* Edited by John Berkman and Michael Cartwright. Durham, N.C.: Duke University Press, 2001.

———. *In Good Company: The Church as Polis.* Notre Dame, Ind.: University of Notre Dame Press, 1995.

Hays, Richard. *The Moral Vision of the New Testament: A Contemporary Introduction to New Testament Ethics.* San Francisco: HarperSanFrancisco, 1996.

John Paul II. *Catechesi Tradendae* (Apostolic Exhortation). 1979.

Kant, Immanuel. *Political Writings.* Edited by Hans Reiss. Cambridge: Cambridge University Press, 1991.

Katongole, Emmanuel. *Beyond Universal Reason: The Relation Between Religion and Ethics in the Work of Stanley Hauerwas.* Notre Dame, Ind.: University of Notre Dame Press, 2000.

Kenneson, Phillip D. *Beyond Sectarianism: Re-imagining Church and World.* Harrisburg, Pa.: Trinity Press International, 1999.

Lasch, Christopher. *The Culture of Narcissism: American Life in an Age of Diminishing Expectations.* New York: W. W. Norton, 1979.

Lash, Nicholas. *Easter in Ordinary: Reflections on Human Experience and the Knowledge of God.* Notre Dame, Ind.: University of Notre Dame Press, 1988.

Leech, Kenneth. *True Prayer: An Invitation to Christian Spirituality.* 2nd ed. Harrisburg, Pa.: Morehouse, 1995.

Lindbeck, George. *The Nature of Doctrine: Religion and Theology in a Postliberal Age.* Philadelphia: Westminster, 1984.

Lischer, Richard. "Preaching as the Church's Language." In *Listening to the Word: Studies in Honor of Fred B. Craddock,* edited by Gail R. O'Day and Thomas G. Long. Nashville: Abingdon, 1993.

———. *A Theology of Preaching: The Dynamics of the Gospel.* Nashville: Abingdon, 1981.

Lovibond, Sabina. *Realism and Imagination in Ethics.* Oxford: Basil Blackwell, 1983.

Luther, Martin. *The Large Catechism.* Translated by Robert Fisher. Minneapolis: Fortress, 1981.

The Lutheran Book of Worship. Minneapolis: Augsburg, 1978.

Lysaught, M. Therese. "Eucharist as Basic Training: The Body as Nexus of Liturgy and Ethics." Paper presented at the College Theology Society annual meeting, St. Norbert's College, De Pere, Wisc., June 5, 1999.

Marshall, Bruce. *Trinity and Truth.* Cambridge: Cambridge University Press, 2000.

Milbank, John. "Postmodern Critical Augustinianism: A Short *Summa* in Forty Responses to Unasked Questions." *Modern Theology* 7, no. 2 (1991): 225–37.

————. "Sovereignty, Empire, Capital, and Terror." *South Atlantic Quarterly* 101, no. 2 (Spring 2002): 305–23.

————. *The Word Made Strange: Theology, Language, Culture.* Oxford: Basil Blackwell, 1997.

Moran, Gabriel. *Religious Education as a Second Language.* Birmingham, Ala.: Religious Education Press, 1989.

————. *Uniqueness: Problem or Paradox in Jewish and Christian Traditions.* Maryknoll, N.Y.: Orbis, 1992.

Neville, Gwen Kennedy, and John H. Westerhoff. *Learning through Liturgy.* New York: Seabury, 1978.

Newbigin, Lesslie. *The Open Secret: An Introduction to the Theology of Mission.* Rev. ed. Grand Rapids: Eerdmans, 1995.

Nicolson, Adam. *God's Secretaries: The Making of the King James Bible.* New York: HarperCollins, 2003.

Norris, Kathleen. *The Quotidian Mysteries: Laundry, Liturgy, and "Women's Work."* New York: Paulist, 1998.

Ochs, Peter, Tikva Frymer-Kensky, David Novak, David Fox Sandmel, and Michael A. Singer. *Christianity in Jewish Terms.* Boulder, Colo.: Westview, 2000.

O'Day, Gail, and Thomas Long, eds. *Listening to the Word: Studies in Honor of Fred B. Craddock.* Nashville: Abingdon, 1993.

Palmer, Parker. *To Know As We Are Known: Education as Spiritual Journey.* San Francisco: HarperCollins, 1993.

Pfatteicher, Philip H. *The School of the Church: Worship and Christian Formation.* Valley Forge, Pa.: Trinity Press International, 1995.

Pickstock, Catherine. *After Writing: On the Liturgical Consummation of Philosophy.* Oxford: Basil Blackwell, 1998.

Ramshaw, Gail. "Pried Open by Prayer." In *Liturgy and the Moral Self: Humanity at Full Stretch before God,* edited by E. Byron Anderson and Bruce T. Morrill, 169–75. Collegeville, Minn.: Liturgical Press, 1998.

Rattenbury, J. Ernest, ed. *The Eucharistic Hymns of John and Charles Wesley.* Nashville: Abingdon, 1947.

Ricoeur, Paul. *Essays on Biblical Interpretation.* London: SPCK, 1981.

Romero, Oscar. *The Violence of Love.* Translated by James R. Brockman. Farmington, Pa.: Plough, 1998.

Rubin, Miri. *Corpus Christi: The Eucharist in Late Medieval Culture.* Cambridge: Cambridge University Press, 1991.

Saliers, Don E. "Liturgy and Ethics: Some New Beginnings." In *Liturgy and the Moral Self: Humanity at Full Stretch before God,* edited by

E. Byron Anderson and Bruce T. Morrill, 15–35. Collegeville, Minn.: Liturgical Press, 1998.

———. *Worship as Theology: Foretaste of Glory Divine.* Nashville: Abingdon, 1994.

Schmemann, Alexander. *For the Life of the World: Sacraments and Orthodoxy.* Crestwood, N.Y.: St. Vladimir's Seminary Press, 1973.

Schmidt, Leigh Eric. *Holy Fairs: Scottish Communions and American Revivals in the Early Modern Period.* Princeton, N.J.: Princeton University Press, 1989.

Smith, Jonathan Z. *To Take Place: Toward a Theory in Ritual.* Chicago: University of Chicago Press, 1987.

Stamps, Mary Ewing. "Lives of Living Prayer: Christomorphism and the Priority of Prayer in *The Rule of St. Benedict.*" In *Liturgy and the Moral Self: Humanity at Full Stretch before God,* edited by E. Byron Anderson and Bruce T. Morrill, 139–51. Collegeville, Minn.: Liturgical Press, 1998.

Steinmetz, David. *Memory and Mission: Theological Reflections on the Christian Past.* Nashville: Abingdon, 1988.

Taylor, Barbara Brown. *The Preaching Life.* Boston: Cowley, 1993.

Teresa of Ávila. *The Way of Perfection.* Translated by E. Allison Peers. New York: Image, 1991.

Theology and Ministry Unit for the Presbyterian Church et al. *The Book of Common Worship.* Minneapolis: Westminster John Knox, 1993.

The United Methodist Book of Worship. Nashville: United Methodist Publishing House, 1992.

Wainwright, Geoffrey. *Doxology: The Praise of God in Worship, Doctrine, and Life.* New York: Oxford University Press, 1980.

Warren, Michael. *Faith, Culture, and the Worshiping Community: Shaping the Practice of the Local Church.* Rev. ed. Washington, D.C.: Pastoral, 1993.

Webber, Robert, and Rodney Clapp. *People of the Truth.* Harrisburg, Pa.: Morehouse, 1988.

Westerhoff, John H. "A Call to Catechesis." *The Living Light* 14, no. 3 (Fall 1977).

———. *A Pilgrim People.* San Francisco: Harper & Row, 1984.

———. "The Sunday School of Tomorrow." *Christian Century,* June 4–11, 1980, 639–42.

———, and William H. Willimon. *Learning through the Life Cycle.* Rev. ed. Akron: OSL Publications, 1994.

Whelan, Matthew. "The Responsible Body: A Eucharistic Community." *Cross Currents* 51, no. 3 (Fall 2001).

White, James F. "Methodist Worship." In *Perspectives on American Methodism*, edited by Russell E. Richey, Kenneth E. Rowe, and Jean Miller Schmidt. Nashville: Kingswood, 1993.

Williams, Rowan. *Lost Icons: Reflections on Cultural Bereavement*. Edinburgh: T & T Clark, 2000.

———. "Poetic and Religious Imagination," *Theology*, May 1977.

———. *A Ray of Darkness: Sermons and Reflections*. Boston: Cowley, 1995.

———. *Resurrection: Interpreting the Easter Gospel*. Harrisburg, Pa.: Morehouse, 1982.

Willis, Susan, Jane Kuenz, Shelton Waltrep, and Karen Klugman. *Inside the Mouse: Work and Play at Disney World*. Durham, N.C.: Duke University Press, 1997.

Wolterstorff, Nicholas. *Until Justice and Peace Embrace*. Grand Rapids: Eerdmans, 1983.

Yoder, John Howard. *The Priestly Kingdom: Social Ethics as Gospel*. Notre Dame, Ind.: University of Notre Dame Press, 1984.

Zizioulas, John. *Being as Communion: Studies in Personhood and the Church*. London: Darton, Longman and Todd, 1985.

ACKNOWLEDGMENTS

Several people have read this manuscript, in part or in its entirety, and I am grateful for their honest and insightful criticism. Ron Anderson, Rodney Clapp, Fred Edie, Stanley Hauerwas, Kathy Jones, Phil Kenneson, Steve Long, Trecy Lysaught, and Jim Murphy were valuable conversation partners at various points during the writing process. I am especially grateful to Phil Kenneson for suggesting that I propose the book to Brazos Press and to editorial director Rodney Clapp, who has been patient, wise, and encouraging throughout. I also owe a special thanks to managing editor Rebecca Cooper for her valuable guidance.

My students over several semesters at Duke Divinity School helped me to imagine and articulate what faithful formation in the context of the church at worship can look like; to them I am grateful. The liturgy task force of the Association of Professors and Researchers in Religious Education, under the leadership of Ron Anderson, also provided a forum for thinking through these matters of worship, discipleship, and Christian education.

Last, I thank my family: My parents, Elmer and Judy Dean, to whom this book is lovingly dedicated; my husband, Jim, whose own witness to the life of prayer and praise is something I continue to aspire to; our son, Drew, who is humble and wise beyond his years; and our son, Patrick, who lives life with the kind of joyful abandon that reminds me daily of the giftedness of life in the kingdom of God.